THE FOUNDING FATHERS, POP CULTURE, AND CONSTITUTIONAL LAW

Applying innovative interpretive strategies drawn from cultural studies, this book considers the perennial question of law and politics: what role do the founding fathers play in legitimizing contemporary judicial review? Rather than promulgating further theories that attempt to legitimize either judicial activism or restraint, this work uses narrative analysis, popular culture, parody, and queer theory to better understand and to reconstitute the traditional relationship between fatherhood and judicial review. Unlike traditional, top-down public law analyses that focus on elite decision making by courts, legislatures, or executives, this volume explores the representation of law and legitimacy in various sites of popular culture. To this end, soap operas, romance novels, tabloid newspapers, reality television, and coming out narratives provide alternative ways to understand the relationship between paternal power and law from the bottom up.

In this manner, constitutional discourse can begin to be transformed from a dreary parsing of scholarly and juristic argot into a vibrant discussion with points of access and understanding for all.

For Kate

The Founding Fathers, Pop Culture, and Constitutional Law
Who's Your Daddy?

SUSAN BURGESS
Ohio University, USA

ASHGATE

Published by
Ashgate Publishing Limited
Gower House
Croft Road
Aldershot
Hampshire GU11 3HR
England

Ashgate Publishing Company
Suite 420
101 Cherry Street
Burlington, VT 05401-4405
USA

Ashgate website: http://www.ashgate.com

British Library Cataloguing in Publication Data
Burgess, Susan
   The founding fathers, pop culture, and constitutional law :
   who's your daddy. - (Law, justice and power series)
   1. Judicial review - United States 2. Popular culture -
   United States 3. Founding Fathers of the United States
   I. Title
   347 .7'3012

Library of Congress Cataloging-in-Publication Data
Burgess, Susan, 1961-
   The founding fathers, pop culture, and constitutional law : who's your daddy / by Susan Burgess.
      p. cm. -- (Law, justice, and power)
   Includes bibliographical references and index.
   ISBN 978-0-7546-7245-6
   1. Judicial review--United States. 2. Political questions and judicial power--United States. 3. Law and politics. 4. Popular culture. I. Title.

   KF4575.B87 2008
   347.73'12--dc22

2007034434

Printed and bound in Great Britain by MPG Books Ltd, Bodmin, Cornwall.

Contents

We can replicate the fundamental political act of the founders only if we are willing to recognize the reality of their act. Stripping them of their right to constitute a government would likewise strip us of our own.

Keith Whittington, Professor of Politics, Princeton University

I can't find anyway to beat them at this point. What can I say? I just tip my hat and call the Yankees my daddy.

Pedro Martinez, pitcher, formerly of the Boston Red Sox

The alarming thing about equality is that we are then both children, and the question is, where is father? We know where we are if one of us is the father.

Patient of D. W. Winnicott, pediatrician and clinical psychologist

Series Editor's Preface

Sometimes a book is so refreshing in its perspective, so innovative, that it promises to revolutionize a field of scholarship. *The Founding Fathers, Pop Culture, and Constitutional Law* is one such book. It is a bold intervention into the field of constitutional interpretation, a field which Susan Burgess argues has reached a kind of scholarly impasse. Rather than tread the well-worked path with another theory of constitutional meaning, Burgess offers us a cultural studies reading of constitutional scholarship. Her reading focuses on the elusive quest to understand the intent of the Framers of the Constitution. In Burgess's hands that quest becomes an avenue to think about the relationship of judicial review and fatherhood.

Drawing on various cultural studies sources, mixing the parodic with serious, sophisticated scholarship, no one can leave this book unmoved. Burgess takes her readers on a journey drawing on soap operas, romance novels, science fiction, and so on to explore the representation of law and legitimacy in popular culture. Her work offers readers a bottom-up approach to a subject all-too-often treated as an exclusively high culture domain. Burgess works her way through a wide variety of contemporary classics to show their generic properties and their unselfconscious search for paternal authority. She re-reads such key cases in modern constitutional law as *Bush* v. *Gore* through queer theory.

All in all, Burgess offers a way of thinking about constitutional interpretation with which not everyone will agree. But, no one can afford to ignore it. *The Founding Fathers, Pop Culture, and Constitutional Law* is both illuminating and enjoyable. And that is a combination rarely found in academic writing today.

Austin Sarat
William Nelson Cromwell Professor of Jurisprudence and Political Science
and Five College Fortieth Anniversary Professor
Departments of Law, Jurisprudence and Social Thought and Political Science
Amherst College

Acknowledgements

Thanks to all the friends and colleagues who offered encouraging and incisive comments about the project, especially: John Brigham, Keith Bybee, Cornell Clayton, Sue Davis, Wayne Fishman, John Gilliom, Howard Gillman, Leslie Goldstein, Bill Haltom, Christine Harrington, Mary Hawkesworth, Ron Kahn, Cricket Keating, Tom Keck, Tim Kaufman-Osborn, George Lovell, Michael McCann, Lynn Mather, Nicole Reynolds, Alisa Rosenthal, Austin Sarat, Sylvia Schafer, Jessica Silbey, Helena Silverstein, Carl Stychin, and Kathleen Sullivan. Thanks also to Beth Manar, Steve Fetsch, and Jen Schomburg Kanke for technical assistance above and beyond the call of duty.

Special thanks to my colleagues in the Department of Political Science and the Women's Studies Program at Ohio University, especially Judith Grant, Lynette Peck, and Julie White, who took time away from their own work to carefully read and thoughtfully comment on the manuscript (more than once).

Extra special thanks to my partner, Kate Leeman, for reading the manuscript (also more than once), often anticipating its argument, and for thoroughly indulging me as I wrote it; no small matter.

In memory of my dear aunt, Cassie Tiogoly. I wish that she was still here with us laughing and telling stories. In lieu of that, I guess I'll just have to tell a few of my own.

*****

Earlier versions of some of the chapters in this book appeared in other publications. Grateful acknowledgement is made to the following journals for permission to reprint portions of the following: "A Fine Romance: Keith Whittington's Originalism and the Drama of US Constitutional Theory," 2001 *Law and Society Review* 35: 931–42; "Did the Supreme Court Come Out in *Bush* v. *Gore?* Queer Theory on the Performance of the Politics of Shame," 2005 *Differences: A Journal of Feminist Cultural Studies* 16 :126–46; "Queer (Theory) Eye for the Straight (Legal) Guy: *Lawrence* v. *Texas*' Makeover of *Bowers* v. *Hardwick*," 2006 *Political Research Quarterly* 59: 401–14; and "Who's Your Daddy? Legitimacy, Parody, and Soap Operas in Contemporary Constitutional Discourse," 2007 *Law, Culture, and the Humanities* 3: 55–81.

Chapter 1

Introduction

Cultural Studies, the Founding Fathers, and Judicial Review

Who's Your Daddy[1] applies innovative interpretive strategies drawn from cultural studies to a perennial question of law and politics: what role do the founding fathers play in legitimizing contemporary judicial review? The concept of governmental legitimacy is grounded in a fear of illegitimacy. In earlier times, this fear was expressed as a concern that the king's heir was truly his legitimate issue, not a bastard (Rubin 2005). In contemporary times, any constitutional issue that is not wedded to the founding fathers risks being labeled illegitimate. Accordingly, leading theories of judicial review typically reference the founding fathers in one form or another, whether that entails embracing them as a basis of authority as in judicial restraint, enlarging the scope of their power as in judicial activism, or resigning to their persistent power as in critical race theory. Rather than offering yet another theory that attempts to legitimize either judicial activism or judicial restraint, *Who's Your Daddy* uses narrative analysis, popular culture, parody, and queer theory to better understand and to reconstitute the traditional relationship between fatherhood and judicial review.

Beginning with the title's use of a phrase that is drawn from popular culture and interrogates legitimacy, *Who's Your Daddy* explores the way that cultural studies can help us to understand "the conjunction of fatherhood and law, [as it] is portrayed in popular culture," and the way in which fatherhood serves as "one of the key terms through which law is mythologized and through which fantasies and anxieties about law are expressed" (Sarat 2000, 8, 3). Unlike traditional, top-down public law analyses that focus on elite decision-making by courts, legislatures, or executives, *Who's Your Daddy* explores the representation of law and legitimacy in various sites of popular culture. To this end, soap operas, romance novels, science fiction, reality television, and coming out narratives provide alternative ways to understand the relationship between paternal power and law from the bottom-up. Keith Bybee has nicely summarized my approach to law and popular culture, saying that it "begins with a specific understanding of American culture and uses that understanding to evaluate the dynamics of judicial decision-making. Instead of considering how law operates on the street, Burgess uses a particular account of the street to explain how law operates in court" (2006, 416).

---

1   *Who's Your Daddy* is the shortened version of title; *The Founding Fathers, Pop Culture, and Constitutional Law: Who's Your Daddy?* which will be used throughout this book as a reference to the title.

Infusing traditional studies of judicial review with interpretive strategies drawn from cultural studies, *Who's Your Daddy* seeks to provide a perspective about law and social change that differs significantly in form and content from the usual fare in contemporary constitutional discourse. Narrative analysis, popular culture, parody, and queer theory provide the tools to challenge the dominance of elite constitutional interpretation, to appropriate and reformulate the terms of the mainstream debate, and to identify a populist basis upon which to fundamentally alter contemporary constitutional discourse. In this manner, constitutional discourse can begin to be transformed from a dreary parsing of scholarly and juristic argot into a vibrant discussion with points of access and understanding for all.

More specifically, *Who's Your Daddy* seeks to reconfigure contemporary constitutional discourse in three ways. First, the book seeks to democratize the debate about judicial review. While jurists and constitutional theorists of various political stripes have long called for a more democratic constitutional discourse, most have concentrated on legislative and executive interpretation as an alternative to judicial decision-making, thus retaining an elite focus (for example, Whittington 1999a). In contrast, *Who's Your Daddy* explores various forms of popular culture as more accessible bases for democratizing contemporary constitutional discourse, following the lead of scholars who have identified popular knowledge and interests as a basis for enlarging the scope of constitutional debates (for example, Brigham 1987; 1990; 1996).

Second, just as scholars such as Jody Baumgartner and Jonathan Morris (2006) have found that viewers of humorous parodies such as *The Daily Show* are not likely to view mainstream politics in the same way as they did when their only source of news was a standard evening news broadcast, each chapter of *Who's Your Daddy* offers a humorous, popularly-based send-up of the relationship of judicial review and fatherhood, which makes it unlikely that the reader will think about constitutional politics and scholarship in the same way ever again. Parodying politics has become very popular in contemporary culture outside of the academy, as evidenced by the enormous success of television shows such as *The Daily Show* and *The Colbert Report* and book-length compilations of satirical political stories from *The Onion*. Written in entertaining and accessible language, *Who's Your Daddy* aspires to offer humor as the basis for a more interesting and hip way of understanding and reconstituting politics. As Baumgartner and Morris suggest, this may lead to increased interest in public debates that otherwise seem specialized and tedious, particularly amongst college students and other younger adults (2006).

Third, *Who's Your Daddy* promises to open up a constitutional debate that leading political scientists and legal scholars have characterized as being lodged at an impasse for the last 25 years (for example, Gillman 2001; Brest 1981). I argue that this is in large part owing to the failure of contemporary constitutional discourse to provide adequate attention to dissenting voices that challenge, rather than seek, legitimacy. Exploring the link between fathers and law provides a basis for better understanding the impasses that exist and opens up the space to consider already existing alternative sources drawn from popular culture. In its current state, contemporary constitutional discourse is similar to music that lacks dissonance—lovely, perhaps, but lacking the tension that is necessary for release and movement.

By integrating populist challenges to legitimacy into the constitutional debate, *Who's Your Daddy* seeks to transform the familiar discussion about the legitimacy of judicial review into a parody that reconstitutes the relationship between fatherhood and law. Because parody typically serves to complicate and confound a familiar narrative, the longstanding nature of the debate about judicial review provides a remarkably rich basis for such an interpretive move.

Structure of the Book

Who's Your Daddy speaks to various scholarly communities interested in judicial legitimacy, law and narrative analysis, law and popular culture, parody as a transformative strategy, and queer theory. Structured to address these concerns, Chapters 2, 3, and 4 each introduce a major theory of judicial legitimacy in contemporary constitutional discourse, subject it to narrative analysis, and compare it with a parallel narrative in popular culture, eventuating in a parody of the original constitutional narrative. These parodies open up space for the alternative narratives of judicial identity and power offered in Chapters 5 and 6.

Chapter 2 explores Keith Whittington's embrace of the founders. It analyzes his theory of judicial restraint as a romantic narrative and compares it to a romance novel to produce a parody of originalist judicial review. Chapter 3 examines Ronald Dworkin's enlargement of the founders' authority. Cast as a comedic narrative and compared to a comic soap opera, the chapter creates a parody of nonoriginalist judicial review. Chapter 4 investigates Derrick Bell's rejection of the founders' authority, interprets his critical race theory as a tragic narrative, and compares his use of science fiction to the parody of mainstream journalism that one finds in the tabloids.

As the book progresses, the constitutional theories explored are more openly narrative in form, and the parodies produced become more ironic. For example, Whittington offers something of a nod to narrative analysis by conceiving popular sovereignty as a metaphor for the constitutional order and by seeking to provide an alternative constitutional narrative that moves the contemporary debate beyond its current impasse. The mild parody of judicial restraint that is produced by way of comparing Whittington's theory to a romance novel is much more reserved than that of Chapter 3. In response to Dworkin's call for a full exploration of law, literature, and popular culture in the form of soap operas, Chapter 3 parodies the role of the founding fathers in relation to judicial activism through the soap opera trope of resurrecting a long-since deceased patriarch. In Chapter 4 Bell's fantastical tabloid-like tales of time travel and alien abduction, rooted in popular culture and self-consciously pitched in a narrative form, are more outrageous even still.

These parodies steadily destabilize the original constitutional narratives to which they refer, and the paternal authority on which they are based, creating the space for two parodies of contemporary constitutional practice, both of which are grounded in queer irony. Chapter 5 presents a parody that rejects the founders' authority, reimagining *Bush* v. *Gore* as a coming out narrative. Chapter 6 reappropriates the founders' authority to a queer end, rendering *Lawrence* v. *Texas* as a makeover of *Bowers* v. *Hardwick*, *à la* the reality television show *Queer Eye for the Straight Guy*.

Below, I discuss in greater detail the scholarly literatures that provide the basis for this work and identify several scholarly communities that would constitute the likely audience for *Who's Your Daddy*.

Scholarly Audiences

Judicial Review and Legitimacy

Judicial legitimacy has long been a central focus of constitutional discourse in the United States, both inside and outside of the academy.[2] Scholars engaged in these debates often assume that judicial review is at base undemocratic, and thus a potentially illegitimate use of judicial power. As the oft-cited John Hart Ely puts it: "The central function is at the same time the central problem of judicial review: a body that is not elected or otherwise politically responsible in any significant way is telling the people's elected representatives that they cannot govern as they'd like" (1980, 4).

The problem of judicial legitimacy is evident not only in academic constitutional theory but also in iconic constitutional cases such as *Brown* v. *Board of Education* and *Roe* v. *Wade*, as well as in more recent cases that are highly contested such as *Bush* v. *Gore* and *Lawrence* v. *Texas*. While scholars and jurists have long sought to resolve this dilemma, offering various arguments to legitimize either active or restrained uses of judicial review,[3] none of these arguments have been widely accepted as the standard upon which to ground judicial review. Thus, the problem of judicial legitimacy and the call for increased democratic input continue to persist in contemporary constitutional discourse.

Debates about judicial legitimacy typically refer back to the founding fathers in one form or another. In the contemporary debate about judicial review, advocates of originalism and judicial restraint such as Whittington (1999a and b) embrace the founders' authority; supporters of non-interpretivism and judicial activism such as Dworkin (1977; 1985; 1986; 1996; 2006) seek to enlarge the founders' constitutional conceptions; and critical race theorists such as Bell (1987; 1992; 1996) reject the founders' basic choices while remaining resigned to their influence on the shape of the debate.

The impasse over judicial legitimacy has led some influential constitutional theorists to claim that the debate is irresolvable on its own terms. More than a generation ago Paul Brest predicted that this impasse would not be resolved "until despair or hope impels us to explore alternatives to the world we currently inhabit"

---

2   Judicial legitimacy has been a focus of debate at least since Federalist 78 and Brutus 15. It can be found in more contemporary discussions in Bork (1990; 1996), Dworkin (1977; 1985; 1986; 2000; 2006), Ely (1973; 1980), Kozlowski (2003), Rosenberg (1991), Sunstein (1984; 1994; 1999; 2005), Wechsler (1959), Whittington (1999a; 1999b) and a host of other conservative and liberal scholars. For a detailed discussion of these debates see Burgess (1992), Gillman (2001), Keck (2004) and Perretti (1999).

3   These include nonoriginalism and originalism, noninterpretivism and interpretivism, maximalism and minimalism, and a host of others.

(1981, 1109). In his well known article "Nomos and Narrative," Robert Cover called for scholars to devise new stories based on new practices in order to bring new worlds into being (1983). Following these leads, recent scholarship suggests that careful attention to narrative analysis and popular culture in conjunction with the use of humor and parody may serve to move contemporary constitutional discourse beyond its current impasse, opening up space for new forms of democratic dissent and transformation.

Narrative Analysis

As Cover has said: "No set of legal institutions or prescriptions exists apart from the narratives that locate it and give it meaning" (1983, 4). Critical race theorists such as Bell (1987; 1992; 1996) and Patricia Williams (1992; 1995) also argue that law is conveyed through narrative, and that form is intimately related to content. They offer narratives that are based in the lived experiences of people of color, in an effort to foreground the persistence of racism in American law. In doing so, they highlight the way that altering mainstream narrative forms may disrupt and thus transform the content of contemporary legal discourse.

In a similar vein, sociolegal scholars such as Patricia Ewick and Susan Silbey maintain that it is possible to articulate subversive stories even though "the structure, the content, and the performance of stories as they are defined and regulated within social settings often articulate and reproduce existing ideologies and hegemonic relations of power and inequality." They argue that such stories can break silence and "bear witness to what is unimagined and unexpressed" (1995, 212). Relatedly, Jessica Silbey claims that understanding the form in which each narrative presents itself is crucial to understanding its substance, or meaning. She argues: "The study of representation—be it discursive legal practices, modern art, or documentary filmmaking—is the study of form...The story being told has little substance independent from its form, and to understand the story—and to judge it—means first to understand its formal qualities" (2002, 162).

Accordingly, *Who's Your Daddy* identifies three major narrative forms prevalent in contemporary constitutional discourse, as a means of analyzing the role that the founding fathers play in legitimizing various practices of judicial review and their outcomes. Whittington's originalist desire to unite the founding fathers with contemporary constitutional debate is cast as a nostalgic romantic narrative; Dworkin's aim to overcome the illiberal politics of the past by enlarging the founders' vision is set as a comedy aiming at a happy ending; and Bell's critical yet resigned rejection of the founding fathers' racism is discussed as a tragic narrative in which no significant change can occur because the die has been cast against African-Americans from the very start of the story. Each narrative has its own set of requirements that drive the plot forward, as well as significant limitations that obstruct transformation of the constitutional debate.

Popular Culture

Popular culture is a potentially rich source of populist understandings that may address narrative limitations. Leading cultural studies scholars such as John Fiske have argued that popular culture offers various representations that can be read both to maintain as well as to challenge dominant power, often in a humorous manner.

> Popular culture is the culture of the subordinated and disempowered and thus always bears within it signs of power relations, traces of the forces of domination and subordination that are central to our social system and therefore to our social experiences. Equally, it shows signs of resisting or evading these forces: popular culture contradicts itself. (1989b, 4–5)

Thus, Fiske looks to popular culture not simply as a reflection of elite power but also as a potential source of dissent and popular interests.

Scholarly work at the intersection of popular culture and the law is burgeoning, as evidenced by the publication of such work in the new peer-reviewed journal *Law, Culture, and the Humanities*. In addition, Richard Sherwin's path-breaking work *When Law Goes Pop* has argued that "any attempt to understand adequately the way law works in contemporary society requires that popular culture be taken into account" (2000, 17). While Sherwin's work focuses largely on the way that popular culture may negatively impact law's meaning, stability, and legitimacy, he remains open to a more affirmative form of postmodernity that would offer a compelling dramatic narrative and challenge the dominant legal order.[4]

Following these leads, *Who's Your Daddy* explores the potentially salutary effects of integrating law and popular culture, arguing that although contemporary constitutional discourse appears to be focused solely on legitimizing judicial review, even it, with the assistance of popular culture, can be seen as containing the seeds of populist dissent, which may well be constructive or transformative with respect to constitutional meaning.

Accordingly, *Who's Your Daddy* pairs each narrative form of elite constitutional discourse with a parallel genre of popular culture, providing a populist understanding of law, legitimacy, and transformation, each of which challenges its elite partner. Thus, Whittington's romantic originalist theory of judicial restraint is paired with a romance novel; Dworkin's comedic judicial activism is paired with a comedic soap opera; and Bell's tragic critical race theory is paired with tragic science fiction stories of time travel and alien abduction. Integrating democratic interpretations of law and legitimacy with elite interpretations in this manner sets the stage for parodies that promise to disrupt the stability of the legitimacy debate and create space for the production of new constitutional narratives grounded in popular forms.

Parody

Popular culture regularly integrates humor into its narratives. At the forefront of this work in critical cultural studies, Mikhail Bakhtin suggests that libratory forms of humor promise to disrupt *status quo* narratives that appear univocal, thus providing

---

4   For a wide variety of views on this issue see Sherwin (2006).

grounds for populist political transformation. For Bakhtin, the laughter occasioned by parody may create a space for "a shift of authorities and truths, a shift of world orders" (1984a, 127). Even if such openings sometimes emerge only temporarily, they nevertheless represent opportunities for dissent and potential transformation.[5]

Bakhtin suggests that parody, a strategy based in humor, can help reveal the paradoxes and problems that underlie the official workings of power. Parody is typically practiced by outsiders subject to the dominant order, as they have more of a vested interest in ridiculing and displacing it than those who continue to benefit from it. Always referential, parody provides a humorous commentary upon another narrative, serving to confound it. It employs double meanings, pretending, with a subtle wink and a nudge, to embrace purposefully implausible and laughable conclusions. The original narrative is typically paralleled in a ludicrous, distorting fashion, to the end of ridiculing, and, potentially, reforming it (Preminger 1965, 600). Operating as a form of dissent, parody typically sends up a serious person, work, or situation by mimicking it in an exaggerated, humorous, and often eccentric or theatrical manner, frequently borrowing costumes, phrases, mannerisms, or voicing from an original in order to alter its content to make it look ridiculous (Cuddon 1998, 64).

Parody asks the audience to laugh at the fact that reality is not merely suspended but constructed, perhaps most especially when it is being represented as natural or given. Yet, reality's constructedness does not mean that it is malleable at will. Parodists are keenly aware of the powerful forces that keep the original dominant, despite whatever criticism, humorous or otherwise, may be leveled against it. In this sense, parody entails a fairly sophisticated understanding of power, as it bespeaks both a strong desire for change as well as an understanding that the ability to effectuate such change at will is typically quite limited, no matter how passionate or charismatic the parodist may be. This does not leave the parodist simply resigned to dominance. Instead, the parodist is committed to working within rather than resolving such contradictions.

Accordingly, parody seeks to transform the audience's consciousness, so that it can no longer view the object of parody in the same way ever again. Thus, the success of parody depends, at least in part, on the audience(s) to whom it is pitched. Because this is so, parody is usually pitched in an accessible and entertaining manner—at least to the audience(s) whose understanding and transformation is (consciously) sought by the parodist. A work may lend itself to parody in a manner seemingly unintended by the original author. Of course, humor and parody may not be received favorably by the original author. In addition, parody itself may reach unintended audiences, who may interpret the parody in a manner not consciously intended by the parodist.

Ohio State Senator Bob Hagan's (D-Youngstown) announcement of his intent to introduce a bill that would prevent Republicans from adopting children offers a good example of the use of parody in contemporary politics. In February 2006, Hagan sent a memo out to his Senate colleagues asking for cosponsorship in order

---

5   In the literature of democratic theory, Iris Young has also argued that humor is central to establishing dissent and the integration of previously excluded voices into dominant narratives (1996, 124, 130).

to "ignore this growing threat to our communities." Explicitly referencing the original that he sought to mock, he stated that his legislation was "modeled after a bill recently introduced in the Ohio House by Rep. Ron Hood (R-Ashville via Carrollton) that would prohibit homosexual, bisexual and transgender people from adopting children." Following the now familiar claims of opponents of gay rights that homosexuals are more affluent than heterosexuals, more emotionally unstable, and more interested in recruiting unwitting outsiders to their lifestyle, Hagan stated: "Credible research exists that strongly suggests that adopted children raised in Republican households, though significantly wealthier than their Democrat-raised counterparts, are more at risk for developing emotional problems, social stigmas, inflated egos, an alarming lack of tolerance for others they deem different from themselves and an air of overconfidence to mask their insecurities" (Nichols 2006). He added several poignant quotations from those afflicted by this scourge, such as a 25-year-old Republican adoptee who "chose to remain nameless" and characterized his adoption as a "nightmare I haven't yet awoken from." Calling the original anti-gay adoption bill homophobic, blatantly discriminatory, and extremely divisive, Hagan said, "We need to see what we are doing." In other words, he hoped to alter his audience's consciousness so that they would never again view an anti-gay bill simply at face value. Perhaps not surprisingly, no one volunteered to cosponsor Hagan's bill. Interestingly, however, the Speaker of the Ohio House, conservative Jon Husted (R-Kettering), blocked the anti-gay adoption bill by coming out as an adopted child himself and noting the enormous need for more people from all walks of life to adopt the large numbers of parentless children across the state of Ohio.

The unruly potential of parody and humor are well-illustrated by jazz musician Joel Forrester's comments about the use of humor by his band, The Microscopic Septet.[6] Music critics had become quite upset with the band because they couldn't figure out who the humor was aimed at. Were they making fun of jazz? The audience? Themselves? Forrester's answer was: all three. Although modern artists had done much to develop jazz into its present form, the band felt that jazz had become much too serious an enterprise, a mere shadow of its former self in the raucous and ribald era of the 1920s and 1930s. In response to this development, jazz audiences had adopted an increasingly expert, serious, and distant style of music appreciation. As a result, the Septet worried that its own performance style had become highly proficient, yet joyless. Their solution was to laugh at the entire enterprise—jazz, the audience, and themselves included—destabilizing the stolid form of performance and reception that had developed over time, in order to make way for something new to emerge. In a similar manner, *Who's Your Daddy* seeks to use humor to reinsert a populist tone into contemporary constitutional discourse. The tongue-in-cheek parodies of various stolid forms of scholarly constitutional work destabilize a well-worn debate, loosening it up to make it more accessible and entertaining for all involved.

Because parody is referential, it invokes familiar narratives that typically assume a shared, stable reality. It seeks to dislodge such assumptions by revealing the shaky grounds upon which firmly entrenched discourses rest. By doing so, parody can open up longstanding debates, particularly those that seem dead-ended, questioning

---

6   Interviewed by Terry Gross, *Fresh Air*, 28 November 2006.

rather than resolving, confounding rather than settling the very terms and shape of the discussion. By breaking down structures and creating disorder, the laughter occasioned by parody may create a space for what Bakhtin has called "a shift of authorities and truths, a shift of world orders" (1984a, 304). Even if such openings sometimes emerge only temporarily, they nevertheless represent opportunities for dissent and potential transformation, in terms of both form and content or performance and substance.

Due to the referential nature of parody, the form of the original narrative must be carefully identified along with its constituent parts. If the parody is to be based in democratic interests, it must be drawn from a populist source. Hence, the narrative analysis and use of popular culture in *Who's Your Daddy* provide excellent taking-off points from which to parody three major stories in contemporary constitutional discourse (romance, comedy, and tragedy) that alternatively embrace, enlarge, and reject the authority of the founding fathers. When the originals are compared to parallel forms drawn from romance novels, soap operas, and tabloids, parodies are produced that send-up both the form and content of contemporary constitutional discourse. Destabilizing the stolid narrative forms available in the contemporary debate, these chapters pave the way for the introduction of two more broadly pitched parodies of constitutional discourse, both of which are based in queer irony.

Queer Theory

Feminist cultural studies scholar Tania Modleski reminds us that if we are always working in an adversarial role, we are always on the defensive, "always, as it were, complaining about the family, but never leaving home" (1982, 103–104). But if the myth of origin is removed, that is, if we leave home, then we might stand a better chance of addressing constitutional politics in our own right, rather than continuing to respond to paternal views in one (narrative) form or another. Removing, or at least decentering, the myth of origin through parody can open up space in which new constitutional narratives and judicial identities can emerge, as Cover, Brest, and others had hoped. The point is neither to idealize nor to malign the founding fathers, but rather to decentralize them, to move on by exploring alternative constitutional narratives that produce different forms of constitutional discourse and judicial identity.

Chapters 5 and 6 offer two such possibilities: both are grounded in queer theory, which foregrounds irony and destabilizes identity, rejecting a stable myth of origin. Rather than centralizing ancestry, queer identity appears to start each generation anew. The question, "who's your daddy?" is much more likely to elicit a narrative about one's own interests, rather than stories like those examined in Chapters 2, 3, and 4, which tend to obscure contemporary power by focusing on paternal decisions made long ago. Chapter 5 provides an ironic account of what constitutional discourse might look like absent the centrality of such a myth to reference in order to legitimate (or resist) constitutional decision-making, while Chapter 6 decentralizes the myth and reconstitutes it along with several other key features of the contemporary debate.

In Chapter 5 *Bush* v. *Gore* is read as a coming out narrative in which the Supreme Court abandons its longstanding attachment to a myth of origin, along with its presumptively legal identity, in favor of a deviant political identity. The chapter is framed in a manner that parallels the standard coming out narrative in which heterosexuality is abandoned in favor of homosexuality. Chapter 6 offers a parodic reading of the narrative forms of contemporary constitutional discourse, inspired by the popular reality television show, *Queer Eye for the Straight Guy*. This chapter evaluates, makes-over, and sends-up romantic, comedic, and tragic narrative accounts of constitutional change as played out in the context of the change in the Supreme Court's treatment of sodomy laws, from *Bowers* v. *Hardwick* to *Lawrence* v. *Texas*. The result, consistent with other parodic readings, is a new way to read and evaluate contemporary constitutional discourse, which transforms the audience's consciousness so that it can no longer view the object of parody, contemporary constitutional discourse, in the same way again.

Chapter 2

A Fine Romance?
Judicial Restraint as a Romance Novel

A fine romance, with no kisses
A fine romance, my friend this is

From *A Fine Romance*
Lyrics: Dorothy Fields
Music: Jerome Kerns

Introducing Originalism

Who's your daddy? For originalists seeking to legitimate judicial restraint, there can be only one answer: the founding fathers. The founders provide a lineage that can legitimate the contemporary practice of judicial restraint, allowing the courts to overturn only those laws that clearly abridge the constitutional text or the founders' views of what the text means. Accordingly, the founders are an intensely sought after object of desire. Originalists seek to join the founding fathers and contemporary constitutional discourse in a lasting union that connects the past with the present in a powerful story of origin. In this chapter, I focus on the work of Keith Whittington, arguably the strongest contemporary advocate of legitimating judicial restraint by embracing the authority of the founding fathers, uniting the past and present in contemporary constitutional discourse. I argue that his theory is best understood as a romantic narrative. In order to better understand the problems and prospects associated with this type of constitutional narrative, I compare it to a parallel narrative in popular culture, the romance novel, producing a send-up of contemporary judicial restraint.

Originalists argue that the Constitution means what the founding fathers intended it to mean. Legitimacy stems ultimately from popular sovereignty, that is, the will of the people, generated through constitutional ratification. Framers' intent serves as a kind of proxy for popular sovereignty, as the people are said to have ratified what the framers' understood the Constitution to mean at that time. Short of constitutional amendment, the founding fathers' views should prevail in constitutional matters.

Establishing a clear lineage between popular sovereignty and the courts through framers' intent is particularly important given the prevailing view that judicial review is a fundamentally undemocratic practice which allows unelected and politically unaccountable judges to overturn laws made by the people's representatives. Without further grounding, judicial review appears illegitimate. Originalists argue that judicial legitimacy depends upon establishing a clear lineage back to the founding fathers. Judges should regularly restrain themselves, overturning only those laws that clearly abridge the original intent of the founding fathers. In lieu of such clarity, laws passed through democratic processes should stand. Thus, most originalists reject the legitimacy of iconic cases of judicial activism like *Brown* v. *Board of Education* and *Roe* v. *Wade* on the grounds that decisions about school desegregation and abortion should be made through democratic processes rather than judicial review, as framers' intent does not clearly dictate the outcomes in these cases.

Originalism has been a persistent force throughout American constitutional history, though it has been more influential in some periods than others (Brigham 2002). Some argue that its dominance was virtually taken for granted from the founding period until the rise of legal realism in the twentieth century, particularly during the New Deal period (O'Neill 2005; Wolfe 1986). They claim that legal realism transformed legal consciousness, ushering in a new era that rejected the belief that framers' intent could produce objective outcomes in constitutional cases.

Since then, the influence of originalism has varied, rising with the resistance to *Brown* v. *Board of Education* in the 1950s (Berger 1977). Another watershed period occurred in the early 1980s; political conservatives created the Federalist Society in order to oppose judicial power, and President Reagan appointed Edwin Meese, a staunch original intent advocate, to serve as attorney general (Hatcher 2006).

Originalism waned in the late 1980s, following the failed nomination of originalist Robert Bork to the Supreme Court in 1987. At the time, some believed that this event signaled "the final victory for the living Constitution," suggesting that "liberal legalism seemed to have weathered the originalist storm" (O'Neill 2005, 184). Despite these dire predictions, the tide of originalism swelled again at the end of the twentieth century, led by a cast of characters that included Chief Justice William Rehnquist on the Supreme Court and Whittington in the academy. The founding fathers are currently enjoying a significant amount of attention outside of the academy as well, with biographies and other accounts of the founding regularly appearing on various best-seller lists over the last several years. In some instances this attention appears to border on devotion, as evidenced by the title of Richard Brookhiser's book, *What Would the Founders Do?*, an obvious play on the phrase currently popular among many evangelical Christians, "what would Jesus do?"

This chapter focuses on the work of Whittington as a prime example of contemporary originalism and judicial restraint. Whittington is currently a Professor of Politics at Princeton University, and his work has been lauded as one of the most sophisticated defenses of originalism offered to date (O'Neill 2005, 201). He has been credited with offering a more theoretically rigorous and less polemical form of originalism than earlier influential scholars and judges such as Raoul Berger and Robert Bork. In addition to being a recognized authority in this area, Whittington is also of particular interest for this study because, unlike most restraintists, he explicitly acknowledges that constitutional theory is grounded in narrative.

Whittington casts popular sovereignty in terms of narrative, characterizing it as a "metaphor for our constitutional order," like a myth, a fiction, or "a label for a story we tell about ourselves, indicating both how we think our system functions and how we think it ought to function" (1999b, 142). Conceding that the story of popular sovereignty isn't "literally true," he argues that it is "true enough that we can adopt it as our regulative ideal" and as a justification for the political system, "as long as the separation between the idea and the reality does not become too great" (1999b, 142). The fact "that the Americans were not really one united people is of less importance than the fact that they could think of themselves as such" (1999b, 144). To be recognized as legitimate, the sovereign must in some way "represent the whole of the people" through majority rule, with limits as specified by the people at the founding, such that "membership is real and significant" (1999b, 145, 142). This includes the minority, who, according to Whittington, is "embraced within the sovereign through the deliberative quality of the constitutional decision" (1999b, 147).

Whittington seeks to provide a narrative that will move constitutional theory beyond the majoritarian dilemma "originally proposed by [noted constitutional scholar Alexander Bickel nearly forty years ago" (1999b, 34). Judicial review presents a dilemma to majoritarianism and appears illegitimate because it is practiced by electorally unaccountable judges and appears to lack a widely accepted standard or uncontroversial constitutional grounding upon which decisions might be based. Although scholars have offered various groundings, Whittington correctly notes that each has been met with "general dissatisfaction," and has yet to result in a theory of judicial review that is "fully persuasive" (1999b, 213). Whittington intends to move the discussion beyond this impasse by persuading both majority and minority populations that his constitutional story is a compelling and persuasive narrative. For Whittington this will mean telling a story in which legitimacy is established by uniting the past with the present, and the founding fathers with contemporary constitutional interpretation.

Judicial Restraint as a Romantic Narrative

Accepting Whittington's invitation to construe constitutional interpretation as a narrative, this chapter suggests that the constitutional story he provides can be understood as a romantic narrative—complete with all the possibilities and limitations that romance entails (see for example, Black 2002; H. White 1973; 1978; 1987; Schafer 1970). In general, romantic narratives seek to reconnect with a simpler time characterized by more authenticity and less corruption. They usually feature a grand quest that harks back to an original and idealized golden age. The hero of this story often feels alienated from his true self and must battle several formidable adversaries who would prevent him from attaining the ultimate goal, the restoration of the edenic natural state, which allows for authentic self-expression and facilitates the long sought after union with the hero's beloved.

Although scholars and public intellectuals often disdain romance novels as pulp fiction unworthy of much attention, the fact remains that at the turn of the twenty-first century they are currently the most popular vehicle for the romantic narrative, accounting for well over half the mass-market and trade paperbacks sold in North America (Regis 2003, xi). Romance novels have been in circulation since 1740, with a legacy that extends to well-respected works such as Jane Austen's *Pride and Prejudice* and Charlotte Brontë's *Jane Eyre*, both of which were enormously popular when they were first published and remain so today. *Pride and Prejudice* continues to be thought of as both the best as well as the most popular romance novel ever written (Regis 2003, 75).

As many scholars have noted, romance novels typically follow a specific formula that features a quest to unite the protagonist and the beloved, despite their flawed society, which presents a variety of barriers to their betrothal (Modleski 1982; Radway 1984; Regis 2003). Accordingly, romance novels usually begin by identifying a beloved and reviewing the corrupt state of contemporary society. Once the protagonist and the beloved are introduced, significant barriers to the union emerge. As Regis puts it, "[t]he barrier drives the romance novel" (2003, 32). Barriers often include a central adversary who opposes the union. They may also involve a tension between the protagonist's desire for the love object on the one hand and a desire to maintain a subjectively grounded basis for the protagonist's continued self-expression on the other hand. The more intense the protagonist's attraction to the beloved, the greater the protagonist fears a loss of self and subjectivity. Despite these barriers, the couple's attraction remains strong, with a dramatic or even desperate declaration of love typically being expressed at some point in the narrative. Eventually, the means to overcome the barriers to union are identified and effectuated. Betrothal typically follows, and the story comes to a close.

Whittington's constitutional narrative can be read as following the form of a romantic narrative and its most popular expression in contemporary culture, the romance novel. His work is strongly nostalgic, seeking to unite an ideal past with a corrupted present; it evokes the founding fathers with contemporary constitutional expression. The founding fathers are clearly the central object of his attention. The central adversary is the corrupt, unrestrained judiciary, which obstructs the union of the founding fathers with popular constitutional expression in contemporary politics. Along the way, tensions arise between the objective status of the founding fathers and the subjective status of contemporary constitutional interpretation. Despite these barriers, Whittington dramatically declares that constitutional expression cannot exist without a connection to the founding fathers. As the story ends, Whittington proclaims that the union has been effectuated and that fidelity to the founders will protect contemporary constitutional expression from an overarching judiciary.

The Founding Fathers as the Object of Desire

Just as an intense desire for romantic union provides the plotline of contemporary romance novels, Whittington's work is also driven by a deep desire to unite contemporary constitutional interpretation with the founding fathers. Paralleling the standard romance novel, Whittington seeks to unite the present and the past, offering a story that features a protagonist that is represented by contemporary constitutional expression, and a beloved that is represented by the founding fathers.

The founders are the one true love of Whittington's constitutional narrative, and, as is the wont of romantics, he idealizes the beloved, presenting it as objective, authentic, and flawless, particularly in comparison with contemporary political society, which has strayed far from the path set down by founders, due in large part to the seductions and obstructions of an illegitimate Court. Whittington's work contains no direct criticism of the founding and no indication of why he supports the founding fathers' substantive political choices, other than that they were their choices, legitimated through ratification. He does, however, indicate why he favors their choices at the level of process: the institutional structures they constructed provide an ongoing venue for authentic and democratic constitutional expression in a contemporary context. Imitation being the highest form of flattery, Whittington's work is characterized by a deep desire to recapture the idealized constitutional expression of the founding and to contest corrupt contemporary practices by uniting the superior norms of the past with the debased but still redeemable norms of present day society.

To this end, Whittington argues that the Court should be limited to exercising judicial review only in cases where original intent is clear. This original meaning is discoverable through the founding fathers' documents, records of drafting conventions, popular debates during ratification, and other relevant commentary from the founding period. Establishing the primacy of the founding fathers, he argues that their intentions "serve as an objective source of law independent of the judicial will," which can be discovered and applied objectively (1999b, 43). For Whittington, legitimacy lies in linking otherwise ungrounded judicial decisions to the founding fathers. "The judiciary gains its authority by objectively applying those principles to which the people consented at the founding. Abandoning originalism allows the judiciary to impose value choices that have not been authorized by democratic action," clearly a corrupt and undesirable outcome (1999b, 112). For Whittington, originalism is the only legitimate mode of judicial constitutional interpretation. He resists multiple readings of the Constitution in principle, arguing "that not only is there a right answer to the construction of an interpretive standard, but also that that answer is fixed in the essential forms of the Constitution and does not change" (1999b, 15).

While the union that Whittington desires does not appear to be sexual, this does not preclude an intense or even erotic relationship.[1] As Radway points out, the desire for union need not be explicitly sexual in romance novels: "It matters little whether that care and attention are detailed in general terms or presented as overtly sexual as long as they are extensively described. However, this focus...is in itself erotic" (1984, 105). Relatedly, in her path-breaking book *Between Men: English Literature and Male Homosocial Desire*, queer theorist Eve Sedgwick describes non-sexual same-sex unions between men as homosocial, by which she means they are intense "social bonds between persons of the same sex" that involve desire, but not overt same-sex sexual behavior, which is connoted by the term homosexual (1985, 1). Similarly, in popular culture, the question "who's your daddy?" can elicit not only information about paternal lineage or sexual partnership, but also stories of intense, perhaps even erotic bonding between men who are not sexually involved. In this sense, "daddy" is anyone whose authority and power is accepted as controlling and superior, as, for example, when former Red Sox pitcher Pedro Martinez couldn't overcome the Yankees during the American League baseball playoffs in 2004 and said, "I can't find a way to beat them at this point. What can I say? I just tip my hat and call the Yankees my daddy" (Farhi 2005, C1).

---

1   In this regard, it seems worth noting that the frontispiece of his book *Constitutional Interpretation* is drawn from *The Phaedrus*, Plato's famous dialogue on *eros*.

Barriers to Union: Judiciary as Adversary

Just as barriers drive the plotline of the romance novel, they are also the engine of Whittington's constitutional narrative. Romantic narratives often feature a strong adversary who obstructs the restoration of an uncorrupted past as well as the idealized union that would be featured in it. Whittington's story is no exception. For Whittington and the originalists, an unrestrained Court is the biggest barrier to uniting the past with the present, the founding fathers with contemporary constitutional expression. Contemporary politics is said to be dominated by an overreaching judiciary that impedes the restoration of an uncorrupted society in which contemporary constitutional expression can be united with the ideals of the founding fathers. Thus, Whittington argues that "the Court has facilitated popular evils through constitutional error." Adding that "[t]he history of the American judiciary is not encouraging," he supports his argument with examples of judicially approved slavery, segregation, oppression of "radical subversives," and "emasculation of private property" (1999b, 139). In his view, errors made by the Court "should serve as a warning of the political possibilities once an unwavering focus on the Constitution's terms and purposes is lost" (1999b, 174). In other words, "the judiciary is a thin reed upon which to rest one's hopes for political salvation in a corrupt world" (1999b, 140).

More specifically, Whittington argues that *Griswold* v. *Connecticut*, the 1965 case in which the Court struck down a Connecticut law that prohibited married couples from using contraceptives, is not good law as "there is general originalist agreement that the broad right to privacy developed by Justice William Douglas in *Griswold* to allow the purchase of contraceptives is unjustified by the discoverable Constitution" (1999b, 37). Following the lead of two icons of originalism, Robert Bork and Raoul Berger, Whittington finds that while the Fourteenth Amendment's Due Process Clause protects privacy, it does not protect sexual autonomy (1999b, 36).

Even though the Court has fallen away from the true path, as evidenced by *Griswold* and a wide variety of other cases, it can still be redeemed by restoring the limits set by framers' intent. Thus, Whittington asserts: "If the Court has corrupted us by seducing us into looking to it rather than to the Constitution, it can also play a role in reversing some of that damage" (1999b, 213). To reverse the damage it has wrought and to prevent further incursions, the Court must return to the founding vision and "rededicate itself to its function as the interpreter of the law" (1999b, 213). In this sense, the beloved founders serve to "protect the Court from itself, and in so doing, to protect us from the Court" (1999b, 218–19). While Whittington sarcastically concedes that "[a]dmittedly, originalist jurisprudence has little to offer those who hope to achieve social change through judicial fiat" he adds that "[s]uch progressive optimism must be tempered with a historical informed skepticism" (1999b, 174).

Despite his desire to reduce judicial power and regardless of his embrace of many individual tenets of judicial restraint (for example, the Court should not operate as a source of fundamental change; the Court should presume legislative action constitutional unless framers' intent clearly indicates otherwise), at times, Whittington's intense devotion to the founders nevertheless serves, however inadvertently, to buttress judicial power. Thus, he calls for judicial "activism in the name of the text plus historical evidence," stating that "when the Constitution is knowable, the Court must act vigorously to enforce the limits it places on governmental action" (1999b, 167, 36). Such activism "advances democratic values not through a majoritarian endorsement of judicial restraint...but through the maintenance of popular sovereignty as a governing idea" (1999b, 153). For Whittington, such originalist judicial activism moves gradually toward "correctly grounded doctrine," that is, doctrine consistent with framers' intent (1999b, 170). Thus, he approves of the court striking down the federal criminalization of guns near public schools in *US v. Lopez* in 1995, because the law was "clearly so marginal to the commerce power" that it did not threaten federal power to regulate manufacturing, which he concedes "would have been far more traumatic to the stability of law and of governmental and economic institutions" (1999b, 171).

The structure of the romantic form helps to understand Whittington's apparent ambivalence about judicial power. The most important feature of the romantic plotline is the quest for union. Yet, actively working to make this happen is the greatest fault that can be attributed to the protagonist. To be active is to be suspect. Thus, the protagonist must appear innocent of power and passive in order to avoid being characterized as lacking virtue. Yet, it is only action that will produce the union. As Modleski argues, "they must try to make themselves *look* innocent, and of course in manipulating appearances, they forfeit the very possibility of innocence" (1982, 52).

In this light, Whittington's limited acceptance of originalist judicial activism may fit quite well with his intense desire to unite the founding fathers and contemporary constitutional expression, even while he continues to advocate for judicial restraint. At times, his desire for union is so strong that he goes even further, embracing not just judicial activism but also judicial finality. "Although the judicial obligation to engage in constitutional interpretation is not unique to the courts, since each branch is bound by the sovereign will, the judiciary nonetheless is functionally elevated above the other branches in terms of its specialized capacity to interpret that will" (1999b, 153, 113). Ironically, this seems to leave judicial power unchallengeable by other branches, suggesting that the checks and balances afforded by the separation of powers will not apply in full force to the judiciary. Judges appear to have the power to make final pronouncements about what the framers intended the Constitution to mean. In addition, the judiciary appears to have the final say over the meaning of the sovereign will, which theoretically serves to limit all the branches of government, including the judiciary. But, can those limits be meaningful regarding the judiciary, if it is the judiciary itself which has the final say? And what does that portend for addressing the main barrier to betrothal—the possibility of an overarching judiciary?

Barriers to Union: Fear of Loss of Identity

Another barrier to union that is common to romance novels is the protagonist's fear of loss of identity. The protagonist is often strongly attracted to her beloved at the same time that she fears losing her self to him. The more intense the attraction, the stronger the fear. In Whittington's narrative, contemporary constitutional expression is the protagonist and the founders are the beloved. While Whittington's idealization of the founding fathers makes it impossible for him to directly acknowledge that the founders might be problematic in any way, his narrative nevertheless must indirectly address the fear of the present being dominated by the past, in order to achieve a successful union of the two. Thus, Whittington seeks to maintain an independent identity for contemporary constitutional expression apart from the founders' influence. To that end, he advocates for adequate space for contemporary constitutional expression through the popular branches; he argues that such expression should not be limited by framers' intent; and he calls for judicial restraint in order to limit the influence of the founders on contemporary constitutional construction. These moves suggest a romantic tension in Whittington's narrative between the desire to unite contemporary constitutional discourse with the founders and a desire to maintain a distinct, politically expressive identity apart from them.

Thus, Whittington is a strong advocate for the significance of continued constitutional expression outside of the courts, that is, beyond the scope of framers' intent. His book *Constitutional Construction* chronicles four detailed case studies that have exemplified this practice in the course of American constitutional development. These are: the construction of judicial power during the 1805 impeachment of Samuel Chase, a Supreme Court Justice who was charged with political bias; the construction of federalism in the 1832 nullification crisis during which South Carolina rejected the authority of Congress to pass a protective tariff that would benefit trade originating in the North; the rise of congressional power when President Johnson was impeached in 1868 for resisting a law that Congress passed to limit his power to remove cabinet members at will; and the affirmation of executive power and congressional deference in the Nixon era prior to his resignation in 1974, during which time President Nixon secretly ordered the bombing of Cambodia and regularly impounded monies appropriated by Congress. Whittington argues that each of these cases of constitutional construction is noteworthy not for its particular political outcome but rather for its long range effect on institutional development. Each illustrates that "the Constitution empowers political actors to alter their social and institutional environment," and "demonstrate[s] how political action becomes constitutive of the political order, reshaping how political problems are conceptualized and restructuring what government actions are possible," "provid[ing] an important vehicle for constitutional development and change" (1999a, 18, 16, 208).

Furthermore, by emphasizing the distinct qualities that characterize judicial constitutional interpretation and constitutional construction in the popular branches, Whittington promotes further separation of popular constitutional expression and framers' intent. Thus, he argues that objective judicial constitutional interpretation grounded in framers' intent is discovered through reason and technical legal skills, above the fray of everyday politics. Subjective constitutional interpretation on the part of the popular branches relies on non-originalist imagination, creativity, and political wrangling. As Whittington asserts: "If construction employs the 'imaginative vision' of politics, interpretation is limited to the 'discerning wit' or primarily judicial judgment" (1999a, 6). While the judicially interpreted Constitution is a set of objective rules that are binding and unchangeable short of amendment or revolution, the Constitution constructed by the popular branches is a set of norms and foundations that offers guidance but also allows for ample subjective expression. Whittington argues that these modes of constitutional expression are complementary, with judicial constitutional interpretation supporting legal stability and the maintenance of law established at the founding, and constitutional construction in the popular branches promoting constitutional development and the ability to adapt to changing political circumstances (1999a, ix).

While contemporary constitutional construction in the popular branches may reference the text and the founding fathers, it is not only permissible but even probable that such debates will move into subjective, nonoriginalist territory that is independent of the framers constitutional thought. Compared with the way that judicial interpretation is strictly limited by founders' intent, constitutional construction in the popular branches is remarkably subjective and enormously wide open. Whittington makes this clear by stating that "[t]he idea of construction helps us understand how constitutional meaning is elaborated even when government officials do not seem to be talking about the Constitution, or are not saying anything at all" (1999a, 7).

In order to further ensure adequate space for vibrant and continued constitutional expression in branches other than the judiciary, Whittington counsels judicial restraint in matters that the founders have not addressed, arguing that "our inheritance" from the founders is "not just a law, but the power to make law" (1999b, 217). The judiciary should do its part by refraining from acting when there are gaps left by the founders, when the founding text does not clearly apply to contemporary circumstances and when judicial decrees fail to resolve issues (1999a, 226).

In this context, Whittington often seems to favor the political branches over the judiciary. Thus Whittington asserts: "Despite the failures of constitutional theory adequately to take into account the elaboration of constitutional meaning outside the courts, political practice bears witness to a continuing effort to resist the judicial monopolization of the Constitution and its meaning" (1999a, 207). Whittington hopes to further promote such resistance by uniting contemporary constitutional expression (that is, democratic authority) with the founding. Accordingly he argues that "[c]onstitutional theory must recognize the multifaceted nature of the Constitution and the importance of divided power for realizing its meaning. In doing so, we can begin to recapture some of the richness of the Constitution and to understand the complexity of constitutional government" (1999a, 228). Increased constitutional construction from the popular branches should disempower the courts: "Judicial review should become less relevant to our political life over time, not more" (1999b, 210).

One might wonder whether characterizing the popular branches as more virtuous than the judiciary is consistent with the (Federalist) framers' general skepticism about human nature and institutional power and with Whittington's own characterization of political actors as especially ambitious and often largely unaware of the constitutional dimensions of their arguments. "Ambitious political actors will ultimately turn to the text in order to find support for their own political interests and will construct a vision of constitutional meaning that enshrines their own values and interests" (1999a, 207). He adds that "those engaged in constructive efforts display none of the objectivity valued in the jurisprudential model. Constructions are made by explicit advocates, not by disinterested arbiters" (1999a, 210). Whittington's support for the political branches, despite this apparent ambivalence, makes more sense in the context of considering Whittington's work as a fundamentally romantic narrative. In romance, the protagonist always struggles to maintain a separate identity from the beloved. Ironically, the fear of being overwhelmed by the beloved persists even more strongly as the desire for the beloved deepens, revealing itself at various points along the way in the quest for union, and suggesting something of a resistance to total union with the founders, lest contemporary popular constitutional expression be completely subsumed by the dictates of the past.

Declaration of Love

The depth of Whittington's devotion to the founders should by now be abundantly clear. He asserts that contemporary constitutional expression could not go on without the founders, which is about as desperate an expression of need as there can be. Arguing that the people must affirm the creation of the founding fathers' power in order to claim the power of self-governance in contemporary politics, he asserts: "We can replicate the fundamental political act of the founders only if we are willing to recognize the reality of their act. Stripping them of their right to constitute a government would likewise strip us of our own" (1999b, 133). In the vernacular of the romance novel, contemporary constitutional expression would be nothing without the founders!

Betrothal

In the standard romance novel, betrothal typically follows the identification of the means to overcome the barriers to union and the declaration of love. In the end, Radway suggests, "all danger has been expunged," leaving nothing but "the promise of utopian bliss" (1984, 97, 100). Thus, Whittington's *Constitutional Interpretation* ends with the belief that originalism will protect contemporary constitutional construction from an overzealous Court, and *Constitutional Construction* ends even more blissfully with a call for an increasingly "integrative approach that connects the Constitution to the actual operation of government institutions and to continuing political conflicts" (1999a, 228).

When the Romance is Over: The Limitations of the Standard Form

There is much to recommend in Whittington's originalism. His theory is far more theoretically and politically sophisticated than the standard originalist fare that can be found in the work of Robert Bork (1990; 1996) or Raoul Berger (1977). His revival of the founders provides an important link between past and present. His form of originalism offers a theory of popular sovereignty that moves beyond the typically flat equation of the legislature with the majority and the judiciary with the minority that one finds in much of mainstream constitutional theory. And, after all is said and done, who doesn't love a good romance? Especially while lovers are still infatuated with each other.

But what happens when the romance is over? Romantic narratives have at least three significant limitations that prevent them from addressing this important question. First, the idealization of the central relationship prevents the romantic narrative from adequately addressing past brutality and contempt or anticipating any possibility of it in the future. Second, because transformation ends with betrothal, romantic narratives cannot acknowledge or anticipate significant change in the future. Third, romantic narratives typically lack the sense of humor that is necessary to make an adequate transition from infatuation to a more complex and developed relationship that will sustain over time.

Brutality

Tania Modleski argues that romance novels typically idealize the beloved in a manner that significantly elides the faults or even the brutality of the beloved (1982, 36). While the beloved is usually "not suspected of being either insane or murderous," according to Modleski, he "*is* more or less brutal" (1982, 40; emphasis in original). During the course of the story the protagonist "is virtuous only insofar as she remains ignorant and confused" about the beloved's seemingly contemptuous behavior. Thus, the heroine must remain (or appear to remain) largely unaware of the beloved's brutality. Any apparent brutality that has been revealed in the course of the story is interpreted to be a result of the deep love that the beloved feels for the protagonist, rather than the product of contempt and hostility (Modleski 1982, 41). That is, the beloved might well have appeared to have treated the protagonist very badly, but only because he had been overwhelmed by the depth of his extraordinarily strong feelings for her. Readers, on the other hand, are typically quite aware of the brutality from start to finish. However, because they are usually intimately acquainted with the stock formula that structures the romance, they know that any apparent brutality and contempt will be transformed into love and commitment by the end of the story (Modleski 1982, 43). Romance provides the fantasy that is the basis of this transformation.

For example, in Jane Austen's *Pride and Prejudice*, Elizabeth Bennett is alternatively attracted to and repulsed by Mr Fitzwilliam Darcy, a rich suitor who appears to be haughty and contemptuous throughout the book. He gives the impression that he is cold and indifferent towards Elizabeth due to differences in their social standing, and he seems to have robbed an alternative suitor, Mr George Wickham, of his rightful inheritance. Yet by the end of the story Elizabeth is convinced that she has been unfairly prejudiced against Darcy from the start, that her judgments have been based on faulty evidence, that his heart is really kind and generous, and that it is Wickham who is really the scoundrel. True to form, the story ends with the betrothal of Elizabeth and Darcy.

The story of *Pride and Prejudice* has been reproduced in contemporary popular culture on many occasions, as for example in Helen Fielding's *Bridget Jones* series, which spearheaded the "chick-lit" explosion in the mid 1990s (Donadio 2006). Following the original romantic form to a tee, in the beginning of each book in the series Bridget Jones believes Mark Darcy to be prideful and disdainful, only to find out by the end of each installment that he is really all that she has been looking for in a man.

Another classic model of the standard romance can be found in Charlotte Brontë's *Jane Eyre*. Throughout the book, Jane wonders about the intentions of the master of the house, the secretive and apparently philandering Mr Rochester. Like Darcy, Rochester is frequently mysterious, brooding, harsh, and even rude. But he is also clever and humorous. Like Elizabeth, Jane is simultaneously attracted to and repulsed by Rochester's character. Due to seemingly insuperable class differences she is unsure of Rochester's attraction to her. (She is, after all, in his employ as a mere governess.) He seems to have many mistresses, as evidenced by his illegitimate child, whom Jane has been called upon to educate. And then there is the matter of a mysterious and violent madwoman who lives in his attic and periodically brutalizes various household visitors. She turns out to be his wife, a Creole he married in Jamaica 15 years prior to meeting Jane. These revelations create much consternation in Jane initially. However, by the end of the story all of this has been explained and reinterpreted. Jane comes to understand that Rochester has had the great misfortune to have married a madwoman. His sense of duty and personal generosity towards his wife lead him to keep her in his house, at great expense and difficulty. Despite this, she eventually burns the house to the ground and jumps off the roof to her death. In this story, Rochester is victimized by her insanity, as he is maimed and (temporarily) blinded by the fire. Once Jane understands this, she is free to marry Rochester, in an apparently happily-ever-after fashion, and then bear him a son.

Similarly, in the popular medical drama *House*, which debuted on the Fox network in 2004, Dr Alison Cameron contemplates the character of her boss, the maimed and misanthropic Dr House. House is brilliant yet eccentric, brutish yet oddly compelling. As a consequence Cameron is simultaneously attracted to and repulsed by him. As House himself comments: "I'm complicated. Chicks dig that" (Millman 2006). Because this series is still in production as of 2007, the final form of their relationship is still in question. However, if the series remains true to form, it will eventuate in union, and House's brutish behavior will be reinterpreted through that lens.

The problem is that this formula works only for readers who are fans of the romantic narrative form. Thus, Whittington has little to offer those who do not share his devotion to the founding fathers. Rather than seriously engaging the exclusion of women and brutality against African-Americans as significant features of the founding fathers' handiwork, as, for example, Leslie Goldstein does in her thoughtful book *In Defense of the Text* (1991), Whittington seems to simply dismiss such concerns, perhaps somewhat defensively, with an arguably contemptuous tone of his own: "[I]n an originalist America, would not the government engage in flogging and branding of criminals, forced sterilization, white supremacy, electronic eavesdropping, silencing of evolutionary teachings and so on?" (1999b, 173). While he concedes that an originalist judiciary would not prevent such evils, he seems content with the conclusion that "it would not impose them, either" (1999b, 173). Continuing in this peculiar tone, he asserts that "[s]uch positive government action requires decisions by political representatives, not by judges, and thus the charge really turns on the willingness of legislatures to issue appropriations for branding irons" (1999b, 173). He rather dismissively concludes, "[t]he adoption of appropriate interpretive standards can only do so much. The rest is politics, and always has been" (1999b, 173). While the goal of self-government may be desirable to majority and minority alike, various critical theorists have made it clear that there is substantial doubt as to whether, to use Whittington's words, that goal "comports well with the actual experience of politics" at the founding, to say nothing of today (Bell, 1987; 1992; 1996; Williams 1992).

So why would Whittington's narrative be compelling to those who no longer are (or perhaps never were) much enamored of the founders given evidence of exclusion and brutality? Put differently, a narrative that seeks union with white patriarchs is not likely to be very compelling to those who are aware that they have been systematically oppressed by "the man." As will be discussed in greater detail in Chapter 4, critical race theorists have long been quite critical of the way that originalism typically extracts from its narrative the founders' brutality and injustice regarding slavery and race.

Whittington seems to be unable to address the problem of brutality adequately, because he has chosen to tell his story in the standard romantic form, which appears to be seriously limited in this regard. His idealization of the beloved founders seems to compel him (and his readers) to adopt a fantasy that elides the apparent brutality of the founders. Consistent with the fantasy about brutality that is so central to the romantic form, does he mean for us to excuse the founders' legitimation of slavery on the grounds that they loved us so much that they could never have intended that level of brutality? Or perhaps that they withheld a judgment against slavery for our own good, so that we could develop fully democratic institutions that would eventually allow us to reject slavery on our own? In either case, the standard romantic form prevents him from fulfilling his goal of solving the majoritarian dilemma in a way that will be acceptable to minority and majority alike. Whittington's romance seems to speak only to true believers and thus falls far short of his own high standard.

Whittington and the originalists could give up the fantasy of recovering an idyllic founding moment that is devoted to an ongoing but uncomplicated union and move to a more complex and disturbing understanding of the birth of American constitutional discourse as well as the relationship between the past and present in its ongoing development. This might be done by retaining, but also reinterpreting, the standard romance.

Along these lines, John Fiske argues that romance may be read in a manner that leads not only to support for the powers-that-be (in this case, the founders), but also in a more populist way that challenges such authority. Speaking of romance novels, he suggests that the relationship between brutality and fantasy may be read in multiple ways: "As a result of the mix of empowerment and self-interested, self-produced meanings of gender relations, the reader is motivated to challenge the patriarchal power exerted through everyday relations with her husband, and to increase her own space within it, to redistribute it, however slightly, towards herself" (Fiske 1989b, 56). Rather than reading the romance novel solely as propagating the view that the price of having a marriage is the acceptance of the patriarchy, Fiske asks us to consider that the complex characters "chicks dig" (according to Dr House) can empower women to be active interpreters of the romance novel, as well as of their own lives (1989b, 119). Of course, Whittington's originalist romance might continue to be read simply as reinscribing the power of the founders through judicial restraint (just as romance novels are often read as buttressing patriarchal power). This might be understood as the price of forging a union between the founders and contemporary constitutional expression. Alternatively, we might take up Fiske's invitation. By revealing the complexity of the relationship between the founding and contemporary constitutional expression that is evidenced in Whittington's originalism, readers are invited to (re)interpret the text in a more subversive manner that is still consistent with romance and look for the ways that Whittington's originalist narrative might empower populist challenges to the founders' power, as I have tried to do throughout this chapter. As Carol Shields notes in her biography of Jane Austen, readers "have always had the power to disrupt the bland surfaces of pedestrian fiction and convert the fluff of romance to something more nourishing" (2001, 38).

The standard romantic form also might be amended in a manner that would allow it to directly address brutality, thus opening up alternative narrative possibilities and political meanings while still being recognized as a romance. Jean Rhys offers an example of this in her 1966 novel *Wide Sargasso Sea*, a "prequel" to Charlotte Brontë's *Jane Eyre*. In *Wide Sargasso Sea*, rather than secretly closeting away Rochester's Creole wife in his attic, however unsuccessfully, as in *Jane Eyre*, Antoinette Cosway is front and center in Rhys' story. The novel is set shortly after the slaves of British-colonized Jamaica have been emancipated. The story alternates between the perspective of Antoinette in the first and third sections of the book and that of her unnamed husband (Rochester) in the second section, thus presenting multiple perspectives in order to tell a complicated story of race and slavery and patriarchy and power in the context of their marriage. In this story, British Rochester's racism causes him to brutalize Antoinette due to her Creole heritage. Sexism obliterates her identity as society compels her to change her surname, and Rochester takes away her first name, substituting Bertha for Antoinette. Bertha descends into madness not necessarily because of personal illness or disability, but rather because of societal dysfunction and disease. This leads Rochester to return to England, and eventually Bertha burns down his house, then jumps off its roof to her death. Rather than Bertha's brutality providing a temporary obstacle to Rochester and Jane's happy and (re)productive union, as in *Jane Eyre*, in Rhys' story it is Rochester's brutality that leads to the tragedy that ends her story. Thus, *Wide Sargasso Sea* offers a much more complicated context, grounded in an analysis of sexism and racism, which provides a very different foundation for the seemingly perfect romantic ending of *Jane Eyre*, the otherwise rather uncomplicated betrothal of Jane and Rochester.[2] Rhys' example suggests that originalists like Whittington might be able to account for the way that the brutality of sexism and racism informs the American constitutional narrative by amending, rather than abandoning, the standard romantic form.

Transformation

In romance, all significant action ends with betrothal. As Radway argues, the protagonist is "required to do nothing more than *exist*" in union with the beloved, union being the only significant point of transformation in the romantic narrative (1984, 97; emphasis in original). Once the union of past and present is achieved, the

---

2   This analysis parallels the path-breaking work of Sandra M. Gilbert and Susan Gubar (1979). They argue that the madwoman represents the author's other, onto whom she projects a variety of rage and anxiety stemming from the rampant sexism endemic to society at the time. Also see the complication of the Jane Eyre romance along sexuality lines offered in Jeanette Winterson (1998).

quest is over. All subsequent events occur in the context of this initial transformation. Romance typically does not acknowledge or anticipate the possibility of further transformation. Yet, however remote it may seem from the perspective of infatuated lovers at the point of betrothal, transformation remains a distinct possibility, the likelihood of which increases as the romance fades. Who amongst us is not familiar with the age-old complaint of the no longer infatuated lover, "you've changed." While the problem of transformation is common in relationships, the standard romance is ill-equipped to address it. To the extent that significant transformations are acknowledged at all in the standard romance, they are thought to be evidence of corruption, which signals the need to restore the superior norms of the past.

Perhaps the most major transformative event that originalists must address in their romantic constitutional narrative is the advent of legal realism in the 1920s and 1930s. For originalists such as Johnathan O'Neill (2005) and Christopher Wolfe (1986) legal realism amounts to a "fundamental rupture" that opens up a whole new form of legal consciousness, tempting judges (and scholars) to renounce their heretofore unselfconscious faith in originalism. Yet, apart from bemoaning such a development, and yearning for a return to an uncorrupted past, standard originalism has little to offer to address this problem. O'Neill, for example, argues that the rupture occasioned by legal realism "undermined nothing less than the traditional rationales for democracy, judicial review based on a written constitution, and the rule of law" (2005, 30). Accordingly, the rest of his book explores various attempts to resurrect originalism and restore tradition, but alas, by the end of the story we are forced to conclude that there is no getting back to the Garden. Legal realism seems to have changed constitutional interpretation forever, as it becomes vastly more plural and complicated East of Eden.

To his credit Whittington concedes that his narrative is theoretically contestable, even though he also insists that, despite contestation, there is one true narrative, and it is his. Thus he confidently asserts: "Though this construction, like all constructions, must be contended for in the political sphere in order to be made good, the arguments presented here indicate the results to which the outcome of that political debate should conform" (1999b, 15). Although transformative elements may be introduced into constitutional debates, their end point is, or rather should be, fixed. Thus, the type of debate that Whittington envisions seems designed to stave off, rather than accommodate, significant transformation, at least when it comes to judicial constitutional interpretation.

As we saw with the problem of brutality, the standard romance might also be amended to address the issue of transformation in a more satisfactory manner. The familiar film *Gone with the Wind* offers an interesting example of how this might be done. Initially written by Margaret Mitchell in 1936, the filmic version was released in 1939 and continues to be regarded as one of the most popular romances ever adapted to the screen. Regis argues that *Gone with the Wind* is not a standard romance, because it does not end with betrothal (2003, 50). However, an amended romance such as *Gone with the Wind* might yield an alternative approach to the problem of transformation.[3]

---

3   For another use of an amended romance see Bonnie Honig's work on gothic romance in *Democracy and the Foreigner* (2003).

The focus of the movie, of course, is the passionate, yet troubled, romance of Rhett Butler and Scarlett O'Hara, set in the backdrop of the Civil War. By the end of the movie, following the death of their daughter, the union of Rhett and Scarlett, always rocky, appears to be headed for divorce. Additionally, the Old South appears to be on the brink of a major transformation. Just as the advent of legal realism forever altered the terrain of constitutional interpretation, so too do various events taking place during the Civil War transform Rhett and Scarlett, to say nothing of the Southern way of life. While Scarlett and Rhett spend a great deal of time and energy resisting this rupture throughout the film, in the end Rhett offers an interesting alternative to the standard romantic response of endless yearning for the past when faced with the possibility of transformation. Thus, while Scarlett responds to Rhett's decision to leave with the questions: "Where shall I go? What shall I do?" he seems completely detached from the fantasy of ever reuniting with Scarlett, responding with his now famous line: "Frankly my dear, I don't give a damn." Thus, Rhett appears to be quite able to embrace the changes to come as positive, or at the very least inevitable, however regrettable they may have seemed during earlier stages of the movie. In addition, Rhett provides an alternative to the Golden Age narrative represented by the gentility of the Old South. Though he remains loyal to the South during the war, Rhett is nevertheless a self-interested businessman intent on making a profit from it. A realist through and through, he predicts before the war has even begun that the South will lose to the industrially superior North.

Scarlett, on the other hand, continues to fantasize that she will somehow be able to devise a scheme that will lead to reunion with Rhett, even after he announces the fundamental rupture between them. Adopting the method of the originalists, she calls upon her dead father for advice. Representing Southern gentility, he tells her to return to the land. And so she decides to go home to Tara, the family plantation, continuing to engage in the fantasy of (re)union, saying: "I'll think of some way to get him back. After all, tomorrow is another day." This last line of the film resonates with her primary approach to difficult situations throughout the movie: avoidance. Each time she is faced with an irreconcilable problem she responds by saying: "I can't think about that now. I'll think about that tomorrow." But of course, tomorrow never quite arrives. Deeply enmeshed in the standard romantic narrative, she refuses to fully acknowledge the difficulties of the present today, tomorrow, or any other day.

Thus, the character of Scarlett can be understood as a cautionary figure who represents the problems associated with embracing a standard romantic narrative framework. In the last scene of the movie, Scarlett is shown resolutely standing in front of Tara, passionately poised to put her plan into effect. The problem is, just as we can all see that the war has destroyed the union of Rhett and Scarlett, so too has it completely decimated Tara and the Old South. Similarly, we might come to understand the standard form of originalism as a somewhat compelling, yet ultimately cautionary, tale. In that light, what may happen after Rhett leaves, discussed below, becomes that much more interesting.

Humor

After the romance inevitably fades lovers must find a way to leave each other or live with each other, brutality and transformational change notwithstanding. Typically, those who stay must strike a balance between attachment and distance. A sense of humor helps. Whittington's originalism, like most romance, lacks proportion and a sense of humor. The seriousness with which he undertakes his quest leads him to idealize his first love, the founding fathers, and to overestimate the strength of his adversary, the unrestrained judiciary. Throughout this chapter I have tried to use humor, mostly of the tongue-in-cheek variety, to disrupt the remarkable seriousness of Whittington's originalism. Using a strategy such as parody could also serve to disrupt the apparent stability of originalism and perhaps lead beyond the problems that are endemic to the standard romance.

Parody always comments humorously on another narrative, usually in an irreverent fashion, revealing the self-seriousness of the original narrative, as well as the multiplicity of interpretations that can emerge from it, despite its best intentions, no pun intended. The object of parody is typically a powerful person or influential narrative that is unconcerned with the perspective of the less than powerful. The original narrative is usually paralleled in a manner that reveals its weaknesses, to the end of reforming it. Parody reveals this by mimicking the original, and exaggerating it, making its ridiculous features more visible. The more serious the original, the more outrageous the parody, as the humor typically stems from the original's often unselfconscious insistence that power is given or natural rather than contingent and constructed. Parody, on the other hand, makes everything much more complicated than it appears to be at first glance.

The Wind Done Gone, the 2001 "unauthorized parody"[4] of *Gone with the Wind*, offers an interesting example of how parody can be used to construct an alternative story, while still remaining within the form of the original, the romantic form in this case. Written by Alice Randall, this literary send-up parallels the story of *Gone with the Wind*, but with a twist. In Randall's parody, the Old South is characterized more by racism and complex power relations than by gentility and simplicity. Brutality and transformation are central to her parody, in which almost nothing is what it had appeared to be in *Gone with the Wind*. Rather than ending with Rhett and Scarlett's divorce, as in *Gone with the Wind*, or harking back to their glory days as in the more standard romance, Randall moves forward to see what might happen in the wake of the transformations wrought by the Civil War, both in terms of their relationship and in terms of race relations in the Old South. In fact, there are no glory days to hark back to in this story, for plantation life is filled with hypocrisy and brutality from the get-go.

This story is written from the first person perspective of Cynara, a mixed-raced slave who is the much maligned and neglected product of a brutal sexual relationship between Mammy and "Planter" (the name given to Gerald O'Hara in this story), making her the half-sister of "Other" (Scarlett O'Hara). Plantation life at "Tata" (Tara) is anything but genteel and simple. Other is favored by everyone, including

---

4   This phrase appears on the cover of the book.

Cynara's own mother with whom she develops a relationship that is at best uneasy. This fosters a life-long competition between the two for the attention of Mammy, as well as for "R" (Rhett Butler). Rather than freeing Cynara to resolve this situation, Planter sells her off, and she winds up in "Beauty's" (madam Belle Watling's) brothel. Despite the clear brutality present throughout, white Southerners in power often seem hapless and shockingly unaware of their persistent self-interestedness, while slaves with seemingly little power often appear rather intelligent and resourceful, if also somewhat manipulative, given the material realities of these power relations.

In the course of the story, both Cynara and the Old South are transformed, emerging on the other side intact, but significantly altered in terms of their possibilities and limitations. After persevering through the brutality of slavery at Tata, Cynara enters into a long-term relationship in Atlanta with R., a Confederate loyalist, eventually marrying him and touring Europe with him. Of course, an interracial relationship such as theirs is laced with complicated power relations on an everyday basis. Reveling in the hope of Reconstruction, Cynara forsakes R. in favor of a black congressman from Alabama. Despite his apparent betrothal to the "gap-toothed girl," the Congressman charms Cynara away while she is accompanying R. on one of his lobbying trips to Washington. Scandal and despair follow as it becomes clear that political and social realities make their relationship (and reconstruction) impossible to sustain. As the book closes, Cynara, now pregnant, decides to give her child (Cyrus) to the Congressman and the gap-toothed girl, cementing their relationship just as she withdraws to live alone on the banks of the Maryland shore. The story does not conclusively resolve whether R. or the Congressman is the father of Cyrus (who Cynara calls Moses).[5] At the end of the novel, Cynara waits for Moses' "color to show or not show" (Randall 2001, 205). The question of paternity is now much more complicated than it might have been, for it has been reconstituted by intertwining it with race. While the open-endedness of this ending recognizes that the problems of paternal power and racial relations will persist well beyond this story, it suggests that both have been significantly reconstituted by the integration of brutality, transformation, and parody into this narrative.

Indeed, paternity and race turn out to be quite complicated for most of the characters in this story. By the end of the book, most of the seemingly white characters are revealed to be mixed race, as are many of the black characters. In a 2001 interview, Alice Randall stated that she was interested in representing how various groups were marginalized in the Old South, explaining "the only positive characters in my book who [are entirely white] are the gay characters. It's part of the parody that when I bring the white characters over, most of them eventually I reveal to be black. But I didn't think it would be fair to transform all of the characters. Not everyone is black, so I decided I would leave two positive characters white—the two gay characters" (Goss 2001).[6] Thus, "Dreamy Gentleman" (Ashley Wilkes) is revealed to be a gay man who

---

5   This is perhaps a reference to the Biblical Moses, who led the Hebrews out of slavery under the Egyptians. Despite persevering for 40 years in a journey through the desert, Moses was never allowed to see the Promised Land.

6   Interestingly, Goss's interview in *The Advocate*, the national gay and lesbian newsmagazine, is the only one that I came across that mentions the gay subplots.

engages in interracial sexual relationships, and Beauty is shown to be a lesbian despite her apparent love for R. and her occupation as a madam.

Thus, *The Wind Done Gone* acknowledges the complexity of power, particularly as expressed across racial, gender, and sexual identity. Rather than offering a romantic if brutal resolution of the problem of power, grounded in the union of past and present, which grinds to a halt once achieved, or deferring to paternity as an authoritative basis of power and interpretation, Randall's parody complicates power's lineage and sends-up the frailties and fantasies of the powerful, as seen from the perspective of those on the margins. The acknowledgement of brutality, the possibility of transformation (however limited), and the laughter of the "powerless" all produce a future in which the complexity and the persistence of power is transformed. Individuals, relationships, and society all continue to develop within, not in spite of, various contradictions, as power persists despite its apparent transformation.

Conclusion

When the infatuation of romance fades, lovers have to integrate their idealized romance into a more complex vision that is proportionate with the rest of the world. Such a vision must look forward into a changing future that encompasses both conflict and transformation with a sense of humor. If Whittington and the originalists would be willing to amend their romance, they could still retain its basic form, as well as the goal of authentic contemporary constitutional expression. However, acknowledging the limitations of the story might alter the confidence and the substance of their expression.

Nevertheless, the limitations discussed above are not unique to Whittington, or even to originalism, so it seems problematic to simply fault them for failing to adequately address them and to leave it at that. As will become clear in subsequent chapters, every narrative form has its limitations. Yet, once the limits of the "original" are acknowledged, it is possible to redirect contemporary constitutional discourse away from its current impasse. Once the givenness of the original is questioned, it (and the focus of the discourse that it perpetuates) are ripe for parody. Rather than continuing to focus on directly resolving the majoritarian dilemma, the usual approach in contemporary constitutional discourse, this book seeks to shift the discussion to understanding the strengths and limitations of each of the major narrative forms available in constitutional theory and the way each form tends, however inadvertently, to lead us back to the same old impasse that has hamstrung the mainstream debate for several generations. Using popular culture and parody to call attention to the relationship between form and content, I seek to dislodge the impasse and set the stage for the emergence of alternative narratives. Without completely abandoning familiar narrative forms, I offer examples of a practice of constitutional interpretation that incorporates transformation as well as stability, a realistic portrayal of brutality as well as the escape of fantasy, and, above all, humor.

To that end, Chapter 3 explores Ronald Dworkin's attempt to provide a comedic narrative of liberal judicial activism that accounts for the possibility of transformation while continuing to centralize the authority of the founding fathers. Yet, like romance, Dworkin's comedic constitutional theory fails to adequately acknowledge and account for brutality and contempt.

Chapter 4 explores critical race theorist Derrick Bell's attempt to provide a tragic constitutional narrative which directly addresses the brutality and contempt associated with racism (1987; 1992; 1996). Bell argues that racism has been a foundational and indestructible aspect of the US constitutional dialogue since the nation's inception, when the founding fathers made the fateful decision to trade African-American rights in order to secure an economically prosperous union.

While Bell regularly incorporates popular culture into his constitutional narrative, relying on science fiction and other forms of fantasy, the tragic form that guides his work seems to rule out the use of humor as a tool of destabilization, thus inadvertently strengthening *status quo* power. A more humorous, perhaps self-consciously ironic narrative might serve to be more empowering and perhaps more destabilizing than Bell's meaningful yet extraordinarily painful tragedy, helping to obviate the criticism that is most often leveled against his work: it is hopelessly enervating to the point of political debilitation.

Chapters 5 and 6 provide two extended examples of populist parodies of power that address this problem while discussing the options of leaving and staying, in the context of a parody of *Bush* v. *Gore* and *Lawrence* v. *Texas*, respectively. Each is grounded in popular culture and laced with tongue-in-cheek humor. Chapter 5 offers a parody of judicial identity, which discusses the Supreme Court's decision in *Bush* v. *Gore* as a (political) coming out narrative. Drawing on queer theory, Chapter 5 explores what constitutional discourse might look like absent a myth of origin to reference in order to legitimate a particular constitutional decision. Chapter 6 summarizes the work of the previous chapters by concluding with a parodic reading of the narrative forms of contemporary constitutional discourse, inspired by the popular reality television show *Queer Eye for the Straight Guy*. This chapter evaluates, makes-over, and sends-up romantic, comedic, and tragic narrative accounts of constitutional change as played out in the context of the change in the Supreme Court's treatment of sodomy laws, from *Bowers* v. *Hardwick* to *Lawrence* v. *Texas*. Chapters 5 and 6 present two of many possible examples that could be imagined, using populist readings to create alternative narratives that parody and challenge the parameters of the standard elite discussion. Designed to destabilize mainstream constitutional discourse and move it past its current impasse, these parodies aim to open up space in which additional alternative narratives might emerge, space that Robert Cover and Paul Brest anticipated over 20 years ago in their path-breaking work on the founding and judicial legitimacy, in which they encouraged scholars to explore and to bring new stories, new practices, and new worlds into being in constitutional interpretation.

Chapter 3

Who's Your Daddy?
Judicial Activism as a Soap Opera

Introduction

Ronald Dworkin's work has long focused on legitimating an active use of judicial review in order to forward a liberal constitutional narrative that would accommodate the previously excluded, to the end of fostering equal rights and tolerance for all. He has been cited as "the most comprehensive theorist" of the living Constitution, forwarding "the idea that the Constitution's abstract rights provisions must be interpreted in light of changing historical conditions and moral understandings" (Keck 2004, 48). He is a chaired professor at both New York University and University College in London and is retired from a chair at Oxford. His faculty profile on New York University's website notes that a recent collection entitled *Reading Dworkin Critically* describes him, as "probably the most influential figure in contemporary Anglo-American legal theory." Dworkin's site also suggests that he is "probably one of the two or three contemporary authors whom legal scholars will be reading 200 years from now."

As discussed in Chapter 2, originalists have long insisted that the founding fathers would have rejected iconic cases such as *Brown* v. *Board of Education* as well as a wide variety of other cases that recognize the equal rights and individual autonomy of those who were previously denied equal protection due to race, sex, and a variety of other longstanding bases of exclusion. After all, in *Brown* Chief Justice Warren declared the intent of the framers' inconclusive, and the decision proceeded from there. Dworkin, however, seeks to legitimize *Brown*, *Roe*, and a variety of other activist cases that further liberal political principles by establishing their lineage to the founding fathers (1996, 13). As a liberal initially concerned with authoritatively grounding the Warren Court's decisions, and later with resisting the conservative challenge to New Deal jurisprudence beginning with the Nixon administration's embrace of originalist jurisprudence and strict construction,[1] Dworkin has spent a good deal of his career trying to reclaim the mantle of framers' intent from the originalists, arguing that they have distorted the founding fathers' views to serve conservative political ends.[2] The problem is the founders seem to be primarily responsible for establishing the very exclusions that Dworkin seeks to eliminate in their name. Thus, Dworkin seeks to offer a constitutional narrative that transforms the founding fathers' illiberal past into a more hopeful and egalitarian future.

---

1   See Brigham (2002) for further elaboration of this point. For a different perspective on the rise and fall of originalism see O'Neill (2005).

2   Although he has written extensively on this topic, Dworkin's early essay, "Constitutional Cases," is perhaps his most famous in this regard (1977, 130–49).

Dworkin is also interesting in that he, like Keith Whittington, whose work was discussed in Chapter 1, is concerned with the relationship between narrative and law. Dworkin goes further than Whittington, however, calling for exploring the connections between law, literature, and even popular culture, in the form of soap operas. His attention to soap operas is perhaps not so surprising when one considers that in the early 1980s they were considered to be perhaps "in the vanguard not just of TV art, but of all popular narrative art" (Modleski 1982, 87). Thus, in the context of a much cited debate with literary theorist Stanley Fish about the relationship between law and literature, Dworkin suggests that "we can improve our understanding of law by comparing legal interpretation with interpretation in other fields of knowledge, particularly literature" (1985, 237). More specifically, Dworkin argues that "judges are like authors jointly creating a chain novel in which each writes a chapter that makes sense as part of the story as a whole" (1996, 10). Cautioning that it is "unrealistic" to think that any constitutional narrative would "miraculously [have] the unity of something written by a single author," Dworkin imagines this chain novel to be multi-authored and somewhat disjointed, likening it to a soap opera (1986, 237). Each author is engaged in the Herculean task of interpreting the "meaning of the work as a whole" in an attempt to show "which way of reading...the text reveals it as the best work of art" (1985, 520–21).

Like most mainstream constitutional theorists, Dworkin is concerned with demonstrating that his method of constitutional interpretation will adequately restrain unelected judges from forwarding their personal political preferences in an unprincipled, and hence illegitimate, manner. Like Whittington and the originalists, he argues that textual integrity and coherence should constrain authors whose work appears later in the chain, and thus that they should be limited in a manner that earlier authors, particularly the first author(s) (that is, the founders), would not have been (Dworkin 1985, 543–5). Although he concedes that there is a range from which judges seek to choose the best interpretation, Dworkin argues that mistakes are possible, that some answers will be better than others, and that ultimately there is one right answer. This is the answer that Hercules, the ideal judge with full information and plenty of time to decide, would give. Actual judges must justify their choices by reference to political theories of, for example, equality and justice, thereby revealing "the value of that body of law in political terms by demonstrating the best principle or policy it can be taken to serve" without reducing interpretation to a subjective "matter of personal or partisan politics" (1985, 544, 527). In Dworkin's view, originalism's failure to offer such a theory exacerbates the problem of judicial discretion. Thus he sets out to show that "originalism cannot save us from judicial power; on the contrary its arbitrary distinctions intensify that power" (1993, 144).

In the course of his debate with Dworkin, Fish proves to be much less concerned about the abuse of judicial discretion, because he is convinced that a good deal of constraint is already built into the system. For Fish, interpretation is itself a structure of constraints that serves to shape subjective preference. Additional external constraints are not necessary, because interpretive practices are so well-defined that any relevant interpretive community would not be able to recognize as "judicial" an opinion that was "really" different.

Interpreters are constrained by their tacit awareness of what is possible and not possible to do, and what is and is not a reasonable thing to say, what will and will not be heard as evidence, in a given enterprise; and it is within those same constraints that they see and bring others to see the shape of the documents to whose interpretation they are committed. (Fish 1982, 562)

He adds that legal interpretation is particularly prone to these constraints as it continually refers to the past in the form of a history of previous decisions (Fish 1982, 558).

[E]ven if one 'decides' to 'ignore' them or 'violate' them or 'set them aside,' the actions of ignoring and violating and setting aside will themselves have a shape that is constrained by those practices. (Fish 1982, 553)

In addition to lessening his concern about judicial discretion, Fish's insights about narrative constraint lead him to be significantly critical of Dworkin's goal of offering a truly transformative constitutional narrative. For Fish, the founding author is every bit as constrained as subsequent interpreters, because the creator of a text is as much embedded "in the context of a set of practices" as subsequent authors and interpreters (Fish 1982, 553). While Fish concedes that "[t]his does not mean that the decisions of the first author are wholly determined," he insists that the field of choice is significantly more constrained by practices governing interpretation than Dworkin's transformative vision admits (Fish 1982, 533).

However, Fish's critique overlooks that which he and Dworkin share, namely, the extraordinarily serious tone that is characteristic of most academic writing. This seriousness prevents both Fish and Dworkin from considering the possibility of humor and parody as an important component of transformative strategy, which leads to an overly sober assessment of the possibility of transforming any legal narrative in the case of Fish and an unsuccessful attempt at transforming a specific legal narrative in the case of Dworkin. In doing so, Dworkin and Fish, both widely known in academic circles for their liberalism and advocacy of a living Constitution, ironically, if inadvertently, wind up lending support to *status quo* legal narratives.

Following Fish, I argue that the comedic narrative form that Dworkin employs in his story of the founding fathers inadvertently stabilizes rather than undermines the originalist narrative of the founding fathers; it thus fails to fulfill his goal of transforming the founders' illiberal past into a more tolerant and inclusive future. Departing from Fish, I argue that transformation may yet be possible if Dworkin is read not as a straight comedy but as a comedic narrative informed by parody. To explore that possibility further, I begin by reviewing the elements of comedy, suggesting that both Dworkin and soap operas can be, and usually are, read as following a comedic narrative form. I then suggest that some comedies may also be read as parodies. Using the soap opera *One Life to Live* (*OLTL*) as a model, I show how Dworkin's comedy can also be read as a parody, furthering his goal of transforming founding authority in contemporary constitutional discourse.

Dworkin's work has been widely read as seeking to defend a version of the legal regime in the United States, admittedly with particular emphasis placed on enlarging the founding fathers' constitutional vision. Such a reading of Dworkin assumes a stable and widely accepted definition of legitimacy. By adopting a strategy of parody that has been modeled in popular culture in general and soap operas in particular, I mean to suggest that, under certain circumstances, contemporary constitutional theorists such as Dworkin can, like popular culture, be read to contain the seeds of democratic transformation of the dominant order rather than simply a defense of it. Read through the lens of parody, as exemplified in the soap opera *OLTL*'s parody of paternity, power, and the law, Dworkin's work has the potential to transform contemporary constitutional discourse by contesting, rather than assuming, the stability of its most basic term—legitimacy—and the role that the founding fathers play in establishing and maintaining it. It may also open up the meaning of other related concepts in contemporary constitutional discourse, particularly judicial activism and judicial restraint. Rather than providing a defense of contemporary constitutional practice as we know it through elite theories such as Dworkin's, my reading seeks to provide something of a populist subversion of both, making it unlikely that either will be viewed in quite the same way ever again.

The Elements of Comedy

Where romance seeks to join the past with the present as protagonists work to establish a union with the fathers, comedic protagonists typically must overcome their fathers in order to enjoy full freedom in the future (Regis 2003, 29). Comedies tend toward an idealized future, while romance yearns for an idealized past. Comedic narratives typically include seriality, a dilemma to be solved, a desire for social change, and a movement toward a happy ending (Cuddon 1998; Harris 1992). They tend to be forward-looking, usually beginning unhappily, with a dilemma to address that obstructs progress toward a happy ending. Comedies also focus on the details of everyday life, often on the ups and downs of family life. I take up each of these features in more detail below, to the end of establishing comedy as the appropriate narrative frame in which to understand and parody Dworkin's liberal judicial activism.

In both constitutional and soap opera narratives, new cases and new story lines are always emerging to create dramatic new enactments of the contemporary political contests that are central to the life of the community. In this sense, both soaps and constitutional interpretation offer ongoing installments in a serial drama that seems to have no definable beginning and no foreseeable ending. While many pinpoint the beginning of the American judicial and constitutional drama at 1803 in *Marbury* v. *Madison*, this remains a contestable matter. As Robert Clinton notes, "there existed before, during, and after the decision of *Marbury*, a generally agreed-upon notion of the reach of judicial power in constitutional matters" (1989, 1). Similarly, the first broadcast of *OLTL* can be specified as July 15, 1968, but viewers who tuned in that day entered into an ongoing drama, set in a specific town and peopled with a variety of characters, possessing a variety of problems and interests. Dworkin's published work premiered in 1966 in the *Yale Law Journal*,[3] and he has offered additional

---

3   This piece has been reprinted as Chapter 10, "Liberty and Moralism" in *Taking Rights Seriously*.

installments on a wide variety of topics ever since (see, for example, 1977; 1985; 1986; 1993; 1996; 2000; 2006).

As Christine Gledhill writes of soap operas, "we probably don't remember or never saw the beginning [and there is] no end in sight" (1997, 352). Soap opera narratives run several story lines simultaneously to keep the serial going, or, as Gledhill puts it, "as one story runs out, another is coming to a boil" (1997, 368). Similarly, the Court ritually references precedent (that is, one or more previous "episodes" of judicial constitutional interpretation) before venturing on to the next installment in that story line. In this sense, the "endings" offered by soap operas and the Supreme Court seem more about continuation than final resolution.

Just as soap operas frequently tease viewers with cliffhanger "endings" that entice regular viewers to imagine what will happen next, the Supreme Court also often releases its most interesting and perhaps most difficult cases near the end of every term in June, during which time court watchers try to predict how the Court will "end" the term. Just as avid soap fans are not often surprised by the result of a particular plotline, seasoned Court watchers such as Dworkin are often quite adept at predicting case outcomes, taking pleasure in anticipating how the story will eventually lead to its predictable *dénouement*. As the term is drawing to a close each year, leading newspapers, court weblogs, and scholarly listservs typically devote a significant amount of time to predicting the outcomes of remaining cases. Speaking about soaps, Geraghty notes, "part of the fun for the audience is to see how the program can get out of the narrative web it has woven for itself and the viewer" (1991, 20). Modleski adds that soap opera narratives make "anticipation of an end an end in itself" (1982, 88).

Comedies also tend to be forward-looking, usually beginning unhappily, with a dilemma to address that obstructs progress toward a happy ending. Thus, Agnes Nixon, the creator of *OLTL*, has said that she was inspired to create the show after being challenged by the dilemma presented at a television conference by Saul Alinsky, the famed author of *Rules for Radicals* (G. Warner 1998, xiii). Responding to Alinsky's claim that "until diverse human beings better understand and respect one another, we can never live in harmony and peace on this planet," Nixon created *OLTL*, a soap opera that tended towards an assimilationist happy ending, with a focus on the trials and tribulations of several characters who cut across and challenge class, race, and gender lines constructed by the patriarchal powers-that-be in Llanview, Pennsylvania, a small town outside of Philadelphia. Not unlike contemporary constitutional discourse, *OLTL* was designed as a vehicle to "fashion stories about richly diverse people as their lives intertwined, as they interacted with one another... To explain the hopes and hardships, the goals, fights, and failures that are ultimately shared by all mankind no matter how disparate their lifestyles" (G. Warner 1998, xiii). Thus, in early plotlines Polish-American Larry Wolek overcomes his working-class roots by becoming a physician and marrying Meredith Lord, the daughter of the wealthy patriarch of the town, Victor Lord. Victor's other daughter, Victoria, the longest lasting and most central character of the show, also marries across class (against her father's wishes), at first resisting, but eventually giving in to the charms of an Irish-Catholic reporter at *The Banner*, Joe Riley. Jewish David Siegel also crosses boundaries, marrying Joe's sister Eileen Riley. Presumptively Italian Carla

Bernari (later revealed to be Clara Gray, daughter of African-American housekeeper Sadie Gray), initially passes as white in order to obtain access to a broader range of roles as an actress, her chosen profession. The wealthy white Buchanan family, the struggling Hispanic Vega family, and the middle-class African-American Gannon brothers are all integrated into the series later in a manner that further destabilizes race, ethnicity, and class lines.

Like *OLTL*, Dworkin is also concerned with forwarding a narrative that would foster equal rights and tolerance for all, just as high profile Supreme Court cases regularly address social change in a dramatic context. Such discourse typically addresses the most topical and dramatically contested issues of the day. As Gledhill notes, soap operas "not only engage with social change but become key sites for the emerging articulation of and contest over change" (Gledhill 1997, 362). Even for a soap opera, *OLTL* has been unusually concerned with social issues, premiering, as it did in 1968, "against a backdrop of student protests, civil rights marches, war, and assassination, a world very much reflected in the heightened social consciousness of the show" (Mumford 1997, 147).

Families figure prominently in all soap operas, *OLTL* included. According to Modleski, they

> ...offer the assurance of immortality...Even though they are always in the process of breaking down, [they always] stay together no matter how intolerable [their] situation may get. Or perhaps more accurately, the family remains close precisely because it is perpetually in a chaotic state. The unhappiness generated by the family can only be solved in the family. (1982, 90)

As in *OLTL*, Dworkin's narrative focuses on the family. He offers a thoroughgoing reinterpretation of the founding fathers and their legacy that seeks to foster their continuing influence in the contemporary debate. This includes a particular concern with the connection between paternity, legitimacy, and law. In this narrative, Dworkin aims "to justify what they [the founding fathers] did...in an overall story worth telling how, a story with a complex claim: that present practice can be organized by and justified in principles sufficiently attractive to provide an honorable future" (1985, 227–8). In other words, Dworkin seeks to legitimize the force of the state generally, and the practice of judicial review specifically, by establishing a clear lineage to the founding fathers in a principled narrative that is based in community practice and that recognizes equal rights and dignity for all citizens. In this manner, Dworkin promises to legitimize cases like *Roe*, *Miranda*, and *Brown* by grounding them in the stately paternity of the founding fathers (1993, 118; 1977, 132). However, he also recognizes that mistakes in need of excising have emerged in the past and may continue to do so in the future—particularly in the area of property rights. Thus, he concedes that the "American constitutional novel includes, after all, the Supreme Court's *Dred Scott* decision, which treated slaves as a kind of property and the 'rights of property' decisions, which nearly swamped Roosevelt's New Deal" (Dworkin 1996, 38). Such decisions must ultimately be rendered illegitimate in Dworkin's constitutional narrative. As in the narrative of soap operas, problems created in the family can only be solved within the family.

Given the enormity of the dilemmas presented by comedies—Dworkin's, the Court's, and *OLTL*'s included—it may sometimes seem as if all will not turn out well in the end. Nevertheless, comedies are typically characterized by remarkable optimism, a fundamental desire for change, and an almost unqualified faith in progress toward a new social order. As Roy Schafer puts it, in comedy

> ...[n]o dilemma is too great to be resolved, no obstacle too firm to stand against effort and good intentions, no evil so unmitigated and entrenched that it is irredeemable, no suffering so intense that it cannot be relieved, and no loss so final that it cannot be undone or made up for. The program is reform, progress, and tidings of joy. (1970, 281)

Louis Kronenberger adds that comedy is "a way of surveying life so that happy endings must prevail" (Harris 1992, 38).

Consistent with the parameters of the comedic soap opera, in which the highest goal appears to be a united and happy family (Modleski 1982, 92), Dworkin confidently maintains that all will inevitably be well in the American constitutional narrative, despite the obstacles that need to be overcome, particularly those that involve reconciling the founding fathers' illiberal past with Dworkin's liberal vision for the future. Both soap operas and Dworkin seek a just conclusion to their respective narratives, however implausible such an ending might seem. Thus, Dworkin argues, "[i]t is the nature of legal interpretation—not just particularly constitutional interpretation—to aim at happy endings" (1996, 38). His optimism is perhaps remarkable in light of the fact that he openly concedes the constitutional story of the United States includes brutality, inequality, and "mistakes," not least of which are decisions that deal with ownership and property rights, including *Dred Scott* v. *Sandford* and *Locher* v. *New York* (1996, 38). Part of Dworkin's resistance to originalism is that it seems to make these mistakes permanent. For originalists, if the founders did not see fit to outlaw slavery, it rightfully (if regrettably) remained legal until the passage of the Fourteenth Amendment changed the very terms of the Constitution. And if, following that change, the framers of the Fourteenth Amendment did not intend to desegregate the schools, then a case like *Brown* is also (however regrettably) illegitimate (Berger 1977), an outcome that is clearly unacceptable to Dworkin (1996, 13). Despite his acknowledgement of brutality, Dworkin persists in his belief that a happy ending is in the offing, insisting that no mistake is too great to overcome. In Dworkin's comedic narrative, brutality is the dilemma to overcome. Thus, he asserts that

> ...political and intellectual responsibility, as well as cheerfulness, argue for optimism. The Constitution is America's moral sail, and we must hold to the courage of the conviction that flies it, the conviction that we can all be equal citizens of a moral republic. That is a noble faith, and only optimism can redeem it. (1996, 38)

He adds that "[t]here is no alternative, except aiming at unhappy ones," which is clearly unacceptable to him.[4]

---

4   Thus, Dworkin opposes Critical Legal Studies scholars on the grounds that they are too cynical (or, to put it differently, not sufficiently comic). He argues that "law is in its worst light not best, for some of these scholars. They suggest roads closed that are open" (1986, 275).

Because the dilemmas presented at the beginning of comedies usually work their way to a happy ending, they are typically enjoyable, if somewhat unbelievable, to encounter. However desirable, the movement from what looks like an insuperable problem to a seemingly unmitigated happy ending is just not plausible at some level. Something has to be left out or some part of the past needs to be undone in order to effectuate the happy ending. As Northrup Frye has said: "Happy endings do not impress us as true, but as desirable and they are brought about by manipulation" (Harris 1992, 36). As will become clear in the analysis of paternity, legitimacy, and law which follows, Dworkin does in fact employ various manipulative devices in a comedic narrative with the intent of effectuating a desirable and happy ending. These include Hercules (his *deus ex machina*-like omnipotent judge), resurrection from the dead, and amnesia. Unfortunately, these very devices serve to obstruct his goal of transforming the founding fathers' vision and influence in contemporary constitutional discourse.

Dworkin's Straight Comedic Narrative

Dworkin has, from the very beginning, focused on retelling the story of the continuing legacy of the (founding) fathers in his narrative. Originalism's dominance of the founding debate and the problem that it creates for liberal constitutional interpretation is particularly acute for Dworkin, since he believes that "almost any constitutional theory relies on some conception of an original intention or understanding" (1985, 57). For him, even noninterpretive theories that claim to move beyond the text and framers' intent "emphasize an especially abstract statement of original intentions (or could easily be revised so as to make that emphasis explicit with no change in the substance of the argument)" (1985, 57). Thus, Dworkin concludes: "The important question for constitutional theory is not whether the intention of those who made the Constitution should count, but rather what should count as that intention" (1985, 57). In short, the founding fathers remain central, but what they stand for is open to (re)interpretation.

In a move designed to both centralize as well as to transform the founders, Dworkin introduced his now famous distinction between concepts and conceptions. For Dworkin, a concept is a general proposition that refers to a principle or abstract intention of the founding fathers, such as equality. Concepts are pitched broadly, and, as such, are capable of accommodating a wide variety of conceptions, or specific views about what each concept might entail in practice (1985, 39). With respect to race, for example, the concept of equality takes on various different conceptions: color-blindness, affirmative action, or a wide variety of other alternatives. To explain the concept/conception distinction in more detail, Dworkin employs a family analogy in three extended examples, each of which focuses on a specific aspect of patriarchal power and legitimate decision-making with Dworkin featured as a father, husband, and son in each successive episode.

In the first installment of his narrative, Dworkin begins by situating himself in a position of power, the role of founding patriarch. Envisioning himself as a father seeking to establish the concept of fairness as a guiding principle for the behavior of his children, he says: "Suppose I tell my children simply that I expect them not to treat others unfairly" (1977, 134). To clarify the meaning of the concept, he adds, he might offer his children some illustrative, but not exhaustive, examples of his expectations about how the concept of fairness might work out in practice. After supplying such examples, Dworkin says that he would then expect his children to apply the concept of fairness to the situations he had discussed with them, as well as to those that he had not discussed or perhaps even thought of in advance. Conceding the possibility that his specific conceptions of fairness might actually be mistaken, Dworkin insists that such mistakes should affect neither his nor his children's attachment to the concept of fairness. Thus, he concludes,

> I stand ready to admit that some particular act I had thought was fair when I spoke was in fact unfair; or vice versa, if one of my children is able to convince me of that later; in that case I should want to say that my instructions covered the case he cited, not that I had changed my instructions. I might say that I meant the family to be guided by the *concept* of fairness, not by any specific *conception* of fairness that I might have had in mind. (1977, 134; emphasis in original)

Dworkin is well aware that his fathers' legacy contains many problematic features that challenge contemporary notions of fairness, many of which center around ownership, including slavery, economic inequality, and disenfranchisement of the unpropertied. As will become clear, Dworkin uses some of the same devices that are used on *OLTL* to deal with these difficulties, such as amnesia and resurrection. He refuses to let the father(s) rest in peace until the seemingly heinous behavior that is their apparent legacy is somehow successfully integrated into his larger constitutional narrative, which seeks to legitimize contemporary judicial activism. Unlike *OLTL*, however, Dworkin assumes that paternity is stable and the authority of the founding fathers is unquestionable. While self-interest is at the heart of patriarchal power in *OLTL*'s Llanview, Dworkin denies the possibility that self-interest might have significantly determined the founder's decision-making: he categorizes problematic past actions as correctable misunderstandings between reasonable people of good will whose only apparent desire is to construct and maintain the best political regime possible. This allows Dworkin to conclude, for example, that racial segregation is "inconsistent with the conception of equality the framers accepted at a more abstract level," and thus that "fidelity to their convictions as a whole requires holding segregation unconstitutional" (1986, 361).

Thus, Dworkin sees his fathers as basically good, if sometimes ill-informed, men who are firmly committed to acting in the self-interest of all citizens. His fathers are authors of laudable guiding principles or concepts, even if many of their specific conceptions are now widely understood to be mistaken and indefensible. Their legacy has been maintained through Dworkin, who in turn is transmitting it to his children through regular, reasoned discourse. In this sense, paternal authority can empower children (or citizens) in a manner that transfers but does not reconstitute or transform paternal authority.

The problem is, this installment of Dworkin's story, like those that follow below, includes neither a complete accounting of the founding fathers' actions, nor a very nuanced understanding of desire and power. Despite their revolutionary challenge to monarchical authority in the name of freedom and self-government, the founding fathers did, after the war, write slavery into the constitutional narrative of the new society that they were building, furthering their economic and nationalist interests. While he does rather abstractly concede that the founders made mistakes, Dworkin fails to weave the reality of the fathers' misuse of power into a more complex, disturbing, and destabilized constitutional narrative that would include revolutionary as well as self-interested behavior on the part of the founders. Rather, Dworkin occludes such complexity through the panacea of reasoned discourse, thereby idealizing the founding fathers as tolerant and inclusive democrats. This narrative move stabilizes the traditional originalist understanding of the founding fathers, thus subverting Dworkin's desire to connect the founding fathers to his liberal cause.

In the second installment of his story, Dworkin situates himself not as a father, but as a husband. He also situates the reader as "you," presumably a friend, who offers to go out and buy sandwiches for lunch. Here Dworkin asks you, in the presence of his wife, to bring him something healthy for lunch. He begins by noting that if you believe what he said about wanting a healthy lunch, you would not bring him a hot pastrami sandwich. But what if, in an attempt to deceive his wife (who apparently is more concerned about Dworkin's health than he is), he winked or made a face at you while she was looking the other way, presumably indicating that you should bring him something that he really wanted, rather than something that was good for him? Dworkin argues that if you brought him back yogurt instead of pastrami in that circumstance he could "rightly accuse you" of disobeying him. He notes further that if he spoke a language similar to, but not identical to English, the word for "healthy" might mean "rich and fatty and briny." In this case you would have blamelessly misunderstood him. It is also possible that even if you and he share the same understanding of the word "healthy," Dworkin might actually believe pastrami to be healthy, and thus expect you to bring him such a sandwich. But if so, he asks, why wouldn't he have just specified that he wanted a pastrami sandwich (1993, 134). Perhaps the presence of Dworkin's wife prevents him from acknowledging this possibility.

In any case, in the second story Dworkin remains in a position of power, an authority figure whose intentions must be interpreted in order for the story to reach a successful conclusion. However, this installment of his story offers a slightly more complicated narrative of power in which Dworkin is being observed and perhaps indirectly regulated by a third party, his wife, who, as such, is explicitly gendered. Dworkin portrays his wife as having a strong interest in really furthering his health; she is thus interested in the concept of "healthy" being read in the best possible light, quite possibly in conflict with Dworkin's own particular wishes and desires. He casts his wife as nurturing and righteous, ready to (indirectly, through her very presence) thwart his plans for immediate gratification (for his own good). Further, in this installment, Dworkin allows for the possibility that he might desire something less than the best for himself, or at least something that furthers his short-term self-interest (a great-tasting, fatty sandwich), at the expense of his long-term self-interest (a healthy and long-lived heart). Even though the only person who might be damaged in this scenario seems to be Dworkin, he does acknowledge the possibility of deception through face-making; in doing so he seems to concede that performance may be more important than words in certain circumstances. While the opportunity is there for Dworkin to provide a more complicated and compelling understanding of power, he nevertheless comes to the same conclusions that he presented in his first scenario. He insists that, logically speaking, despite the complications that arise from conflicting appetites and their regulation through gender, reason dictates that you would best follow his intentions by bringing him back a yogurt rather than a pastrami sandwich for lunch.

Dworkin ties this example into his constitutional narrative by applying a similar logic to the founding fathers' intent as regards the Eighth Amendment maxim that cruel and unusual punishment is unconstitutional. Arguing that "[t]here is no evidence whatsoever that the politicians who enacted these amendments were so deceitful or so linguistically incompetent, or spoke a language so different from contemporary English," he infers that "[w]e can only conclude that the Constitution's authors meant to say what they did say" (1993, 135–6). Just as bringing back something healthy requires a yogurt rather than a pastrami sandwich, the founding fathers, rightly understood, would deplore cruel and unusual punishment such as the death penalty and approve of the use of judicial activism to strike down such excess.

In the third installment of the story, Dworkin situates himself as a son trying to follow his deceased mother's intention that he should refrain from unfair business practices. Seeking to follow her intent, Dworkin finds himself faced with a dilemma. While his mother was alive, she engaged in practices such as price gouging, which, while widely understood as fair at the time she was in business, are now thought to be unfair by Dworkin and many others. Thus, Dworkin must decide whether to follow his mother's specific (and in his view problematic) conception of what fairness entails or her general dictum that he act fairly. Noting that the originalist maxim "follow her intentions" will not prove useful, because, in this instance, his mother seems to have had "at least two relevant convictions," Dworkin adjudicates this conundrum by arguing that following the concept of fairness is most important, as "her intention can accurately be described only as the intention that I do what is in fact fair, not what I think fair, even though, of course, I can only carry out her intention by acting on my own convictions" (1993, 36, 137).

In this third installment, Dworkin situates himself for the first time not as (founding) father or an authority figure, but as an heir to a founder—in this case his (founding) mother. Only in this scenario does he discuss a founding practice that is explicitly problematic and damaging to others. Following the pattern of the "bad woman" that is ubiquitous in soap operas, Dworkin's mother is ready and willing to actively further her self-interest, even at the expense of others, in this case by practicing ruthless price-gouging in order to drive her competitors out of business. As Modleski points out, "there is only one character whom we are allowed to hate unreservedly [in the soaps]: the villainess, the negative image of the spectator's ideal self," the manipulative mother who "tries to interfere with her children's lives" (1982, 94, 92). For Dworkin, the question is, should he continue to respect his mother's wishes now that she is dead, even if he finds practices like price-gouging reprehensible? Diverging from the pattern of the soaps, Dworkin asserts that his mother, the bad mother, will ultimately be redeemed by reason (by him). Thus, even though Dworkin recognizes that his mother's behavior remained morally problematic to her death, he still argues that "if she had become persuaded that [price gouging was unfair]—as she might very well have been had she lived longer and encountered a different business climate—then she would no longer have wanted or expected me to do so" (1993, 137).

In sum, presented with several opportunities to provide a nuanced understanding of power, particularly as it relates to unfair, appetitive, and acquisitive acts of the founding fathers, Dworkin instead continues to suggest that reason will intervene and save the day, thus furthering the happy ending of his comedic narrative. Supposing a strong familial attachment, it is perhaps understandable that Dworkin might hope that his mother might have changed her mind in the matter, as he claims to with his own children in the first installment of his story. However, it is equally possible, perhaps even likely, that both her acquisitiveness and property holdings might have grown over the years and that she might have conjured up new, ever more successful strategies for disadvantaging business competitors for whom she had presumably no love lost. That is, her growing gains might have occasioned her to use reason to justify, rather than forgo, past decisions. However, Dworkin seems unable to engage these possibilities as regards his mother or the founding fathers. This seems oddly idealizing, because even Dworkin conceptualizes the founders as both private fathers and public politicians. In addition, Dworkin's most doggedly self-interested founder is his mother, whom he portrays as both a (private) mother and a (public) businessperson. Even though Dworkin reshuffles power along gender lines to some extent in this story, he ultimately does so to the end of propping up rather than destabilizing founding authority. Thus, while his mother's ruthless (economic) ambitions may misguide her, thereby temporarily obstructing the story's movement toward a happy ending, she is ultimately, in Dworkin's view, thoroughly redeemable, once shown the error of her ways. Even her death does not prevent Dworkin from this happy, but in Frye's words, manipulative and implausible, narrative conclusion. While such a comedy may entertain, its stabilization of paternal power in conjunction with its occlusion of the founder's attachment to their own self-interest at the expense of others serves to subvert Dworkin's desire to legitimize liberal judicial outcomes by convincingly connecting them to the authority of the founding fathers. The comedic narrative form that Dworkin employs ultimately undercuts the liberal legal-political content of his project, obstructing his ability to argue persuasively that equal rights and tolerance for all are the founders' true legacy.

Popular Culture as a Reflection of the *Status Quo*: *The Patriot*'s Straight Comedy

This problem can perhaps be seen more clearly through a parallel comedic portrayal of paternal authority in the filmic representation of the founding fathers that can be found in *The Patriot*. Just as Dworkin attempts to connect the founders to liberal ideals through reason, and just as the concept/conception distinction seems to be an implausible if perhaps desirable narrative, the movement from dilemma to happy ending in *The Patriot* seems contrived and stabilizing, with reason occluding the visibility of interests and events that should be integrated into the story in order for it to become truly persuasive. In the comedic narratives of both Dworkin and *The*

Patriot, founders of various types are presented as selfless democrats who, however harmlessly misguided they may be about what is best for us, are able, through the earnest use of reason, to reform their mistaken notions, seemingly even at their own expense. Read in this manner, both these narratives are entirely devoid of humor or parody. They suggest that, if left to their own devices, certain sites of popular culture, like certain constitutional narratives, may fail to provide a source of democratic transformation, serving simply to legitimize power as we know it. Of course, many scholars have long been concerned that popular culture is much too commodified to offer a real alternative to dominant interests and power. While this worry was first articulated by critical theorists such as Theodor Adorno and Max Horkheimer in the post-World War II period, more recent works by Richard Sherwin and others continue to reflect a concern that the integration of law and popular culture "is having a particularly pernicious effect" (Sherwin 2000, 37). *The Patriot* is certainly worthy of this type of concern and criticism.

As "the Patriot," Mel Gibson plays a former French and Indian War-hero with some dirty deeds in his past. He heads up the colonial's ragtag militia (which includes his rather zealous son), despite his concern that a revolution may destabilize his family. While the Patriot signs up new recruits, his son sews a flag and talks to a slave whose master has allowed him to join the militia. Meanwhile, one new recruit, a white man, loudly decries the new practice of arming slaves and granting them freedom if they fight for a year in the militia. Following the classic comedic format of introducing a dilemma, and foreshadowing social change toward a happy ending, the Patriot's son, who is also white, tells the slave to ignore such contempt, because the new society ushered in after the war will be based on equal rights for all. "Sounds good," says the slave.

By the end of the movie, right before the big battle that will finally turn the war to the colonials favor, the Patriot formally establishes his legacy by handing a written document for his children to a colonel in the regular army. Directly after this scene, we see the (formerly) contemptuous militia man standing in the ranks alongside the slave, telling him that it's been more than a year and that he's a free man now. "I know," says the slave, "I'm here by choice now." The formerly contemptuous militia man responds, "It's an honor to serve with you. An honor." In this respectful exchange amongst men who are equals despite racial differences, we see a microcosm of the new society and the implausible, yet seemingly desirable, happy ending that it promises to usher in. This, presumably, is the Patriot's legacy for his children. The initially resistant white militia man has come full circle regarding racial equality, and the newly freed slave has chosen to support the state (rather than resist it) as a soldier (with the promise of full masculinity that such a position holds). The relationship between the white soldier and black soldier serves to stabilize the patriarchal power that underlies state power, even in the midst of an otherwise revolutionary context. No wonder the white man is honored! The unspoken subtext is that patriarchal authority will be held firmly in place long after the founding fathers' embrace of slavery dissipates the promise that so captivates the black soldier in this scene. Additionally, the Patriot has a secret past characterized by brutality and violence, which threatens to surface at several points throughout the story (but never quite does) in a manner that would mar the Patriot's claim as a leader with moral authority.

In order to further the goal of transforming the founding fathers' illiberal past into an egalitarian and inclusive future, both *The Patriot* and Dworkin must be read in a manner that effectively dislodges, rather than supports, patriarchal authority as we know it. Without a detailed acknowledgment of brutality and the addition of parody and humor, the straight comedic narratives offered by *The Patriot* and the standard comedic reading of Dworkin are not well suited for this task.

Popular Culture as a Challenge to the *Status Quo*: *One Life to Live*'s Parodic Comedy

In the following sections I suggest that adopting parody as a populist strategy might provide a better basis for a more transformative constitutional narrative than Dworkin's very serious comedic narrative. Using *OLTL* as a model, I offer an alternative, parodic reading of Dworkin that destabilizes paternal power, and thereby offers a much more promising basis for his transformative project. Soap operas such as *OLTL* present a very different kind of comedy that may also be read, in part, as an acknowledgment of the brutality of dominant power as well as a parody of it. Offering parody in place of a straight comedy, *OLTL* suggests that considerations of power and desire run through both familial (private) and business (public) relations, often trumping reason and obstructing the redemption of various characters. In this regard, *OLTL* offers an alternative to Dworkin that advances important lessons about how popular culture and parody can contest the apparent stability of paternity, legitimacy, law, and power, thereby opening up new narrative possibilities.

Soap operas such as *OLTL* have a great deal of transformative potential, because they integrate comedy and parody, consent and dissent, both revering and mocking paternal and legal authority even as they acknowledge the difficulty, perhaps even absurdity, of stabilizing an alternative source of authority. Employing elements of both comedy and parody, *OLTL* can be read as glorifying as well as contesting the traditional family structure in a manner that is consistent with John Fiske's suggestion that popular culture may typically be read to support as well as to challenge the *status quo*. As such, it offers an interesting alternative to the standard reading of Dworkin's founding narrative in that it includes a populist interpretation that contests his elite understanding of the family in general and paternal power in particular. Family life is the central narrative in *OLTL*, even though legitimacy is regularly contested throughout the series. Paternal power is both represented in traditional as well as destabilized forms on a regular basis. Fathers are often very powerful in the soaps, but, despite their seemingly overwhelming power in the community and in their families, soap opera patriarchs often are unable to successfully control their unruly and unstable families as well as the strong matriarchs who often informally govern them. Since its first airing 35 years ago, the relationship between Victoria Lord and her father, the late Victor Lord, has been at the center of *OLTL*. Victor is the powerful and ruthless founding patriarch of the show who, as the publisher of the local newspaper *The Banner*, has a huge influence over the shape of popular opinion on a wide variety of issues. Victoria's relationship to her father is fraught throughout.

From the beginning of the show, *OLTL* has both revered and destabilized the legitimacy of patriarchal authority and its uninterrupted transference. Although Victor naturally desires a son, a legitimate heir who will one day take over his empire, as luck would have it, he fathers two girls, Victoria and Meredith. Both eventually marry across class lines, over his repeated objections and obstructions. Determined, as always, to control the unruly and inconvenient circumstances of family life, Victor is bent on making Viki into the son he never had. Despite her gender, he grooms her to take over his business. To this end, he "demand[s] perfection from Victoria" and "heap[s] mental and physical abuse upon [her]" (G. Warner 1998, 218). Due to Victor's repeated attempts to squelch any inkling of feminine desire that she might have, Viki eventually learns to repress interest in all (other) men, so that she can more effectively follow in her father's footsteps. In various ways Viki, at least for a time, crosses gender lines and becomes the (somewhat) legitimate son that Victor desires in a manner that contests fixed gender identity. Over time, however, despite his enormous power, Victor once again is unable to exert the desired control over his family, as Viki falls in love and eventually marries working-class newspaperman Joe Riley against her father's wishes.

Over the years, *OLTL* has employed various devices such as split personalities, amnesia, and resurrection from the dead to address the seemingly irresolvable problems created by its comedic narrative, particularly as regards Viki's need to somehow come to terms with the legacy of the brutal behavior of her father. However, rather than following a Dworkinian model and employing such devices to rationalize Victor's self-interested exploits, *OLTL* parodies his patriarchal behavior and the consequences of it, exaggerating and mocking his desire for control and stability. Thus, Viki does cross class and marry Joe Riley, contrary to her father's wishes, but not before Niki Smith, a fun-loving floozy and Viki's alter ego, emerges. This split personality allows her to escape, at least temporarily, the circumscribed identity that Victor compelled her to occupy within the family and to "forget" much of her father's ruthlessness. Much later in the series, when it becomes clear that Victor repeatedly sexually abused Viki when she was a child, viewers learn the even greater extent of the brutal behavior Victor was willing to engage in to control his family and further his own self-interest, as well as the depths of Viki's need to forget and escape through Niki. Until Viki fully integrates her father's abuse of power into her personal narrative, and into the narrative of the community, Niki Smith and a variety of other personalities emerge to shield her (and the community) from that knowledge, including the hyper-rational, cool, and calculating Jean Randolph, who "serve[s] as the gatekeeper, controlling the emergence of each of the multiple personalities" (G. Warner, 1998, 224). In her suit and horn-rimmed glasses, Randolph looks very much like a professor taking herself perhaps more than a bit too seriously.[5]

Law plays an important part in transmitting the property of Victor to his legitimate heirs, thus maintaining the patriarchal lineage. However, the contestation of paternity, legitimacy, identity, and even mortality that characterize these narratives often serve to undercut whatever stability the law might otherwise provide. In February 2003, two characters thought to be dead for years, Victor Lord and Mitch Laurence,

---

5   For a picture of Jean Randolph, see G. Warner (1998, 224).

were resurrected. Viewers learn of these developments when Viki, who has been searching for one of her progeny who has been missing, comes across her father Victor in an old warehouse. Although he is in a wheelchair, very frail with a failing heart and in need of oxygen periodically, his very presence serves to destabilize. Viki cannot believe Victor is alive (because she thought she killed him). Underscoring the outrageousness that typically characterizes parody she repeats over and over "this can't be happening" and "this is unbelievable."

Victor explains that he is searching for "the heart of a true Lord," which he needs to survive and which will come from one of Viki's twin daughters (by different fathers!). Victor plans to rewrite his will, that is, change the law, in a manner that promises to undo over thirty years of plotlines. This includes a redistribution of Victor's estate to Mitch Laurence, in return for which Mitch, the new legitimate heir to the Lord fortune, will transplant "the heart of a true Lord," into Victor. In addition, Victor insists that Viki will have to choose which of her daughters will sacrifice her heart so that Victor can be saved. In order for Victor's legacy to be passed on successfully, Viki must sacrifice the maternal and make a heartlessly rational calculation about which daughter to give up. As Viki looks from daughter to daughter, she resists her father's taunts to become a true Lord, challenging his (and the situation's) rationality, shouting at him "you're insane" and "this is crazy."

Of course Victor's planned redistribution has ramifications not only for the wealth and property of Viki, but also for many community members whose livelihoods depend upon the Lord empire. It also has import for Viki's self-understanding, as she had long believed (but clearly in error) that she had suffocated Victor to death many years ago in revenge for his brutality. While Mitch Laurence decides to deliver the heart of Viki's daughter Jessica Buchannon to Victor, the instability of paternity foils his plans. Becoming aware that Jessica is actually his own daughter via a rape that Viki had long repressed, Mitch rescinds his decision to sacrifice Jessica and instead offers up Jessica's twin Natalie, fathered by Viki's second husband, Clint Buchannon, knowing full well that Natalie does not possess the rare blood match required for Victor's transplant to be successful. In this scenario, Victor would die immediately on the table, leaving Mitch a fortune. Obviously, without a heart Natalie would also die immediately, thus furthering Mitch's (and Victor's) reign of terror on Viki, and Mitch and Jessica would be left as the foundation of a new dynastic tradition. However, Mitch, the would-be patriarch of this new regime, is ultimately foiled by law (enforcement), which, just in the nick of time, crashes into the old warehouse, rescuing both Viki and her two daughters before Mitch's devious plot can be executed. As a consequence, Victor dies (or so it would appear) for the lack of a heart (of a true Lord).

It is hard to understand this story as anything but parody—with due reference, of course, to the standard comedic narrative that governs family life. Twin daughters by different fathers? Victor Lord, patriarch and pillar of the community, withdraws from power and from view for 20 odd years only to reemerge at death's door in search of the heart of a true Lord? Mitch Laurence, the former leader of a Christian cult, will successfully perform heart transplant surgery? Matriarchal power will serve as the basis for a stable new political community? All of these events seem unbelievable to the point of absurdity. Their fantastic representation mocks the reality of family life and paternal authority as we know it, that is, as it is represented in traditional comedy. Thus, patriarchal heir-apparent Mitch Laurence's crazy and bombastic hunger for power is portrayed as patently absurd and ultimately self- and other-destructive, as is Victor's pathetic, delusional, and failed attempt to hold on to power to the point of defying mortality in order to find the heart of a true Lord.[6]

Parody in popular culture generally, and, in soap operas and *OLTL* more specifically, can offer a pleasant moment of escape from power as we know it in patriarchy, offering a populist alternative to elite interpretations of the authority of fathers. Viki's character provides a point of dissent from paternal power. However, *OLTL*'s parody of paternal power cautions against seeking an easy and stable solution in its antagonist, Viki, and the matriarchal line that she represents. Rather than simply calling for a reshuffling of power along gender lines, *OLTL*'s narrative challenges the very stability of gender, transforming the parameters of the discussion. The contestation of paternity, legitimacy, and gender that are a staple of soaps creates the possibility of undermining both patriarchal power and the strong matriarchs who subvert them. Even mortality is destabilized through parody, as nothing, not even death, is ever certain or final.

In short, power is reconstituted through parody in *OLTL*. Even though Mitch's abuse of power certainly seems to qualify him as Victor's heir-apparent, and even though this reality is reflected in Victor's rewritten will, the judge (that is, the law) nevertheless declares Viki the rightful heir of Victor's estate. The judge's recognition of Viki signifies a new (matriarchal) dynastic foundation in the community that is based upon a more complicated, but not necessarily more stable, reconstitution of power. After all, it is now clear that it is always possible that her (dead) father may return and (try to) reset the terms of his legacy. Regardless, these events cause Viki to rethink her relationship to power—her father's as well as her own. For years, Viki believes that she suffocated her father in revenge for the abuse that he had heaped upon her as a child. However, seeing Victor alive makes it clear to Viki that she has not really killed her father. Rather, it is Victor's self-interested conniving, particularly with Mitch, that ultimately leads to his (apparent) demise. Seeing Victor alive (and then dead) again compels Viki to create a new understanding of the extent of her father's abuse of power and the damage he has wrought in her community, her family, and her self. In this narrative, Viki is not the murderer she thought she was. Rather, she is both a victim and a powerful community leader. As a character whose upbringing is grounded in the ambiguities of gender and power, Viki's power is neither completely self-interested (as in the case of Victor and Mitch) nor entirely selfless (as is the case when Viki's earlier victimization causes her to flee her self through the creation of multiple personalities, such as the hyper-rational Jean Randolph).

In contrast to the serious, orderly, and reasonable representation of family life that is usually attributed to Dworkin's work (it is not for nothing that his first book is

---

6   For a televisual representation, see the episodes initially aired on 21, 24, 25, and 26 February 2003. These episodes are summarized on the *One Life to Live* website at <http://abc.go.com/daytime/onelifetolive/episodes/2003-04/20030102.html>. Videotape of the scenes discussed above are on file with the author.

entitled *Taking Rights Seriously*), the fantastic representation of paternity, legitimacy, law, and power in *OLTL* mocks and offers an escape from the reality of power and desire as we know it—even as it recognizes that this position may be impossible to maintain over the long haul. In this sense, *OLTL*'s narrative holds greater potential for transformation through democratic authority than a straight comedic reading of Dworkin. The parodic reading of Dworkin which follows, based on the narrative provided in *OLTL*, might further his goal of connecting the founding fathers to a reformed agenda better than the comedic, yet serious, form in which his work is typically framed.

Taking Soaps Seriously: Parodying Dworkin's Defense of Judicial Activism

There certainly seems to be room for parody in the founding narrative. The very men who excluded the rabble from the halls of power are the same men who are going to fling the doors wide open to all? The same men who constitutionalized slavery in order to further nationalist and economic interests have at heart the best interests of the disenfranchised? Even the Federalist founders acknowledged ambition in hoping that competing ambition might serve to check it![7] Federalists and Anti-Federalists alike mocked and parodied their opponents and perhaps even themselves. Jay, Hamilton, and Madison adopted "Publius" as their pen name, comparing their project to the grandeur of the Roman Republic and suggesting that they were representing a unified "people," presumably knowing full well that they fell well short in both regards. Anti-Federalists were no less outrageous, adopting "Brutus" and other grandiose pen names. To say nothing of the fact that the "original" Roman stories were mythic in their own regards (Rand 1995, 29).

Ironically, the super-serious tone that characterizes Dworkin's work compels us to question how seriously we should take his remarkably sanguine understanding of power, brutality, and self-interest. What if we took the soaps seriously and used *OLTL* as a guide to reading Dworkin's constitutional narrative as a parody? The result would need to be referential, commenting in a mocking and exaggerated manner on the standard founding narrative in order to confound it, borrowing characters from the original to reveal the impossibility of stabilizing the legitimacy of paternal power.

Picture this: Victor, in his first incarnation as the founding patriarch, could represent the founding fathers in a manner that fully acknowledges their concern for their progeny and an interest in their legacy as well as their self-interested abuses of power in the name of the public good. The uncontrollable, female, somewhat legitimate heir of the founder, Viki, could represent the new, more liberal, and inclusive regime of the New Deal and the early post-World War II period. Just as Victor was for years thought to be dead, founding authority was thought to be dead—or at least in decline—with the rise of legal realism and the advent of a new kind of practice of judicial activism. Decisions rendered in this period might temporarily convince liberals that they, like Viki, had vanquished their illiberal father(s), and rightly so, given their long train of abuses. However, like Viki, liberals might also

---

7   See *The Federalist Papers*, Numbers 51 and 10.

come to learn that their initial understanding was mistaken, and that they had not destroyed the influence of the founding fathers in any sort of permanent fashion. Thus, in his second incarnation, Victor could represent the originalist reemergence in the Nixon and Reagan years, complete with the threat to reestablish the old regime and to cut out the heart of the progeny of the centerpieces of Dworkin's liberal regime, namely *Brown*, *Roe*, and *Miranda*, just as Viki's children are under threat to have their hearts cut out so that Victor (representing the earlier, less inclusive regime) can survive. Just as Victor's reemergence destabilizes legitimacy in *OLTL*, so too might the reemergence of the founding fathers destabilize the very foundations of contemporary constitutional discourse.

This new reading of Dworkin seems to offer some escape from the brutality of the founding fathers or, at the very least, contestation about their ongoing relevance for legitimizing contemporary constitutional decision-making. Power could be reconstituted such that originalism might be vanquished—at least somewhat—just as Mitch Laurence's self-serving claim to be the true heir to Victor's fortune is thwarted by a judge who names Viki the true and legitimate heir. The hero of the new regime would be different from the heroes currently featured in Dworkin's straight comedic regime, because she would be unwilling to sacrifice her progeny to retain power and legitimacy for herself, her family, or her community, just as Viki was unwilling to do so in *OLTL*. Yet, while the new hero might contest her father's abuses of power, she might still be incapable of killing him, just as Vicki was not capable of killing off her father. Because this is so, the new regime would necessarily remain unstable—after all, interpreters of all stripes would be aware that the founding father(s) could return at any moment (just as Victor had) to try to reset the terms of their legacy.

Parodying Judicial Activism: Scalia in *Lawrence*

Just as parody can be used, as outlined above, as a strategy to dissent from originalism's challenge to liberal judicial activism in the post-World War II period, so too can parody be used as a means to contest the legitimacy of liberal judicial activism's periodic dominance during the same era. This is apparent in Justice Scalia's dissent in *Lawrence* v. *Texas*, which ridicules the (apparently) longstanding hegemony of modern judicial activism and its many contradictions.

In this regard, Scalia's recent dissent in *Lawrence* v. *Texas*[8] provides an excellent use of parody from a position of relative power to contest the legitimacy of judicial activism. It is referential, commenting upon the majority's opinion in order to confound it. Asserting that "[m]ost of the rest of today's opinion has no relevance to its actual holding," Scalia rewrites the Court's very serious opinion through parodic and satirical humor. While Scalia's dissent adopts a classic parodic form, it varies significantly from *OLTL*'s example in at least two ways. First, it fails to employ popular culture as the source of its critique, relying instead on a presumptively superior understanding of the law itself rather than any sort of populist challenge. Second, Scalia's parody offers a good deal more satirical bite. Both of these variations are

---

8   539 US 558 (2003).

perhaps owing to his position of power and authority as a judge, albeit a dissenting judge. Both may also prevent his dissent from being as transformative as it otherwise might be. True to elite interests, Scalia strives, however unsuccessfully, to restabilize the law ever more forcefully once he has revealed in detail how liberal jurisprudence has been its undoing. Scalia imitates, exaggerates, and sends-up the majority's style of argumentation. He borrows phrases from the original opinion and alters their intended meaning to reveal the groundlessness and absurdity of the majority's position. He also mocks the opinion's serious tone with the aim of entertaining, and, ultimately, transforming his audiences' view of the outcome in *Lawrence* and the result-oriented liberal judicial activism more generally. In this sense, Scalia does indeed succeed at opening up the debate between activists and restraintists, achieving, perhaps unwittingly, somewhat more than he may have bargained for by revealing the instability of seemingly all legal interpretation, his included. Scalia, who is deeply invested in stabilizing the law, instead offers a dissent that does much to unhinge it.

In *Lawrence* v. *Texas*, decided in 2003, the US Supreme Court struck down a Texas law criminalizing same-sex sodomy and overturned the 1986 case of *Bowers* v. *Hardwick*. Comparing the *Lawrence* majority's active use of judicial review in overturning a law that criminalized same-sex sodomy with the *Casey*[9] plurality's restraint in upholding *Roe* v. *Wade*, Scalia mocks these differences as inconsistencies that typify the politically-oriented, and thus illegitimate, practice of liberal jurisprudence. Mimicking the majority's serious stance, Scalia notes the *Lawrence* Court's "surprising readiness to reconsider" *Bowers*, decided a "mere 17 years ago" (*Lawrence* 2003, 586).

Underscoring the outrageousness that typifies parody, Scalia initially appears simply unable to believe what he is seeing. Yet, he is also well aware of the fact that 17 years is also roughly the amount of time that lapsed between *Roe* and *Casey*, and he plays this to full effect, reminding his audience that the *Casey* plurality relied heavily on *stare decisis* to the end of preserving "judicial invented abortion rights" (*Lawrence* 2003, 587). Bitingly referring to *Roe* as "rock-solid" and "unamendable," Scalia mocks the majority's lack of concern for the destabilizing consequences in *Lawrence*, particularly in light of the central role that concern for stability in law played in the opinion of the *Casey* plurality: "What a massive disruption of the current social order, therefore, the overruling of *Bowers* entails. Not so the overruling of *Roe*, which would simply have restored the regime that existed for centuries before 1973" (*Lawrence* 2003, 591). Dropping his mock astonishment fully, he reveals that his apparent surprise has been entirely parodic, to the end of revealing the contradictions that are sown into contemporary liberal jurisprudence:

> To tell the truth, it does not surprise me, and should surprise no one, that the Court has chosen today to revise the standards of *stare decisis* set forth in *Casey*. It has thereby exposed *Casey*'s extraordinary deference to precedent for the result-oriented expedient that it is. (*Lawrence* 2003, 592)

---

9   505 US 833 (1992). *Casey* offers another excellent example of Scalia's use of parody in dissent.

Exaggerating the original in a manner that typifies parody, Scalia disputes the *Lawrence* majority's view that the prosecution of same-sex sodomy has actually been minimal across time. Noting that even the *Lawrence* majority concedes that "homosexual sodomy was criminalized" in the past, Scalia argues that the *Lawrence* majority's reconstruction of history relies upon a pointless distinction between private and public sex. Thus, in response to the majority's position that the law was rarely enforced against private acts of same-sex sodomy, Scalia responds: "I do not know what 'acting in private' means; surely consensual sodomy, like heterosexual intercourse, is rarely performed on stage. If all the Court means by 'acting in private' is 'on private premises, with the doors closed and windows covered,' it is entirely unsurprising that evidence of enforcement would be hard to come by" (*Lawrence* 2003, 597). Ironically, Scalia seems to unwittingly provide the grounds for parodying his own position by exaggerating the *Lawrence* majority's argument in a manner that occludes the fact that these are precisely the circumstances under which the prosecutions did occur in both *Bowers* and *Lawrence*!

Surely Scalia does not mean to imply that the distinction between public and private sex is without meaning! Even sex radicals like Pat Califia who defend public sex still recognize a distinction between public and private (1994). While it might be somewhat surprising that the majority fails to exploit this opportunity for parody, it is more understandable when one recalls that parody typically serves as a form of dissent and destabilization. Thus those in relatively stronger positions of power rarely adopt it themselves as a conscious narrative strategy, even though their narratives may be read parodically by others.

Scalia also mocks the majority's interpretation of liberty and sexuality, referring to the majority's very serious discussion of liberty as "the dictum of its famed sweet-mystery-of-life passage" (*Lawrence* 2003, 588). Here Scalia is directly referring to the following passage from the majority opinion: "At the heart of liberty is the right to define one's own concept of existence, of meaning, of the universe, and of the mystery of human life" (*Lawrence* 2003, 574, 588).

He argues that the *Lawrence* majority "simply describes petitioners' conduct as 'an exercise of their liberty'—which it undoubtedly is—and proceeds to apply an unheard-of form of rational-basis review that will have far-reaching implications beyond this case" (*Lawrence* 2003, 586). He also characterizes the majority as cooing, or speaking lovingly and softly, presumably to homosexuals and their liberal allies, much as enraptured lovers might:

> [I]f, as the Court coos (casting aside all pretense of neutrality) 'when sexuality finds overt expression in intimate conduct with another person, the conduct can be but one element in a personal bond that is more enduring'; what justification could there possibly be for denying the benefits of marriage to homosexual couples exercising 'the liberty protected by the Constitution.' (*Lawrence* 2003, 604)

Like all good parody, Scalia's dissent reveals the groundlessness of the constituent elements of the discourse being ridiculed, contesting the legitimacy of the pursuit of a predictable and stable ending. Revealing law's groundlessness is about as destabilizing as it gets in a legal opinion. To this end, Scalia announces that the majority's rejection of traditional morals as a legitimate state interest as a basis for criminalizing "immoral and unacceptable" behavior "effectively decrees the end of all morals legislation"! (*Lawrence* 2003, 599.) In addition, he claims that Justice O'Connor's concurring opinion further undermines the basis not only of morals legislation, but of all law, by arguing that the Texas sodomy law should be struck down because it is targeted not at conduct, but at "gay persons as a class," and therefore unfairly discriminates against them. In classic camp style, he refers to discrimination as "discrimination" (*Lawrence* 2003, 603). As Susan Sontag has noted, "Camp sees everything in quotation marks. It's not a lamp it's a 'lamp'; not a woman, but a 'woman'" (1990, 280). This, she argues, signifies that rather than naturally Being, everything is construed as "Playing-a-Role" (1990, 280). Directly referencing and mocking the content of O'Connor's opinion, he states: "Of course the same could be said of any law. A law against public nudity targets 'the conduct that is closely correlated with being a nudist,' and hence 'is targeted at more than conduct'; it is 'directed toward nudists as a class'" (*Lawrence* 2003, 601).

The problem for Scalia, and for all parodists, is that revealing the groundlessness and illegitimacy of opponents' arguments will typically also serve to destabilize other positions—including their own—if, as is usually the case, such positions are grounded, at least in part, on the stability of constituent elements of the discourse, such as law, history, liberty, paternity, and so forth. As a rule, parodists are not indifferent to outcome, and Scalia is no exception. Not simply resigned to being besieged by persistent power, parodists typically retain some attachment to their own positions, and thus often fail to distance themselves enough to level on their own arguments the same parodically critical eye that effectively destabilized the original text.

Thus, Scalia's parody of the *Lawrence* majority's historiography is marred by his attempt to firmly establish an "utterly unassailable" history of criminalizing sodomy as established in *Bowers* (*Lawrence* 2003, 597). His parody of the majority's use of liberty is similarly scarred by his desire to restabilize liberty through *Bowers'* dictum that the Due Process Clause clearly does not contain a fundamental right to sodomy. Finally, his parody of law's groundlessness is tarnished by his desire to restabilize law in order to provide adequate resistance to same-sex marriage, despite protestations to the contrary: "Let me be clear that I have nothing against homosexuals, or any other group, promoting their agenda through normal democratic means" (*Lawrence* 2003, 603). (Perhaps he should have added that some of his best friends are homosexuals!) Nevertheless, neither tolerance nor parody prevents him from railing against the "so-called homosexual agenda" that dominates the "law-profession culture" or from asserting:

> [H]aving laid waste the foundations of our rational-basis jurisprudence the Court says that the present case 'does not involve whether the government must give formal recognition to any relationship that homosexual persons seek to enter.' Do not believe it. (*Lawrence* 2003, 602)

One could only believe that, Scalia concludes, if "principle and logic have nothing to do with the decisions of this Court. Many will hope that, as the Court comfortingly assures us, this is so" (*Lawrence* 2003, 605). But Scalia, despite all that his dissent has done to reveal the groundlessness of law, clearly does not envision himself in that crowd—at least not when same-sex marriage is at issue. In that regard, he falls back into the standard debate that dominates contemporary constitutional discourse, staking his claim through the familiar terms of judicial restraint, namely: democratic majoritarianism and deference to state prerogatives. That such a strategy might lead to stabilizing his favored outcome seems dubious over the long haul given the persistence of power as expressed in the longstanding pull and tug between judicial activism and judicial restraint in contemporary constitutional discourse.

The very best parodists recognize that the entire discourse, including their own dissent, is a constructed yet potentially playful and entertaining performance. Thus, even though they cannot fully sever attachment to their own position, they can offer their audience a wink and a nod to let them know that despite this, all things remain fundamentally in play. In this Scalia seems to fail, as he merely seeks to reinstate the previous regime of sexuality regulation represented by *Bowers*.

Perhaps Scalia might have been better off had he winked at his audience through some other means, such as when Chief Justice Rehnquist, another strong advocate of judicial restraint, seemed to do when he was inspired by (high) culture, to add four gold stripes to his judicial robes by the character of the Lord Chancellor in the Gilbert and Sullivan operetta *Iolanthe*. The plotline of *Iolanthe* focuses on illegitimacy and the problems of law, paternity, and democracy that arise when fairies want to marry! The title character, Iolanthe, is a fairy who was exiled many years earlier for marrying a mortal. Her secretly half-fairy and half-mortal son Strephon wishes to marry purely mortal Phyllis. Phyllis's guardian, the Lord Chancellor, refuses to allow the union, partially because he has designs on her himself. The Queen of the Fairies takes revenge by casting a spell that makes Strephon a member of parliament who can pass any bill without opposition, a turn of events which eventuates in the fairies taking over Parliament! In the midst of all this, the source of Rehnquist's inspiration, the Lord Chancellor sings the following lines: "The law is the true embodiment/Of everything that's excellent/It has no kind of fault or flaw/And I, my Lords, embody the Law." Accordingly, when Phyllis's true paternity is revealed—she is in fact the product of Iolanthe's earlier marriage to the Lord Chancellor himself—the Lord Chancellor changes the law such that it is no longer a crime for fairies to marry mortals. What an unusual source of inspiration for a dyed-in-the-wool judicial restraintist like Rehnquist![10]

Scalia's own parody of the *Lawrence* majority's activism, particularly when read alongside the reconstruction of Dworkin's constitutional theory as a parody of judicial restraint, suggests that judicial restraint and majoritarianism will not stabilize the law any more than Dworkin's judicial activism will. The irony, of course, is that Scalia's parodic narrative further reveals this, thus undermining his ability to offer a persuasive nostalgic and romantic narrative that seeks a return to a more idyllic past (that is, *Bowers*). This contradiction, intended or not, holds the potential of making him, or perhaps more likely, some part of his audience if they're reading and listening

---

10 See <http://www.c-span.org/questions/week136.asp>. Note that C-Span chalked Rehnquist's stripes up to "whimsy."

carefully, much more savvy about the persistence of power as it is expressed through the ongoing tension between judicial activism and judicial restraint in contemporary constitutional discourse.

Conclusion

My aim in this chapter has not been to provide a conclusive interpretation of either Dworkin or Scalia, but rather to suggest that many readings are possible, including those that undermine rather than stabilize mainstream constitutional theory and practice. In doing so, I seek to offer a strategy for reading their narratives in a manner that may open up contemporary constitutional discourse, contrary to Fish's rather depressing contention that all constitutional narrative is hopelessly nontransformative. By regularly referencing the constituent elements of well-entrenched discourses, parody addresses Fish's fear that truly subversive narratives will literally not be recognized in well-defined genres such as contemporary constitutional discourse, or in two of its major sub-narratives, judicial restraint and judicial activism.

The parodies of comedic judicial activism that I have provided from the work of Dworkin and Scalia represent dissenting readings of the continuing drama of contemporary constitutional discourse, with the dominant storyline being the ongoing conflict between judicial activism and judicial restraint created by the quest to resolve the problem of judicial legitimacy. There is no question that contemporary constitutional discourse has reached a serious impasse. The question is how to dislodge it. Further analysis of parody, on and off the Court, provides excellent (and entertaining) opportunities in that regard.

Given the apparent proclivity of scholars and jurists to focus on arguments that defend judicial legitimacy, it may be initially difficult for some to read constitutional discourse parodically, even with the help of the examples provided in this and the previous chapter. Interpreters may choose to continue to read the Constitution as either a straight comedy or romance. Yet, as Fish points out, the superiority of one narrative over another cannot be settled simply by appealing to the text because "they are names for ways of reading, ways which when put into operation render from the text the 'facts' which those who are proceeding within them then cite" as the justification that "only he is continuing the novel in the direction it has taken so far and that others are striking out in a new and unauthorized direction" (1982, 555).

Readers who are wedded to interpreting the Constitution as a comedy that legitimizes equitable and progressive outcomes or as a romance that longs to return to a more idyllic and enlightened past may remain unpersuaded that parody is the most useful strategy for their particular purposes. While that may or may not prove to be accurate, my point is to suggest the viability of parody as a strategy that can be used to acknowledge the brutality of the founders in a manner that allows us to laugh at the pretensions of the powerful in a potentially transformative way. By contesting legitimacy, parody may provide an opportunity to achieve a better balance between consent and dissent than that which seems currently available in contemporary constitutional discourse. As is the case with movement in music, such a balance can provide the creative tension that is necessary to foster the movement and transformation that both judicial activists and judicial restraintists such as Dworkin and Scalia appear to be so deeply in search of in their work.

Integrating both dissent and instability alongside consent and legitimacy, the possibilities offered by a parodic rendition of power seem to be endless rather than conclusive, including newly transformed storylines that might (or might not) serve to further Dworkin's goal of locating a more egalitarian and tolerant constitutional narrative and Scalia's goal of reestablishing a more democratically grounded rule of law. After all, each interpretation is just one episode in an ongoing series. Many, if not all, of the problems of paternity raised by attempts to tie contemporary constitutional discourse to the founding fathers are addressed in soap operas, suggesting that paternal identity may be as unstable in constitutional discourse as it is in the soaps. Who are the real fathers? What is their legacy? Who are their legitimate heirs? Must these heirs continue to follow the dictates of their fathers, even after they are (apparently) dead? Accordingly, a good (soap) writer might cast representatives of romantic judicial restraint such as Whittington and of comedic judicial activism such as Dworkin as protagonist and antagonist in a fabulously absurd evil twin plotline: Who is the legitimate heir and rightful bearer of the founding father's legacy? Can anyone successfully stabilize paternity and lineage in a manner that proves, once and for all, that he and only he is the true and rightful heir of the founding fathers and that the other is an illegitimate evil twin who, if followed, would destabilize the rule of law and lead the country to ruin and despair? Of course, being twins, neither would be readily identifiable as evil, given their very similar appearance. They would appear to be locked in an apparently unending, yet deeply destabilizing, struggle for power in the family.

An alternative possibility lies in the work of critical race theorist Derrick Bell, whose work is discussed in Chapter 4. Uninterested in embracing either comedic judicial activism, romantic judicial restraint, or becoming embroiled in the ongoing struggle for dominance between them, Bell rejects the founding fathers as a source of legitimacy. Instead, he opts for a narrative rather than the prosaic form that typifies mainstream constitutional theory. Drawing from popular culture in the form of science fiction narratives of time travel and alien abduction, he constructs a tragic narrative that accounts for the persistence of unacknowledged brutality and self-interest in contemporary constitutional discourse.

Chapter 4

Space Aliens Save Country from Ruin? Critical Race Theory as Tabloid Science Fiction

Introduction

Tragedy provides a major alternative to the romantic and comic narratives that dominate mainstream constitutional discourse. Where romance nostalgically seeks to reconnect with an idealized past, and comedy seeks to reconfigure the less than desirable effects of the past, tragedy accepts the past as unchangeable, however undesirable it may be (Harris 1992, 36). Challenging the ideology of integration, Critical Race Theorists argue for "the necessity of moving beyond the comforting belief that time and the generosity of its people will eventually solve America's racial problem" (Bell 1992, 13). They maintain that the Constitution is irreparably flawed when it comes to race. Whereas romance and comedy both avoid discussing brutality, Derrick Bell's work provides a tragic narrative that frankly accounts for the brutal exercise of power in the context of the Constitution and race. In doing so, he challenges the construction of reality in mainstream constitutional discourse, paving the way for the subsequent emergence of alternative constitutional narratives.

This chapter explores tragedy in contemporary constitutional discourse, as developed in the work of Derrick Bell, Critical Race Theory's "intellectual father figure" (Delgado 2001, 5). A former civil rights attorney who worked for the Department of Justice, Bell left when he was pressured to sever his relationship with the National Association for the Advancement of Colored People (NAACP). He then worked for the NAACP Legal Defense and Education Fund in the era immediately following *Brown* v. *Board of Education*, fueled by the passionate belief that law would affect significant social change, effectively eliminating racism and its remaining vestiges. When the changes he expected did not come to pass, Bell left legal advocacy somewhat dismayed and entered the academy in 1971, becoming the first black law professor at Harvard. In 1981, he became the first African-American Dean of the Law School at the University of Oregon. The legal academy proved unsatisfactory as well, as Bell found that racism persisted there also. Bell left Oregon in 1985 after being ordered not to hire an Asian-American to fill a faculty position. Returning to Harvard, he took a leave of absence in 1990 to protest the lack of women of color on the law faculty. Harvard dismissed Bell when he refused to return after two years on the grounds that nothing had been done to address the problem. Since that time, he has taught law as an adjunct professor at New York University and published a wide variety of writings that appeal to academic as well as popular audiences; several of his works have appeared on the *New York Times* bestseller list. Unlike the comedic and romantic constitutional narratives examined in earlier chapters, Bell's work is written in a first person dramatic form designed to appeal to a wider audience than the small community of scholars and judges to whom most constitutional analysis is addressed.

In this chapter I will argue that Bell's work follows a tragic narrative form. Tragic narratives tend to be epic in scope and quite sober in tone, with the hero resisting powers well beyond his or her control. While small victories might result from battles won here and there, the war will inevitably be lost, and the tragic hero knows it. Due to a fundamental error in judgment and a design set in motion long in the past, the tragic hero is limited in his or her ability to effectuate substantial change in the present and the future. The protagonist's role is neither to reconnect with the past nor to resolve conflict in the present by reformulating the past. Rather, he or she is fated to make meaning in the present by accepting the permanence of past injustices and embracing the inevitability of continued struggle in the future. As a consequence, tragedies tend to be extremely sober in tone.

Although tragedy initially entails more of a challenge to the current order than romance or comedy, the hero's inability to undo the mistakes of the past serves to affirm the power of the *status quo*, perhaps even more strongly when all is said and done. As Herbert Weisinger argues, "Tragedy occurs when the accepted order of things is fundamentally questioned only to be the more triumphantly affirmed" (Harris 1992, 419).

Tragic narratives are typically defined by an error in judgment leading to inevitable downfall. Despite the fact that the hero is often tremendously accomplished and seeks to challenge the powers that be, fate inevitably has crushing blows in store, which typically result in a defeat of "exceptional calamity," often including death (Harris 1992, 417–18, 419). The tragic hero typically defies the current order, only to find himself ultimately destroyed by it. This failure leads not only to the hero's personal resignation to his own fate, but also serves as a warning as to what is in store for all would-be challengers to those in power. As Northrup Frye puts it, "tragedy must lead up to an epiphany of law, of that which is and must be" (Harris 1992, 419–20).

Nevertheless, the hero continues to fight the good fight in a courageous fashion, providing a model of how to find meaning in struggle for others who, like him, are fated to be subject to dominant power. Tragic heroes realize themselves most fully through adversity, finding courage to persevere even in the face of certain defeat (Schafer 1970, 285). Heroes are admirable not because they can win; they can't. Rather, they are admirable because they are able to bear the worst that heaven and earth have to offer, and, having lived to tell the tale, they are able to make great meaning for themselves and their communities. Meaning is found not in winning, but in resisting despair as they continue to fight the good fight, even as it leads inevitably to defeat (Schafer 1970, 285). In this sense, Krook notes, tragedy serves to affirm "an order of values transcending the values of the human order" (Harris 1992, 421). Yet, this does not simplify matters for heroes, as they remain painfully aware that life presents "inescapable dangers, terrors, mysteries, and absurdities of existence." No matter what they do in this life, there will be, at best, "elements of defeat in victory and of victory in defeat" and "guilt in apparently justified action"

(Schafer 1970, 285). Thus, the "protagonist is inevitably divided within himself, some of his rights, values, duties, and opportunities necessarily clashing with others, and his choices consequently always entailing sacrifice, ambivalence, and remorse, if not guilt" (Schafer 1970, 286).

In tragedy, time is linear and irreversible. Unlike romance and comedy, there is no possibility of either affirming or reconfiguring the past. As Schafer puts it, "choices once made are made forever; a second chance cannot be the same as the first" (1970, 286). The consequences of past choices are keenly felt, no matter how much they may be reviewed and reinterpreted. Ultimately, life is a progression towards death. There is no going back, and rebirth, at least in this life, is an illusion. At best, the hero can find transcendent meaning in understanding the deeper significance in the struggle.

Thus, the protagonist's response is ultimately geared less towards action and more toward "deep empathy, sober contemplation, and containment of tension, working the experience over in one's mind and heart, and humility acting as a brake on hubris or grandiosity, all in the face of the awesome power, complexity and unpredictability inherent in human affairs" (Schafer 1970, 288). Despite its defiant origins, a strong sense of resignation informs tragedy, and this, ironically, serves to reaffirm the very order that the tragic hero initially set out to challenge.

Bell presents an epic tragic narrative about the persistence of power and the permanence of racism from the founding to the turn of the twenty-first century that includes three stories which represent the beginning, the end, and the postscript of his narrative of race in American constitutional development. The stories incorporate popular culture by using themes of time travel, alien visitation, and alien abduction. In the first story, a contemporary African-American woman travels back through time to the Constitutional Convention of 1787 to try to persuade the founding fathers not to constitutionalize slavery. In the second, space aliens visit Earth, offering valuable natural resources in exchange for all African-Americans. And in the third, abducted African-Americans decide that they would rather return home to racial oppression and struggle in the United States than go to the aliens' planet, which, though unfamiliar, is guaranteed to be utterly devoid of such discrimination.

Bell's sober story suggests that African-American heroes who adopt civil rights strategies and rely on judicial review to better their lot are ultimately doomed to failure, earnestly but errantly thinking that law can effectuate meaningful social and political change. Consistent with the parameters of tragedy, the heroes of Bell's story who resist oppression are ultimately doomed to fail due to the consequences set in motion by the founders' fateful decision to constitutionalize slavery. Try as they might, Bell's tragic heroes are unable to alter the symbiotic relationship between racism and constitutional democracy that has permeated American politics from the very start.

While Bell offers a much more compelling account of the role of racism in American constitutional development than the comedic and romantic narratives that have long dominated US constitutional discourse, his work has been faulted by many for lacking hope and failing to provide a productive alternative to the current political and legal context that it criticizes so incisively. Yet Bell's tragedy reserves hope for spiritual redemption in the next life rather than offering a story of political and legal transformation in this one; despite certain calamity, potentially meaningful change eventuates. Consistent with the tragic form, Bell's story suggests that meaning comes from understanding and persisting in a struggle that can never be fully won. Although his work is powerfully challenging to the representation of reality that can be found in mainstream constitutional discourse, his work has often been read as affirming the power of the *status quo*. I argue instead that he leaves us suspended in space, confronted with the question of whether to stay and work within the parameters of contemporary constitutional discourse or to leave in order to explore alien worlds that may offer new and exciting possibilities. Bell experiments with the relationship between form and content, offering a constitutional narrative that has the potential to transform fantasy into reality. Employing fantasy, Bell provides an alternative reality that opens up the choice to embrace or abandon contemporary constitutional discourse as we have known it. By doing so, Bell's tragic narrative contributes to a transformative future much more than his critics give him credit for.

The Roots of the Tragedy: Time Travel to the Founding

Bell begins his story with a recollection of the excitement around *Brown* v. *Board of Education* and the widespread belief that law would foster racial justice. He recalls that many thought that most of the significant work had been done, as reflected in a popular slogan at the time, "Free by 1963." He concedes that "[n]ot even the most skeptical...could have foreseen that, less than three decades later, that achievement would be so eroded as to bring us once again into fateful and frightful coincidence with Jeremiah's lament," which is referenced in the title of his book *And We Are Not Saved* (Bell 1987, 3). Taken from Jeremiah 8:20, this biblical verse suggests that Bell has come to believe that racism is not curable through law: "The harvest is past, the summer is ended, and we are not saved." Racism persists in the wake of the heyday of the civil rights movement. As a consequence of the deep symbiosis between American liberal democracy and racism, brief periods of hope are typically followed by a pattern of sacrificing black rights (Bell 1987, 10). To explore the question of why optimism would be followed by defeat over and over again in the course of American constitutional development, Bell offers a fantastic story in which Geneva Crenshaw, a contemporary black woman, travels back through time to the Constitutional Convention of 1787 in an attempt to persuade the founding fathers that constitutionalizing slavery is a mistake.

While Bell's experimentation with form and content, particularly his contributions in the area of narrative, have rightly been hailed as path-breaking by many scholars, his use of popular culture is not often discussed, despite the fact that he often integrates it into his work, for example, with stories of time travel. Time travel as a pop culture narrative has often included racial themes, although not necessarily in a politically progressive manner. The outcome of such stories is largely dependent on form, which influence the time traveler's ability to alter the past and present.

In 1985's *Back to the Future*, which takes a romantic view of time travel, white teenager Marty McFly returns to his parents' high school years in the 1950s. This story suggests that black doo-woppers stole the secret of rock and roll from McFly, and that a seemingly hapless black soda jerk would never have become mayor of the town years later without McFly's suggestion that he do so. While inserting a contemporary character like McFly into the past does not change actual outcomes, it does lead to a radically different story about how those outcomes came to pass. In addition, it leads McFly to understand and identify better with his father. Just as was the case in Whittington's romantic story, *Back to the Future* suggests that reconnecting with the past makes for a purportedly better story in the present.

The 1998 film *Pleasantville* offers a more comedic narrative. In this story, two white teens living in a broken family in contemporary California are sent back into the set of the *Leave it to Beaver*-like television show, *Pleasantville*. Rather than affirming the romantic notion that the 1950s were a simpler, less corrupt time, this brother and sister duo find that the mythic past is much more complicated than they ever would have guessed. Authentic feeling and desire bring color and change to the thoroughly bland and predictable world of *Pleasantville*. Prejudice and violence follow the advent of difference, with the knowing siblings from the future resolving the ensuing conflict for the uninitiated citizens of Pleasantville. In this story, characters from the present can change the past for the better. In the process, the present is improved as well, as the teens return from the context of having lived in a 1950s style nuclear family with a much deeper appreciation and affection for their divorced mother who is struggling to keep their family together as best she can in the 1990s. Consistent with Ronald Dworkin's comedy, change and happy endings follow a period of intense conflict.

Finally, Octavia Butler's 1979 science fiction novel *Kindred* offers a tragic narrative that parallels the story line in Bell's work. Butler's story features Dana, a black woman who through a mysterious force is taken from modern-day California and sent back into the antebellum South in order to save the life of Rufus, a white plantation owner whom she discovers is one of her distant ancestors. While her intervention serves to perpetuate the bloodline that leads to Dana's own birth years later, saving Rufus's life is fraught with ambivalence and guilt as it also entails capitulation with the racist practices of the past, including complicity in Rufus's habitual rape of Alice, one of Rufus's slaves and one of Dana's most trusted allies on the plantation. In the course of the story, Dana finds it to be much more difficult, if not impossible, to change the course of the past than she had ever imagined from the vantage point of the comfortable home she shared in California with her white husband. At the end of her journey she also finds lineage and familial fidelity to be much more tragic and complicated than she thought at the start.

Although each of these examples offers a very different story about race, each is based on a recurring issue in time travel: whether the past can be changed by an intervention from the future or whether once the past is done, it's done, and in that sense controls the future. As we have seen this is also a major theme in contemporary constitutional discourse, as a central question there is whether decisions rendered in the past by the founding fathers control the present and the future. Romantic narratives, as exemplified by the work of Whittington, yearn for an edenic past and seek to recapture it, while comedic narratives such as that offered by Dworkin present a narrative in which obstacles of the past are overcome in order to affect a happy ending of accommodation, peace, and integration. In either case the past is a central problem. Bell's story of time travel offers a third alternative, a tragic narrative that is neither optimistically comedic nor nostalgically romantic.

Despite moments in Bell's story in which the question about whether to constitutionalize slavery still seems open for debate, in the end this story suggests that the founders erred in favoring order and economic development over rights and justice at the inception of the nation; that non-elite whites have erred in identifying with prosperous whites rather than with their black class counterparts at the founding (and continue to do so today); and that civil rights advocates have erred in thinking that law can effectively alter a racist past, present, or future. The tragic errors made at the founding stem from character flaws grounded in narrow self-interest, which lead to the development of an irredeemably flawed Constitution. Bell's fantastic story of time travel cannot overcome the racism that has been and will continue to be a permanent feature of constitutional discourse in the United States. Ironically, this realization seems to reaffirm the power of the *status quo*.

The story begins with Bell frustrated and bored at a civil rights conference. Geneva Crenshaw, the hero of the story, offers an alternative, inviting him to interpret a number of stories, which he suddenly finds in the reading materials for the next day of the conference. These stories, or, as she calls them, Chronicles, have the effect of changing both the form and content of Bell's narrative.

Consistent with the dictates of tragedy, death figures prominently for Geneva. A former civil rights lawyer like Bell, she had been run off the road in Mississippi during Freedom Summer and has never been the same since, having had a near death or perhaps an actual death experience (the text does not completely clarify this matter). As Bell puts it:

> We identify with and hail as hero the man or woman willing to face even death without flinching. Why? Because, while no one escapes death, those who conquer their dread of it are freed to live more fully...Beyond survival lies the potential to perceive more clearly both a reason and the means for further struggle. (Bell 1987, 12)

Because of her experience, Geneva's consciousness has been altered. After the crash Geneva's "mind wandered in realms where medical science could not follow" (Bell 1987, 21). Since then, she seems to have occupied a supernatural place, but has now "folded [her] wings for a little while and returned to this world" (Bell 1987, 22). Consistent with the tragic form, she offers a transcendent vision that may sometimes seem fantastic when viewed from the perspective of the world as we know it (Bell 1987, 244). She is filled with "allegorical visions that, taking [her] out of our topsy-turvy world and into a strange and a more rational existence, have revealed to [her] new truths about the dilemma of blacks in this country" (Bell 1987, 22). Disillusioned with the outcome of the civil rights movement, she states that her "worst fears have been realized: We have made progress in everything yet nothing has changed" (Bell 1987, 22).

Geneva's story of time travel presents the possibility that the tragedy of constitutionalizing slavery in the past might be averted through an intervention from the future. Bell confesses to having a longstanding fantasy about time traveling back to the Constitutional Convention with the best lawyers from the *Brown* era to "reason with the Framers before they decided to incorporate slavery into the Constitution" (1987, 24). After Geneva laughingly notes that Bell would first have to explain to the founders why he had the nerve to think that he could teach white men anything, she confides that through the power of "extraordinary forces" she has already done just that (1987, 24, 26).

She then recounts the story of her time travel, beginning: "At the end of a journey back millions of light years, I found myself standing quietly at the podium at the Constitutional Convention of 1787" (Bell 1987, 26). Telling the founders that she is there "to test whether the decisions you are making today might be altered if you were to know their future disastrous effect on the nations' people, both white and black," Geneva suggests that at least initially she believes that it is possible for her to change the course of the past (Bell 1987, 26). In contrast, even though they are about to live through the moment when the fateful decision about slavery will be made, the founders treat it as if it were already a done deal. Their exchange with Geneva reveals that they believe that the constitutionalization of slavery is both necessary and inevitable.

As she enters the room where the founding fathers are meeting, an "angry commotion" ensues, and they move to eject Geneva. "Extraordinary forces" in the form of a "transparent light shield" protect her, shocking and knocking down each man who tries to reach through it and sounding like a bug zapper. Undaunted by their aggression, she urges them not to ignore Thomas Jefferson's emphasis on the importance of life, liberty, and pursuit of happiness in the Declaration of Independence, noting that some of her ancestors were his slaves (Bell 1987, 28). As predicted, they respond by questioning her authority to participate in the discussion: "[H]ow dare you insert yourself in these deliberations?" (Bell 1987, 28).

Utilizing her vantage point in the future, Geneva suggests that, contrary to their stated expectations, slavery will expand rather than wither, exacerbating the conflict between northern and southern states. Arguing vigorously that slavery is evil and a threat to the basis of liberty, which is dehumanizing to both slaves and owners, she appeals to their desire for fame, asking: "Is this, gentlemen, an achievement for which you wish to be remembered?" (Bell 1987, 29).

Consistent with the dictates of tragedy, the founders highlight the impossibility of change and the inevitability of their decision. One delegate begs her to "be reasonable" and to recognize that "compromises have been reached, decisions made, language drafted and approved" (Bell 1987, 29). When several other delegates also insist that the matter has been settled, Geneva again attempts to use her knowledge of the future to change the past, replying, "the matter of slavery will not be settled by your compromises. And even when it is ended by armed conflict and domestic turmoil far more devastating than that you hope to avoid here, the potential evil of giving priority to property over human rights will remain" (Bell 1987, 29). In this manner, Geneva begins to define the errors that inevitably lead to a series of tragic consequences.

For Geneva, the founders' fatal flaw lies in their inability to see the contradiction between their ideals and their actions in regards to slavery. The very title of this story, "The Chronicle of the Constitutional Contradiction," highlights their inability to see a contradiction between what is right on the one hand and constitutionalizing slavery on the other. Calling it the "basic contradiction" in their position, Geneva connects this contradiction to the founders' desire to further their own interests at seemingly any cost, accusing them of "protecting [their] property interests at the cost of [their] principles" (Bell 1987, 31). They argue that the basic end of government *is* to protect property, including slaves, and continue to highlight the necessity of that decision, arguing that the South would not join the Union without assurances that such property would be protected (Bell 1987, 30). In response to her warning that the gap between "what you espouse and what you here protect will be held against you by future citizens of this nation," a delegate responds that "unless we continue on our present course...there will be no nation whose origins can be criticized" (Bell 1987, 31). Order is necessary, he argues, because "the country is teetering between anarchy and bankruptcy" (Bell 1987, 31). The founders fail to acknowledge any contradiction, insisting that the decision is inevitable in order to foster national unity (Bell 1987, 29). Geneva's tragic contradiction is, for them, a necessary compromise.

As the story unfolds, it becomes clear that nothing could have changed the founders' minds. Not intervention from the future into the past. Not the ability to foresee the tragic persistence of the problem of race into the future, including the destruction wrought by the Civil War. Not the insertion of the fantastic into a serious reasoned discourse. Nothing can persuade the founders that trading rights for the hope of union is a bad idea. As is typically the case with tragedy, the die has already been cast. Predictable and unchangeable consequences will flow from decisions made in the past. Time is linear, and the past cannot be undone.

George Washington is the first delegate identified by name who responds to Geneva. He again lays out the arguments for compromise to the end of preserving the union. Geneva notes that she is aware that he is against slavery (despite the fact that he owns several slaves), and that he has said little throughout the convention so as not to influence and thus impede unity in the proceedings. Washington argues that the proposed Constitution is the best possible at this time and that dissolution is an unacceptable alternative. Others, including James Madison, concur, contending that it is the best that could be, given conflicting state interests. Again emphasizing the contradiction, Geneva directly discusses the long-term consequences of forging unity at the price of freedom. "Such sacrifices of the rights of one group of human beings will, unless arrested here, become a difficult-to-break pattern in the nation's politics" (Bell 1987, 32).

Citing Luther Martin, she wonders why the only kind of commerce that is exempted from regulation under the Constitution is that which is unjust by nature, namely slavery. While the delegates continue to insist that the situation necessitates it, she again notes the contradiction between the Constitution's aspirations and the practice of slavery, saying that she "cannot believe...that even a sincere belief in the supremacy of the white race should suffice to condone so blatant a contradiction of your hallowed ideals" (Bell 1987, 36). Once, again, her authority is questioned, this time by a delegate who had actually shot at her earlier: "It should be apparent by now...that we do not care what you think. Furthermore, if your people actually had the sensitivities of real human beings, you would realize that you are not wanted here and would have the decency to leave" (Bell 1987, 36).

When Geneva refuses to leave, several delegates state that they are willing to live with the contradiction, because of the depth of their commitment to the nation, reiterating that without slavery, the backbone of the economy, there can be neither nation nor freedom for anyone. Being men of good breeding, they prefer not to address this difficult issue directly. "Surely we know, even though we are at pains not to mention it, that we have sacrificed the rights of some in the belief that this involuntary forfeiture is necessary to secure the rights for others in a society espousing, as its basic principle, the liberty of all" (Bell 1987, 36). After much discussion, some delegates concede the economic benefits that will accrue to both the North and South due to slavery. They continue to insist that such economic stability is in the national interest. Thus, one delegate forthrightly admits that "slavery has provided the wealth that made independence possible," noting that the crisis they are facing amounts to preserving slavery in order to save the Constitution. For him, the preservation of slavery "is essential if the Constitution we are drafting is to be more than a useless document" (Bell 1987, 34).

Seeming to recognize at least the possibility of making a different choice, another delegate asks, "more out of frustration than defiance," what better compromise she could offer them. Highlighting the agency of the founders, she argues that they should follow the pattern of the North in abolishing slavery, suggesting that "[w]hat is lacking here is not legislative skill but the courage to recognize the evil of holding blacks in slavery" (Bell 1987, 37). Asserting that such an evil would be recognized and abolished immediately if it were whites being bought and sold, she argues that the "racial contradiction," ironically, will lead not to stability but rather will "mean that the nation's survival will always be in doubt" (Bell 1987, 37).

At the very point that moral choice and agency are introduced into the discussion, Alexander Hamilton argues that the inevitability of slavery and its consequences justifies their decision, suggesting that Geneva's challenge actually serves to reinforce the power of the founding fathers. Beginning by saying that he "resent[s] to [his] very soul the presence in our midst of this offspring of slaves," referring to Geneva as "the negress who has seized our podium by diabolical force," he argues that if her predictions about race are indeed accurate, they might as well go ahead with their plan for the fate of the slaves appears to be sealed (Bell 1987, 38).

In addition, Hamilton underscores the seduction of the white working class, asserting that slavery has provided more solid grounds for white racial solidarity by reducing the importance of class differences between farmers and plantation owners. "Wealthy whites, of course, retained all their former prerogatives, but the creation of a black subclass enabled poor whites to identify with and support the policies of the upper class" (Bell 1987, 40). For him, even abolition inadvertently supports slavery, as it would benefit those who already own slaves, because their market value would increase if the free-flowing supply of such labor were to be terminated.

Cutting through the earlier idealistic talk about nationhood with a thoroughly unromantic and uncomedic dose of realism about economic self-interest and stability, Geneva acknowledges his argument: "You are saying that slavery for blacks not only provided wealth for rich whites, but, paradoxically, led also to greater freedom for poor whites" (Bell 1987, 41). From this point of view, slavery presents a solution rather than a contradiction. Blacks serve to stabilize society. Hamilton, dazed by her restatement, thanks her for clarifying the situation so well for him.

Others delegates ask her whether racial problems persist in her own time. Before she can answer, a cannon aimed at her from outside the convention hall is fired. Though the shield saves her from peril, her mission abruptly ends, and she is returned to the twentieth century.

Consistent with the dictates of tragedy, Geneva notes in subsequent conversation with Bell that the conclusion of the story was inevitable: "The Chronicle's message is that no one could have prevented the Framers from drafting a constitution including provisions protecting property in slaves" (Bell 1987, 43). In her view, they simply did not take themselves or their ideals seriously.

> The men who drafted the Constitution, however gifted or remembered as great, were politicians, not so different from the politicians of our time and, like them, had to resolve by compromise conflicting interests in order to preserve both their fortunes and their new nation. What they saw as the requirements of that nation prevented them from substantiating their rhetoric about freedom and rights with constitutional provisions—and thus they infringed on the rights and freedom not only of the slaves, who then were one-fifth of the population, but ultimately, of all American citizens. (Bell 1987, 50)

To this the founders could only respond, tragically, that their hands were tied, or, as Geneva puts it, "'That's the way the world is. We did not make the rules, we simply play by them, and you really have no alternative but to do the same. Please don't take it personally'" (Bell 1987, 44). When Bell argues that she at least was able to get Hamilton and other delegates to think through their motivations, Geneva notes, in a manner consistent with tragedy, that such reflection wound up reaffirming the *status quo* by leading Hamilton and the others to think that slavery was even more important and inevitable than they had initially believed.

Finally, Geneva also reveals the fatal flaw of lawyers in the civil rights movement who continue to have an enduring but misguided faith in the ability of law to serve as a tool of social change that would overcome these profoundly racist and self-interested beginnings. She chastises Bell and the civil rights community for continuing to believe in "the nation's Fourth of July fantasy" despite having "lived to see your faith betrayed, your hard work undone" (Bell 1987, 45). For his part, Bell still seems to put a great deal of faith in reasoned discourse. Despite hearing this story, he continues to wonder whether the founders might have changed their minds had they been aware of the "dire human consequences" of their actions (Bell 1987, 49). For Geneva, "the real problem of race in America is the unresolved contradiction embedded in the Constitution and never openly examined, owing to the self-interested attachment of some citizens of this nation to certain myths" (Bell 1987, 49).

These myths continue to be explored in the middle of Bell's story, which remains consistently tragic. Together with Geneva, Bell explores various strategies designed to undo the racism set in motion by the founders' fateful decision, each to no avail. He repeatedly discusses the failure of both judicial and legislative activism in the form of the Civil Rights Act, the Voting Rights Act, school desegregation, reparations, affirmative action, and the equal protection clause. In addition, he examines strategies to undermine racism, including emigration, separatism, and nationalism. Each leads Bell to conclude that no different strategy could have changed the course the founders set in motion. Despite acknowledging that "the civil rights movement was the greatest social reform movement America had ever known," Bell nevertheless concludes that law is unable to effectively challenge the permanence of racism, whether it is created or affirmed by an active or restrained legislature or court (Bell 1987, 150). This leads to the tragic ending of Bell's story of race in the United States.

Tabloid and Critical Race Challenges to the Mainstream

The ending of Bell's narrative is perhaps even more fantastic than the time travel featured at the beginning of his work. Drawing on alien visitation themes prominent in popular culture, Bell offers "The Space Traders." In this story, contemporary political leaders prove every bit as willing as the founders were to trade African-American rights and liberties for the promise of economic prosperity and stability. As the story of race in the United States comes full circle, Bell reveals the consequences of the founders' fateful decision to constitutionalize slavery, highlighting the white elite's continued willingness to trade the rights and liberties of African-Americans in order to further their own interests and (their perception of) the national interest, as well as the willingness of white non-elites to go along. The "hero" of the story, Gleason Golightly, a conservative black economics professor who has influence with the president and his cabinet, offers an innovative resistance strategy designed to make whites think that the trade would further black interests. Golightly's failure to persuade the civil rights community to take up his strategy reinforces the inevitability of the tragic ending of the complex story of race in the United States.

In popular culture, stories of alien visitation regularly appear in tabloids (Bird 1992). Such stories are based on alternative sources of knowledge that challenge firmly entrenched mainstream beliefs. Jodi Dean notes that alien abduction narratives contest the legitimacy of the government and the stories about reality that it presents. By their very existence, Dean argues, "abductees bring to the fore the government's failures, its inability to protect, its schemes and conspiracies, its relationship to aliens and the otherness it denies" (1998, 23). While successful moon launches and space shuttle missions may support the notion of the superiority of the American way of life, alien visitation and abduction stories offer an alternative that challenges the legitimacy of the former narrative (Dean 1998). Tabloid stories implying that the government is covering up alien visitation include a headline of "Alien Backs Clinton," complete with a picture showing the two shaking hands. More than that, some tabloid stories suggest that government officials are aliens, as in the story, "Twelve US Senators Are Space Aliens," which lists 12 prominent officials in this group, including Orren Hatch (R-UT), Christopher Dodd (D-CT), John Rockefeller IV (D-WV), and John Glenn (D-OH) (Perel 2005; Glynn 2000, 150; Dean 1998, 157). Although some stories in the tabloids purport to be deadly serious, many contain an element of tongue-in-cheek humor. Indeed, much of the entertainment value of the tabloids lies in their ability to poke fun at the powers that be. They also offer readers a chance to laugh at themselves and the ridiculous situations that they find themselves in *vis-à-vis* official power.

Because stories of aliens contest the *status quo* and are based on a firm distrust of the government, Dean argues that stories about alien visitation can be understood as political metaphors for other social issues, including race. She argues:

> Ufology is political because it is stigmatized...It is this stigma attached to UFOs and UFO belief that enables the alien to function as an icon for some difficult social problems, particularly those located around the fault lines of truth, reality, and reasonableness. And it is also what makes aliens and UFOs interesting for critical social theory, not whether they are real, not whether the claims about them are true. (Dean 1998, 6)

Interestingly, the first abductee account, recorded in 1961, is the story of an interracial couple, Barney and Betty Hill.

Viewed from a mainstream perspective, stories of alien visitation and abduction are conspiratorial, unbelievable, and fantastical. As Dean points out, "participants think they speak and reason like everyone else, but...everyone else finds what they are saying to be incomprehensible and irrational" (Dean 1998, 16). However, as Dean points out, even stories once thought to be fantastic or paranoid by the mainstream can subsequently become widely regarded as true, including stories that the government introduced syphilis into unsuspecting black subjects in Tuskegee, and that the evidence in the O.J. Simpson case was tampered with. The eventual legitimization of such stories lends more credence to other "paranoid" stories about, say, the government introducing AIDS into black bodies or crack into Los Angeles in order to obtain guns for the Contras. As Dean puts it,

[s]ome African-Americans believe, in other words, that America has systematically oppressed black people, denied them jobs and opportunities, established separate and unequal procedures and criteria for justice, beaten, imprisoned, and killed black men, subverted African-American leaders, devalued black bodies, and denied basic necessities of humane physical and medical care to African-American citizens. (1998, 142)

Stories of alien visitation and abduction may not be all that far outside mainstream belief. While official government sources deny that there is any truth to alien abduction stories, a 1990 Gallup poll shows that a full 50 per cent of Americans believe in aliens, while roughly 33 per cent believe that aliens have visited earth. These include President Carter, who officially reported a sighting of a UFO, and Louis Farrakhan, who claims to have been abducted (Dean 1998, 25). Such stories may well have revolutionary potential. When Dean visited Roswell, New Mexico for the fiftieth anniversary of the alleged landing of the first alien aircraft to visit Earth, one speaker heralded the anniversary as a second American revolution focused on resisting the authority of those who would claim a monopoly on truth. In his view, Roswell represented "a reenactment of that original resistance which constituted America" (Dean 1998, 190).

There are many parallels between tabloids and Bell's critical race theory. Just as tabloids could easily be read as a parody of the mainstream or "real" news, Bell's stories could be read as a parody of contemporary constitutional discourse. Although each presents its alternatives as unproblematic truth, most readers know that such material isn't quite true in the conventional sense, in part because of the fantastic and excessive ways in which it is presented. As Fiske points out, tabloids offer a "sensational example of the inability of 'the normal' (and therefore the ideology that produced it) to explain or cope with specific instances of everyday life. The world it offers the readers is a world of the bizarre, the abnormal," which causes readers to question mainstream norms and frameworks (Fiske 1989b, 116).

Similarly, Bell's tragedy presents an alternative view of constitutional development that contains elements of both realism and the fantastic, to the end of exploring the hypocrisy of government and the failure of the civil rights movement. One of the strengths of Bell's work lies in his ability to use form to challenge the accuracy of reality as portrayed in mainstream constitutional discourse. According to Bell, fantasy is central to his narrative. He explains: "I have chosen in this book the tools not only of reason but of unreason, of fantasy" (Bell 1987, 5). To that end, Bell's *Chronicles* "employ stories that are not true to explore situations that are real enough but, in their many and contradictory dimensions, defy understanding" (Bell 1987, 7). Highlighting the need to depart from mainstream forms in order to devise a critique of mainstream content, Bell cites Kimberly Crenshaw (the apparent namesake of his hero Geneva Crenshaw): "'Through allegory, we can discuss legal doctrine in a way that does not replicate the abstractions of legal discourse'" (Bell 1987, 6–7). In this manner, what was once regarded as mere fantasy can become the basis of a legitimate alternative vision of reality. That is, fantastic stories can come to be seen as true, and realistic stories can come to be seen as fantastic.

Just as Bell offers something not often found in mainstream constitutional work, "the tabloids clearly offer millions of Americans something they do not find in other media" (Bird 1992, 7). Like Critical Race Theory, tabloids are "seen as an alternative, a way of knowing about the world" (Bird 1992, 138). Like Bell, the tabloids offer a "radical alternative" to the mainstream "that may be valuable to people who feel alienated from dominant narrative forms and frames of reference" (Bird 1992, 133). Even if tabloids do not always offer a radical alternative, they "may still offer a space within [the dominant] ideology, through which there may be some limited appropriation of and dispute over conventional constructions of reality" (Bird 1992, 160).

Like Bell, tabloids "deny the integrity of official epistemological categories," basing much of their material on the lived experience of people who claim to have had experiences that folks in the mainstream have not had (Glynn 2000, 148; Dean 1998, 109). Because tabloids recognize and encourage populist challenges to elite knowledge, they "challenge both the substantive content of conventional journalism and the stance toward knowledge on which it relies" (Glynn 2000, 144). Tabloids legitimate populist stories of alien visitation and abduction, causing scientific and governmental dismissal of the same stories to seem incredible. As Glynn puts it, the eruption of plural knowledges destabilizes the *status quo*, creating new political possibilities. He argues:

> Discursive power is up for grabs in the anything-goes world of the fantastic tabloids. A wide range of knowledges compete for control over the meaning of events, including popular knowledges that are generally discredited and excluded altogether from mainstream journalism. (Glynn 2000, 155–6)

Tabloids continue to thrive due to proven popular demand for such stories (Bird 1992, 28). They parody dominant narratives, including mainstream journalism and the reality it presents, often with a good deal of tongue-in-cheek humor. Satirical newspapers like *The Onion* pick up where the tabloids leave off, parodying mainstream journalism and the news presented there. Although it was once thought (however errantly) that the tabloids appealed solely to an older, conservative, uneducated audience, this is certainly not the case with *The Onion*, whose audience includes a large number of young, college-aged progressives. It regularly features stories that parody the Supreme Court.¹ In any case, the broad appeal of newer satirical outlets such as *The Onion* and *The Daily Show*, to say nothing of the fact that Bell's work has reached the *New York Times* bestseller list, all suggest that there is a strong demand for parodic alternative stories about political and constitutional power in a variety of alternative and mainstream media formats.

The End of the Story: Alien Visitation

Bell begins his story of alien visitation by recounting the many weeks of announcements preparing Earth for the visitation of over 1,000 alien ships, which land on the east coast from Massachusetts to North Carolina on the dawn of the new millennium—1 January 2000. As is common with alien narratives, the visitation begins with a "fantastic display of eerie lights and strange sound," as the aliens land (Bell 1992, 159; Dean 1998; Glynn 2000). The aliens speak English in the voice of Ronald Reagan and appear genderless, the latter being another feature common to visitation narratives. Emphasizing that no force will be used, the aliens offer the government gold to pay off the national debt, chemicals to clean the environment, and a safe, new energy supply, in exchange for all the African-Americans in the United States. In less than three weeks, on 17 January, Dr Martin Luther King Jr's birthday, the space traders deal is accomplished. The government agrees to the trade, tragically coming full circle with the story of race in America, which began with slave traders and will now end with space traders.

From the very start, whites and blacks have different perceptions of the trade. By and large, white people find the aliens unthreatening, while black people find them "unpleasant, even menacing in appearance" (Bell 1992, 161). While most blacks feel outrage that is "discounted in this crisis...[and that] they had, as usual, no credibility," most whites regard the trade as "the ultimate solution to the nation's troubles" (Bell 1992, 161). Accordingly, the President views the trade as "a chance to correct the excesses of several generations" as well as a solution to "the great American racial experiment" (Bell 1992, 164). His cabinet emphasizes the importance of the trade for economic stability. Several cabinet members assert that blacks should be willing to sacrifice for their country, and that whites would do so if they were similarly situated. Accordingly, the Attorney General proposes to draft a bill like the Selective Service Act, which would compel African-American participation in the trade.

Sitting in on the cabinet meeting as a special advisor to the administration is Gleason Golightly, who is alternatively described as a good soldier or an Uncle Tom, depending on the speaker's perspective. He claims that the trade amounts to group banishment "without either due process or judicial review" (Bell 1992, 167). Echoing Geneva's statements to the founders, he argues that if it were any group other than blacks that was being considered, "a horrified public would order the visitors off the planet without a moment's hesitation" (Bell 1992, 167). In a statement that would have applied equally well to slavery, he asserts that it is wrong to trade liberty for economic

---

1   See for example "Supreme Court Reaches Landmark 'It Depends' Ruling," *The Onion*, 28 May 2007.

advantage: "You simply cannot condemn twenty million people because they are black, and thus fit fodder for trade, so that this country can pay its debts, protect its environment, and ensure its energy supply" (Bell 1992, 167). Echoing Geneva, he appeals to their desire for fame, arguing that "what today seems to you a solution from Heaven will instead herald a decade of shame and dissension" (Bell 1992, 169).

After the cabinet discussion is over, Golightly realizes that he has succumbed to the error he so often had criticized civil rights movement activists of falling prey to, namely trying "to get whites to do right by black people because it was right that they do so" rather than appealing to their self-interest (Bell 1992, 171). Ironically, the Secretary of the Interior privately appeals directly to Golightly's self-interest, asking him to pitch the trade to other blacks on the basis of sacrifice for country, in recompense for which he would allow Golightly to take 100 black families out of the country before the trade occurs.

The anti-trade coalition, a group of white liberals, black civil rights representatives, and progressive academics, immediately urges opposition by using traditional forms of political resistance including constitutional challenges, direct action and boycotts, kidnapping, and massive disobedience. Golightly speaks to them at a mass meeting, acknowledging that black rights and interests have always been fit for sacrifice in order to further white needs and wants. He argues that unlike the great majority of blacks who know better and are thus resigned to their fate, civil rights groups time and time again mistakenly assume "that whites really want to grant justice to blacks, really want to alleviate onerous racial conditions" (Bell 1992, 175). Highlighting the tragic inevitability of the situation, Golightly argues that the efforts of the anti-trade coalition and other civil rights groups "will simply add a veneer of face-saving uncertainty to a debate whose outcome is not only predictable, but inevitable" (Bell 1992, 175).

Urging them to begin with a more realistic assessment of the situation, he begins to lay out an alternative strategy based on "cunning and guile" rather than earnest persuasion. Golightly urges civil rights groups to modestly propose acceptance of the trade, on the grounds that whites will reject the trade if blacks appear to want it or if whites come to believe that it is in the self-interest of blacks. Arguing that "[a] major, perhaps the principle, motivation for racism in this country is the deeply held belief that black people should not have anything that white people don't have," he recommends spreading the story that the aliens will be taking blacks to a land of milk and honey (Bell 1992, 175). He predicts that this will cause whites to challenge the trade in court, by contending that it is "unconstitutional discrimination against whites" (Bell 1992, 176).

In the end, these civil rights leaders cannot trust Golightly enough to go along with his idea, as they have been on the opposite sides of so many issues in the past. Golightly accuses them of "confusing integrity with foolhardiness," unlike rank-and-file blacks who, he argues, typically understand that employing duplicity is to some degree necessary for survival (Bell 1992, 178). Ironically, it turns out that Golightly's story is not far from the truth. In the epilogue to this story, Bell reveals that the alien's planet *is* a land of milk and honey of sorts, a place where African-Americans would be respected, admired, and studied for their perseverance in the face of severe oppression. However, as we shall see, even when this alternative is revealed, blacks will once again fail to trust in it, opting to go back to certain struggle at home rather than risk possible victory in an alien land.

In any case, as the days leading up to the space trade roll by, the President publicly acknowledges both sides of the argument, adding that even though only one group is being singled out, there is no apparent discriminatory intent. Although he emphasizes that the trade would solve the economic crisis, others, particularly corporate leaders, are not as sure that the trade is in their best interests. They recognize that black consumption is an important part of the economy and that real estate markets have long been energized by the fear of "tipping" neighborhoods (Bell 1992, 181). Others add that economic and political stability might be challenged if poor whites become inflamed about their own situation and begin to notice "gross disparities in opportunities and income" in the absence of a favorable comparison with less advantageously situated blacks (Bell 1992, 181). All too willing to behave duplicitously, business leaders quietly begin an expensive media campaign designed "to exploit both the integration achieved in America and the moral cost of its loss" (Bell 1992, 181).

Arguing that the framers designed the Constitution to accommodate programs like this, supporters of the trade follow their example and convene a special constitutional convention in Philadelphia in order to pass a constitutional amendment that allows Congress to call for selective service "to protect domestic interests and international needs" (Bell 1992, 185). Supporters of ratification assert: "The Framers intended America to be a white country" (Bell 1992, 187). Arguing that integration has failed, they follow the example of the founders and prioritize national stability over rights and liberties, stating:

> After more than a hundred and thirty seven years of good-faith efforts to build a healthy, stable, interracial nation, we have concluded—as the Framers did in the beginning—our survival today requires that we sacrifice the rights of blacks in order to protect and further the interests of whites. The Framers' example must be our guide. Patriotism, and not pity, must govern our decision. (Bell 1992, 187–8)

Echoing the founders' arguments for stability and union, they assert that "[w]ithout the compromises on slavery in the Constitution of 1787, there would be no America," and thus no emancipation. They ask: "where and how might slavery have ended had a new government not been formed?" (Bell 1992, 189). On this basis they conclude that while "[t]he role that blacks may be called upon to play...is, however regrettable, neither immoral nor unconstitutional" (Bell 1992, 189).

It eventually becomes clear, even to the opponents of the trade, that the law offers no meaningful basis of resistance. The Supreme Court refuses to intervene to halt a planned referendum on the question, saying that the issue is a political question not a legal matter. Citing *Korematsu* (the case in which the Supreme Court upheld the internment of Japanese-Americans during World War II) and other relevant precedents, the court consistently finds that the "standard of national necessity" applies in this case, overriding any arguments that race is a suspect classification worthy of greater constitutional protection. The referendum passes by a resounding 70 per cent/30 per cent margin, a result that Bell characterizes as the standard "fate of minority rights when subjected to referenda or initiatives" (Bell 1992, 191).

In the end, Golightly is granted safe passage to Canada for his years of loyal service to the administration, but even he is stopped at the border. While he kicks himself for not heeding his own warning about trusting whites in power, he comes to realize that there was never any real alternative to the tragic ending about to be played out. As his wife points out, if the trade had been rejected, and blacks had been allowed to stay, they would inevitably have been blamed for the unresolved problems that would ostensibly have been successfully addressed by the trade. Thus he realizes that the conclusion to the narrative is inevitable, beginning with the founders' decision to trade African-American rights and liberties for national stability. The book ends with resignation to this fate, bringing the beginning and the end of the story together into a tragic conclusion that testifies to the profound betrayal of the civil rights movement's hope of full citizenship and assimilation with equal rights and liberties under the law: "There was no escape, no alternative. Heads bowed, arms now linked by slender chains, black people left the New World as their forebears had arrived" (Bell 1992, 194). Ironically, they are taken away at dawn on Martin Luther King's birthday, stripped nearly naked with no escape or alternative.

Epilogue of the Story: Alien Abduction

In the wake of this tragic ending Bell calls for a new, hopeful narrative that would find humanity in the midst of inhumanity, meaning in the midst of extreme adversity. Such a narrative would speak to the persistence of power as well as "the indomitable human spirit" (Bell 1992, 197). It would include heroic acts of defiance as well as the ordinary resistance of everyday African-Americans who have produced cultural meaning through art, music, and poetry; reshaped the Christian religion; and unified many peoples into a single community. Yet this new narrative that Bell imagines still seems tinged with tragic complexity and fatalism. Speaking of the "dilemmas of committed confrontation," he concludes: "We can go forth to serve, knowing that our failure to act will not change conditions and may very well worsen them" (Bell 1992, 198).

In *Gospel Choirs* Bell offers a sequel, or what might be thought of as an epilogue, to the story of the space traders. This installment of Bell's narrative initially suggests a pulling back from resignation and its tragic ending, as African-Americans are given the option to live in peace on the aliens' planet. Resisting the idea that his early stories were grounded in resignation, Bell insists that "[t]he 'permanence' [of racism] theme was not, as some thought, a signal of surrender, but a tardy recognition of racism's deepest roots" (Bell 1996, 13). Yet African-Americans' rejection of the option to leave suggests that the hold of racism cannot be broken in this or any other world, even when racism and its consequences are directly acknowledged.

The story begins where it left off; the government's willingness to engage in the space trade suggests that "the rights and even lives of black people, even as citizens, have always been a commodity subject to barter by white people for their own needs and self-interest" (Bell 1996, 17). Bell picks up the story onboard the alien spacecraft. Following the usual pattern of alien abduction narratives, the pulsating lights and colors flash, but the hidden voice now speaks in a warm, non-gender-specific, black voice, rather than in the voice of Ronald Reagan as was the case on Earth. The chains fall off the African-American abductees and they become clothed in robes.

A period of darkness follows, and time is suspended for two months, time loss being another theme common to stories of alien abduction. When the flashing light reappears, the voice explains that they, the aliens, are studying the United States' experiment with democracy and the "blot" on it, namely the government's long refusal to grant African-Americans full rights of citizenship equal to those of white citizens. The voice relates that black experience from slavery to the space trade suggests that "white people consider you—as they considered you from the beginning—no more than their property, to be sold to the highest bidder" (Bell 1996, 20). The aliens find that while they can replicate African-American voices and expressions, they cannot recreate the "robust warmth and humor...the emotional and spiritual strength whereby you have sustained that humanity through all your travails...[and] your ability to transcend suffering—to sing through it, as you yourselves might say" (Bell 1996, 20). Despite their advanced technology, the aliens have not been able to relieve the suffering of their own people, so they seek to integrate African-Americans into their society, "to mingle with our citizens as equals and full partners in our development and growth" (Bell 1996, 20).

The aliens initially believe that African-Americans will be glad to leave and make a new start in a new world, particularly in light of the government's willingness to send them off to an unknown fate. During the journey away from Earth, however, the aliens detect a more complicated set of emotions, which include "a longing to return to the land that you call home" during the period when time is suspended (Bell 1996, 20). Because they want the African-Americans to enter their world without coercion, they ask them to vote on the question with the full knowledge of the circumstances they will face if they decide to return home to the United States. Accordingly, the aliens disclose that the United States has been receiving the scorn of the world for accepting the trade. At the same time, it has already used up almost all the new resources, with no racial scapegoats on whom to deflect the blame.

The heroes of Bell's earlier stories, Geneva Crenshaw and Gleason Golightly, each ask to speak to the group before the vote. Golightly favors returning home to the United States, while Geneva favors moving to the alien planet. Embracing a tragic fate characterized by oppression and injustice, Golightly would rather return to a shared history and to the civilization African-Americans helped create than embrace an alien world populated by technologically superior beings. While Golightly concedes that he cannot guarantee that their situation will be better than it was before they left, he recalls that their ancestors provided an example which suggests that it is "through struggling against evil that we achieve our salvation" (Bell 1996, 24).

For Geneva, returning home would divert white folks' attention from their current crisis, without any promise of racial justice. Asserting that "four hundred years is enough to convince me that America will never change—indeed, is incapable of change," she rejects the tragic narrative that home offers, arguing that the space trade has finally fulfilled the longstanding racist hope that African-Americans would cease to exist (Bell 1996, 23). She argues that African-Americans have at long last been freed and are now being offered a land of their own, just as the children of Israel had been following their bondage in Egypt. She urges them to create a new narrative, consistent with the one that Bell anticipated in his postscript to the space traders' story.

As Geneva finishes her speech, a light again begins to flash, and the vote ensues, resulting in 70 per cent wanting to go ahead with the aliens and 30 per cent voting to return to Earth. However, by monitoring the thoughts of the abductees, the aliens determine that the abductees would favor whoever was speaking last by this margin. From this they deduce that Geneva's position won because she spoke last, but that Golightly would have won by a similar margin had he been given the last word. Consistent with the tragic narrative, the complexity of the situation eventuates in ambivalent action on the part of African-Americans. Noting that "[s]uch ambivalence is very disturbing to us," the aliens argue that such "commitment to that land of your enslavement defies rationality" (Bell 1996, 26).

Several of the abductees start singing the hymn "Soon and Very Soon," but instead of concluding with "we're going to see the Lord," they substitute "we're going to see our home" (Bell 1996, 27). The aliens detect that 70 per cent are now ready to return to Earth and that the number is rising. Saying that they cannot risk "disrupting our more advanced world with immigrants who could not accept it wholeheartedly," they elect to circle Earth's galaxy until they decide what to do with the abductees (Bell 1996, 27). Geneva starts singing "Amazing Grace," written by former slave ship captain John Newton, and the rest join in, with the story ending with the line "and grace will lead me home."

Conclusion

Rather than seeking either a romantic stabilization or a comic liberation from the past, Bell offers a tragic reading of the Constitution that questions romance's nostalgic yearning for the past and comedy's cheery optimism about the future. His detailed account of the persistence and brutality of racism challenges the foundations of both the romantic and comic constitutional narratives, providing an important narrative of dissent from mainstream constitutional theory. Despite all the disagreement in mainstream constitutional discourse about whether judicial restraint is preferable to judicial activism, mainstream constitutional discourse has largely (and quite reasonably) been read as trying to legitimize judicial review and establish consent to the dominant order. Bell offers an alternative method of reading constitutional discourse, grounded in narrative analysis, popular culture, and fantasy, which eventuates in dissent rather than consent, resistance rather than legitimacy.

Bell's work suggests that from the very start US constitutional discourse has contained the seeds of resistance in addition to the standard defense of the dominant order, even though that resistance may often be overlooked, misunderstood, or drowned out in the mainstream discourse. In this he runs parallel to popular culture theorists such as John Fiske, who argues that while popular culture often appears blithely to support the *status quo*, it can also serve as the basis for a democratic challenge to the dominant order.

Even though he offers a strong narrative of dissent, Bell is far less confident than Fiske regarding the political efficaciousness of such challenges. While Bell openly calls for a new narrative to replace the old one, and while his own stories go a long way in fostering the dissent necessary for such a transformation, the tragic form he adopts ultimately prevents him from realizing it, as it seems to inadvertently support dominant power.

Every dramatic form has its limitations, political and otherwise, and tragedy is no exception. While tragedy offers a much more compelling account of the role of racism and brutality in American constitutional development than the comedic and romantic narratives that have long dominated constitutional discourse, it nevertheless has serious limitations. By definition it leads to the affirmation of the dominant order, fostering resignation to the *status quo*. By characterizing resigned resistance to oppression as tragically heroic, Bell's tragedy reproduces an oppressed/oppressor binary across racial lines, thereby reinscribing power as we know it. In addition, tragedy typically ends in death, an irreversible and permanent ending. Thus, Bell's *Gospel Choirs* ends with the savior figure Geneva Crenshaw disappearing into thin air (or perhaps ascending into heaven, depending on one's perspective), not having solved or perhaps even altered the problem of racism, either in our world by time traveling to convince the founders of the error of their ways or in any other world as evidenced by the story of the space trade. In this sense, tragedy seems to have foreclosed the location of a new, more democratic narrative in contemporary constitutional discourse.

And yet, the question remains as to what will happen with the African-Americans still suspended in space between this world and the next. *Gospel Choirs* ends with Bell acknowledging Geneva's disappearance and saying, "It is up to us now to do what we can for one another" (Bell 1996, 214). That is, it is not up to the founders, or Geneva, or any other savior figure that we could imagine. It is up to us, the people, to figure out how to move forward into a more democratic constitutional discourse that foregrounds equality. In a sense, like the African-Americans in Bell's stories, we are all suspended in the spaceship, struggling with our attachment to the world that we know and the alien world that might offer a much better alternative.

Should we stay or go? The beauty of Bell's work is that it opens up this important question by using fantasy to challenge constitutional reality as we know it. Bell's frank and tragic discussion of the brutality of racism allows us to move beyond constitutional meaning as we know it. Without it, we are stuck at an impasse between romance and comedy. With it, we are suspended between this constitutional world and the next. But it makes all the difference to know that other worlds exist and that we have a choice as to whether we stay or go. By focusing on his extremely sobering account of the persistence and brutality of power, Bell's critics overlook the ways in which his tragic acknowledgment of brutality may, ironically, be the only thing that can lead us beyond our current impasse. While his work does not hold out the promise of an idyllic future, it does foreground the relationship between form and content which in turn can foster the generation of new and creative narrative possibilities that have yet to be imagined.

The addition of parody and humor to alternative stories like Bell's may lead us even closer to transformation. Of all the narrative forms we have explored thus far, tragedy may be the least amenable to humor, and for good reason. Bell's tragic reading of the Constitution emphasizes the deadly seriousness of power, often in all its brutal and murderous detail. He notes that humiliation, by which he means humor at the expense of the oppressed, is part and parcel of this country's constitutional story, including a long and continuing history of racial oppression. In this frame, humor can seem to be a disrespectful and painful reminder of power and its consequences. Thus Bell resists the integration of humor into his work, fearing that laughter will give more power to voices that already dominate, while he aims to give voice to marginalized groups.

However, it is precisely this dilemma that a parody of power seeks to address and negotiate: how can those with little formal power outfox the powerful, even as they continue to remain, by definition, subject to the dictates of power? Rather than further humiliating those with little power, an effective parody of power aims primarily to ridicule the powerful, including their self-serious pretensions and outrageous abuses, thus giving more voice to those with little power and allowing them to form an entirely different understanding of power and its ridiculous consequences.

Despite his stated reticence to use humor, Bell's work acknowledges the realities of power by providing a narrative that is rooted in the populist genre of science fiction and by including voices that power typically suppresses. And the tabloids seem to provide an example of a populist form that uses humor in a manner that seems friendly to many of Bell's themes. Yet, the tragic form of Bell's narrative rules out the use of humor as a tool of destabilization, at least on his account, leaving us suspended in space deciding whether to return home or to leave for an alien world.

A more humorous, perhaps self-consciously ironic, narrative might serve to be more empowering and perhaps more destabilizing than Bell's meaningful yet extraordinarily painful tragedy, helping to obviate the criticism that is most often leveled against his work: that it is hopelessly enervating to the point of political debilitation. If power is in fact as far reaching as Bell suggests, there is all the more reason to explore every tool possible to escape or at least undermine it, even if temporarily. Such a narrative should directly confront the choice with which Bell leaves us: should we stay or should we go? Should we abandon constitutional discourse and its attachment to the founding fathers, legitimacy, and all the limitations that such devotion entails, in favor of some other more unique way of thinking about constitutional meaning and judicial identity? Or should we embrace mainstream constitutional discourse as it is, fraught with the tension between romance and comedy? Do we accept its inability to address brutality, to provide moments of transformation, and to laugh at the ridiculous persistence of power? This is the choice that Bell's work leads us to confront.

The following chapters provide two extended examples of parodies of power that explore the limitations of mainstream constitutional discourse. Each parody is grounded in popular culture and laced with tongue-in-cheek humor. Drawing on the rather alien and ironic form offered by queer theory, Chapter 5 explores what constitutional discourse might look like if we left behind the myth of origin that drives mainstream constitutional theory and is regularly referenced in order to legitimate various constitutional decisions. Instead, it offers a parody of judicial identity that discusses the Supreme Court's decision in *Bush* v. *Gore* as a (political) coming out narrative.

Chapter 6, on the other hand, stays with the narrative forms currently available in mainstream constitutional discourse, along with its myth of origin, while at the same time challenging its limitations and stretching its boundaries as far as possible, from the inside out. Inspired by the popular reality television show *Queer Eye for the Straight Guy*, this chapter centralizes parody, offering a unique reading of each of the narrative forms of contemporary constitutional discourse as we know it. In doing so, it evaluates, makes over, and sends up romantic, comedic, and tragic narrative accounts of constitutional change as played out in the context of the change in the Supreme Court's treatment of sodomy laws, from *Bowers* v. *Hardwick* to *Lawrence* v. *Texas*. Following Bell's example of altering form as a means of altering content and Robert Cover and Paul Brest's exhortation to open up space in which other alternative narratives might emerge, these chapters offer two of many possible examples that could be imagined which use populist readings to parody and challenge constitutional reality as we know it.

Chapter 5

Did the Supreme Court Come Out in *Bush* v. *Gore*? The Instability of Judicial Identity

Introduction

This chapter offers a different take on the question "who's your daddy?" than the previous chapters. Rather than focusing on a myth of (paternal) origin and seeking to reconnect to it in a deferential manner as in romance, to reformulate it in an active manner as in comedy, or to reject it in a resigned manner as in tragedy, this chapter explores what constitutional discourse might look like absent a myth of origin to reference in order to legitimate (or resist) judicial review as practiced in a controversial constitutional decision, *Bush* v. *Gore*. As we've seen, the myths of origin that inform romance, comedy, and tragedy each lead to a specific constitutional narrative and a particular understanding of judicial identity, foreclosing rather than opening up innovative ways to conceptualize constitutional interpretation. Whittington's romantic originalism leads to judicial restraint, Dworkin's comedic take on the founding leads to judicial activism, and Bell's tragic view of the founding leads to resignation to judicial decision-making as a tactic that the powers that be employ to diffuse political dissent.

While previous chapters suggest that there is much to be gained from parodying the narratives that dominate contemporary constitutional discourse, Tania Modleski reminds us that if we are always working in an adversarial role, we are always on the defensive, "always, as it were, complaining about the family, but never leaving home" (1982, 103–104). Perhaps if the myth of origin is removed, that is, if we leave home, then we might stand a better chance of addressing constitutional politics in our own right, rather than continuing to respond to paternal views in one (narrative) form or another. Removing, or at least decentering, the myth of origin can open up space in which new constitutional narratives and judicial identities may emerge. The point is neither to idealize nor to malign the founding fathers, but rather to decentralize them, to move on by exploring alternative constitutional narratives that produce different forms of judicial identity.

This chapter and the following chapter offer two such possibilities; both are grounded in queer theory, which emphasizes parody and destabilizes identity and thus challenges a stable myth of origin. Because queer identity does not centralize ancestry, each generation appears to start anew. Accordingly, the question, "who's your daddy?" is much more likely to elicit a narrative about one's own desires and interests in a context that directly acknowledges the persistence of power, rather than narratives like those examined in previous chapters, which tend to obscure self-interest by focusing on paternal desires. These responses to "who's your daddy?" are reflected in popular culture. Compare, on the one hand the Fox reality television show entitled "Who's Your Daddy?," which centers on adoptees discovering their authentic paternity as they consider several possible fathers, with country singer Toby Keith's song, "Who's Your Daddy?" which highlights desire, self-interest, and power:

> And who's the one guy that you come runnin' to
> When your love life starts tumblin'?
> I got the money if you got the honey
> Let's cut a deal, let's make a plan...
> Who's your daddy, who's your baby
> Who's your buddy, who's your man?

This chapter explores judicial identity in *Bush* v. *Gore*, using insights garnered from queer theory's rejection of the myth of origin as well as its parodic take on sex and gender identity. *Bush* v. *Gore* decentralizes the paternal authority of the founding fathers. In the course of six opinions spanning 61 pages, the founding fathers are mentioned only once, in the dissenting opinion of Justice Breyer. This reference is not addressed in any of the other opinions and does not otherwise play much of a role in this case. Hence, the *Bush* v. *Gore* case offers an interesting opportunity for exploring alternative forms of judicial identity absent a central myth of origin.

In this chapter I read the performance of judicial identity in *Bush* v. *Gore* as a coming out narrative in which the Court abandons a presumptively normative legal identity in favor of a deviant political identity, in a manner that parallels the standard coming out narrative in which heterosexuality is abandoned in favor of homosexuality. By reading the opinion in *Bush* v. *Gore* as parallel to an open secret in a classic coming out story, I parody the Supreme Court's straight-faced insistence that their work is legal, not political, and offer an alternative narrative about judicial identity. With tongue firmly in cheek, I also parody the seriousness of the straight form of academic writing that is adopted by so much of the Lesbian, Gay, Bisexual, Transgender (LGBT) work on the topic of coming out, by systematically delineating six aspects of the coming out narrative and meticulously applying each one to the Court's opinion in *Bush* v. *Gore*. By playfully parodying the Supreme Court's attachment to a rigid division between law and politics, the coming out narrative that has been so central to LGBT studies, and the ultra-serious performance of academic theorizing, I offer an alternative narrative of judicial identity in an innovative form that reimagines contemporary constitutional discourse in a manner that seeks to move beyond its current impasse.

The Gay Coming Out Narrative

While there has been an enormous amount of discussion about *Bush* v. *Gore* since the Supreme Court decided the case on 12 December 2000, no one has analyzed the case as a classic coming out narrative. Much, if not all, of the debate about *Bush* v. *Gore* has focused on (and reproduced) the conflict between conservatives and moderates on the Court about the correct outcome of the case, particularly as to whether the recount in Florida should have been allowed to continue. Replicating the split on the Court, conservative scholars have welcomed the Court's decision to halt the recount, characterizing it as based on sound legal reasoning, above the political fray, and hence legitimate, while liberal scholars have characterized it as politically motivated, lawless, and hence illegitimate.[1] The focus on conflict seems to have caused scholars to overlook the assumption, which is widely shared regardless of their conflicting views about the appropriate outcome in the case, that it is illegitimate and thus shameful for the Court to behave politically, be it openly or otherwise.[2] Though conservatives and liberals may disagree about whether the Court actually was political in *Bush* v. *Gore*, closeting and shaming any and all judicial political behavior seems to be the order of the day.

Gay and lesbian studies have much to add to the debate about *Bush* v. *Gore*, due to expertise in analyzing closeting and coming out narratives.[3] This sort of analysis has been done primarily in relation to sexual identity. Recently, however, queer theorists have argued that analyzing closeting narratives may be useful for understanding not only gay and lesbian politics, but also for understanding legal, cultural, and political discourses more generally. For example, Eve Sedgwick has argued that "the epistemology of the closet" has marked Western conceptual systems at least since the dawn of the twentieth century, even those that seem to have nothing to do with sexuality (1985, 1). Michael Warner adds that "the logic of the sexual order is deeply embedded by now in an indescribably wide range of social institutions, and is embedded in most western accounts of the world" (1993, x). Elsewhere I have argued that the persistent habit of closeting sexuality in mainstream constitutional theory has had a profound impact on the parameters of scholarly constitutional discourse (Burgess 1999; 2002). Here I extend this work by analyzing a constitutional case that seems to have nothing to do with sexuality, *Bush* v. *Gore*, as a coming out narrative.

The opinions in *Bush* v. *Gore* parallel a classic gay and lesbian coming out narrative—complete with all the prospects and problems that such a narrative typically entails. Just as gay and lesbian sexual behavior and identity are the focus of the standard coming out narrative, so too are political behavior and identity the focus of the Court's coming out narrative. Just as heterosexuality is default until one comes out as gay or lesbian, a legal identity is default for the Court until political behavior suggests an alternative identity. In both cases the default identity is valorized, while the identity that requires outing is typically thought to be undesirable or an aberration from the more legitimate default identity. Just as homosexuals often strive for the legitimacy that accrues to heterosexuals as a matter of course, judges who exhibit political behavior struggle to regain the legitimacy that they enjoyed when their legal identity was not in question.

---

1 Compare, for example, Richard Posner (2001) and Howard Gillman (2001).

2 For an exception see Fish (2000).

3 See for example, Berube (1990), Blasius (1994), John D'Emilio (1983), Shane Phelan (1994).

Just as gays and lesbians have long struggled with the difficulties associated with both closeting and revealing a purportedly shameful sexual identity, the opinions in *Bush* v. *Gore* exemplify a parallel set of narratives in which the Court is struggling to maintain its legitimacy by closeting politics and resisting the shame associated with "coming out" as political. Coming out of the closet has been a central narrative of gay and lesbian life at least since the early 1970s, following the famous Stonewall riots.[4] The closet serves as a metaphor for invisibility, which is largely a reaction to a longstanding assumption that gay and lesbian sexuality is deviant or illegitimate, and thus worthy of ridicule, punishment, and perhaps violence. In this context, the closet offers gays and lesbians a measure of safety in return for keeping sexual identity a secret. It also offers a measure of shame and isolation, as closeted gays and lesbians are taught that it is necessary to hide their sexuality in order to survive physically, personally, and professionally.

In general, the gay and lesbian coming out narrative can be characterized as moving sexual identity from the closeted private sphere into the political public sphere. Several features characterize the lesbian and gay coming out narrative, including drama, passing, and a "moment of truth" in which the shameful identity in question is directly discussed and, as a result, clarified. Friends, relatives, and professional colleagues typically offer a variety of reactions to the disclosure(s) offered by the moment of truth. These include contempt, tolerance, and fear of loss of approval. The opinions in *Bush* v. *Gore* contain all of these features, offering a political coming out narrative that parallels the gay and lesbian coming out narrative, particularly that part of the narrative commonly known as the open secret, under which individuals behave in a manner consistent with a shameful identity even though they continue to deny all such association.

The Judicial Coming Out Narrative

Drama

What is coming out as gay or lesbian if not an extended opportunity to engage in protracted drama? Similarly, the backdrop of *Bush* v. *Gore* is one of high drama that is ripe for a coming out analysis. 24/7 coverage on cable news networks offered up a number of dramatic developments as they broke during the 36 days between the 2000 presidential election and the United States Supreme Court's decision to halt the recount. Every day brought a new development, many of which would have been unthinkable in mainstream analyses of US politics prior to this election. The dramatic context of the 36 days during which the US presidency seemed up for grabs following Election Day 2000 was topped only by the Supreme Court's dramatic and split resolution of the election controversy in *Bush* v. *Gore*. Would the Florida Secretary of State review improperly marked ballots for possible inclusion in the recount? No! Would the Florida Supreme Court do so? Yes! Would it extend the

---

4   For an argument that suggests that the centrality of this narrative is in decline, see Wilson (1996).

12 December "safe harbor" deadline?[5] Yes! Were African-Americans in selected counties of Florida systematically disenfranchised during the 2000 presidential elections? Depends on who you ask! Were large numbers of liberal Florida Jews hoodwinked into voting for ultra-conservative Pat Buchanan by confusing butterfly ballots? Again, depends on who you ask! Would the United States Supreme Court decide to hear a case that would determine a contested presidential election? Yes! Would a conservative majority decide to halt the recount, thus legitimating the election of conservative George W. Bush? Yes! Would Al Gore accept the US Supreme Court's decision and concede the election? Yes!

In addition, just as the gay penchant for drama and theatre in all its varieties has been well documented, so too have several Justices publicly indicated their love of drama. As discussed in Chapter 3, Chief Justice William Rehnquist's passion for theatre was so strong that he very visibly integrated it into his professional identity. Inspired by the Gilbert and Sullivan operetta "Iolanthe," he altered his professional appearance by adding four gold stripes to the sleeves of his judicial robe sleeves in 1995. In addition, the unlikely pair of Justices Ruth Bader Ginsburg and Antonin Scalia have regularly been seen attending the theatre together in various Washington venues, confirming what gays and lesbians have long known, namely that drama can make for extremely strange bedfellows.[6]

Passing

Just as gays and lesbians can closet their sexuality and pass as straight, the Court can closet its politics and pass as legal. This has long been a standard feature of mainstream US constitutional theory, with judicial activism often serving as a stand-in for politics, leaving judicial restraint as the default legal position.[7] Justices regularly offer legal reasoning to ground their decisions, largely avoiding a direct discussion of the role that politics and activism play in their rulings. The majority opinion in *Bush* v. *Gore* is no exception. It is structured to try to downplay questions of politics and judicial legitimacy. It begins with the facts of the case and focuses largely on legal doctrine to undergird its decision to halt the recount. However, judicial restraint normally entails deference to state law as produced and interpreted by state legislatures and state courts, respectively. Therefore, in order to avoid the appearance of judicial activism, the majority repeatedly takes great pains to explain why it is intervening in a matter that seems to be controlled by Florida law. This is especially necessary since the majority concedes that there is no federal constitutional right for individuals to vote in presidential elections. In addition, the Constitution gives states plenary power to decide the manner in which presidential electors are chosen. However, the majority opinion argues that when states vest the right to vote in the people, that right becomes fundamental and invites enforcement through

---

5   The safe harbor deadline refers to the Florida Legislature's determination of when the recount needed to be concluded.

6   See <http://www.usatoday.com/news/court/nsco1082.htm> and <www.cpan.org/questions/week136.asp>.

7   For more on this point see Perretti (1999).

federal judicial intervention. Attempting to further downplay the unrestrained nature of their dramatic intervention into the presidential election debacle, the majority also attempts to ground its decision in law by citing settled precedent. The cases cited are two instances in which the Supreme Court actively intervened in state electoral systems, *Harper* v. *Virginia Board of Elections* and *Reynolds* v. *Sims*. In one sense, the decision to cite such cases is unsurprising given the *Bush* v. *Gore* majority is attempting to legitimate its active intervention into Florida's electoral system. However, from the standpoint of passing, these two cases are quite problematic as they are both prime examples of the type of Warren Court activism into state electoral systems that conservatives and advocates of judicial restraint have long characterized as illegitimate judicial intervention into the political realm. As is commonly the case when (gay) sexuality (or political behavior) is an open secret, the actor in question behaves in a manner that suggests that he or she is gay, while continuing to insist that he or she is not. Thus, despite the fact that the majority's behavior in *Bush* v. *Gore* seems decidedly political, the majority continues to insist that their decision is grounded in law rather than politics.

Moment of Truth

Needless to say, passing is not a foolproof tactic. Edmund White suggests that at some point in the coming out process there is typically a "moment of truth" that reveals (gay) sexual identity. He explains: "Since homosexuals are never brought up to be gay and discover their sexual identity and declare it (at least to themselves) at a precise moment in their young years, the first time has become a sacrosanct topic in gay life. There's always that moment (usually just after sex) when a new partner asks, 'So, when did you first figure out you were gay?'" (E. White 2002, 20). Of course, White's analysis assumes a fairly large degree of self-acceptance of one's sexual identity. Those who are not as far along in the coming out process would be more likely to continue to exhibit shame about their gay behavior, perhaps claiming that they were seduced or forced to engage in the behavior by a bona fide homosexual.

Similar to gays and lesbians with regard to sexuality, Justices on the Court have not been socialized to think of themselves as political. How they address politics, particularly in a highly visible case such as *Bush* v. *Gore*, is a "moment of truth" for the Court that is likely, in one way or another, to clarify the Court's judicial identity. If White is correct, this would be most likely to occur directly after the Court has engaged in political behavior. This is precisely what happens in *Bush* v. *Gore*. In order to overturn the Florida Supreme Court's ruling, the majority must openly practice activism and behave politically. Evidencing shame regarding their political behavior, while still never directly discussing it, they instead offer an immediate explanation for judicial intervention, characterizing their activism as unusual and claiming that the actions of the truly lawless Florida Supreme Court forced them into it.

By openly rejecting deference (with only one exception that is peripheral to the Court's decision),[8] and thus openly embracing activism, the majority outs its politics. However, following the classic open secret pattern, the majority claims that they were forced to act politically due to the actions of others. Thus, in the much quoted concluding paragraph of the opinion, the majority faces its moment of truth and admits its activism, but blames it on others:

> None are more conscious of the vital limits on judicial authority than are the members of this Court, and none stand more in admiration of the Constitution's design to leave the selection of the President to the people, through their legislatures, and to the political sphere. When contending parties invoke the process of the courts, however, it becomes our unsought responsibility to resolve the federal and constitutional issues the judicial system has been forced to confront. (*Bush* 2000, 533)

Elsewhere, the majority blames its activist behavior on the Florida Supreme Court, claiming that they never would have been required to take the case had the Florida high court halted the recount. Following the classic open secret pattern, the partially-out, partially-closeted majority cannot help but acknowledge its visible political behavior, while still claiming to have been forced into it by others (George W. Bush, Al Gore, and the Florida Supreme Court) whose politics are already out of the closet. The visible politics of the others compels the Court also to behave politically, ostensibly only in response to the obviously political others. On this basis, the majority reasserts its legal identity, even as it acknowledges, at least somewhat, that it has behaved in a manner that suggests the emergence of a political identity.

Much as White might have predicted, Chief Justice Rehnquist's concurring opinion (joined by Justices Scalia and Clarence Thomas) immediately follows the majority's political behavior, opening with a direct explanation of said behavior. Rehnquist's concurring opinion begins by indirectly outing the Court's activism, conceding that while "[i]n most cases, comity and respect for federalism compel us to defer to the decisions of state courts on issues of state law" there are some exceptions, such as this case, "in which the Constitution imposes a duty or confers a power on a particular branch of a State's government" (*Bush* 2000, 533).

Rather than forwarding its own political agenda, Rehnquist insists that the majority halted the recount in service to the Florida State Legislature's agenda. Thus, Rehnquist claims that the Florida Supreme Court substantially departed from the Florida Legislature's scheme by eliminating the original deadline for the recount and disregarding Secretary of State Katherine Harris's decision not to accept recounts beyond that deadline. In this view, therefore, it is the Florida Supreme Court that is responsible for illegitimately altering the law and raising a federal question that necessitated (seduced?) the US Supreme Court into acting. Thus, like the majority opinion, Rehnquist reveals the majority's political behavior while denying political identity, claiming once again that the majority was forced to act. Attempting to maintain the Court's legal identity, Rehnquist insists that the majority offers "an independent, if still deferential, analysis of state law" (*Bush* 2000, 534).

---

8   As Howard Gillman points out, the majority defers only once to the Florida Supreme Court on the issue of the 12 December safe harbor deadline (2001, 159).

Having addressed the (political) moment of truth, Rehnquist immediately attempts to reassert his own fidelity to judicial restraint and deference, contending that "the clearly expressed intent of the legislature must prevail," despite the lawless ruling of the Florida Supreme Court and the fact that the Florida statute does not require improperly marked ballots to be read. Rehnquist claims that by authorizing recounts that could not be completed by 12 December, the Florida Supreme Court "jeopardizes the 'legislative wish' to take advantage of the safe harbor" provisions, and requires improperly marked ballots to be read even though the Florida statute does not require it, thus "significantly depart[ing] from the statutory framework in place on Nov. 7" (*Bush* 2000, 537, 538).

Contempt

Those who claim to have been forced out by others (that is, the true homosexuals, the truly political) often exhibit a variety of behaviors that signal contempt for the alleged outers including name-calling, sanity questioning, and associations with other problematic behavior. These accusations are designed to undercut the credibility of the alleged outers. Ironically, this visible posturing often leads the accusers even further out of the closet. *Bush* v. *Gore* follows these classic patterns.

Rehnquist offers a biting concurring opinion that seems designed to undercut the credibility of the Florida Supreme Court. Calling into question the rationality of the Florida Supreme Court, he asserts that its search for "certainty as to the exact count of six million votes" is "elusive—perhaps delusive" (*Bush* 2000, 538). In addition, Rehnquist is openly contemptuous of the Florida Supreme Court, comparing it to other state courts that upheld segregation and resisted black civil rights in the South. However, this accusation has the effect of further outing Rehnquist and the others as political, as it aligns the concurring opinion with cases like *NAACP* v. *Alabama ex rel. Patterson* which, like the aforementioned *Reynolds* v. *Sims* and *Harper* v. *Virginia Board of Elections*, political conservatives and advocates of judicial restraint have long criticized as prototypical examples of judicial activism and illegitimate political maneuvering from the bench. Nevertheless, Rehnquist concedes: "What we would do in the present case is precisely parallel: Hold that the Florida Supreme Court's interpretation of the Florida election laws impermissibly distorted them beyond what a fair reading required" (*Bush* 2000, 535). Whether or not the civil rights cases that Rehnquist cites are "precisely parallel" to *Bush* v. *Gore*, the visible affiliation with judicial activism and its purportedly open politics becomes even more striking when it is set alongside Rehnquist's contemptuous critique of the Florida Supreme Court's lawless activism.

Tolerance or "Not that there's anything wrong with that"

Another common response to coming out is that of tolerance. Rather than reacting with anger and derision, the tolerant react with acceptance, tempered by distance.[9]

---

9   Tolerance can also imply that something untoward, deviant, or even disgusting is being magnanimously forborne by a more accepted or privileged individual or group. See Brown (2006).

In popular culture this stance has been captured well by a classic episode of *Seinfeld*, the most popular television show of the 1990s. Entitled "The Outing," and first aired in 1993, in this episode two New York University coeds writing a story about Jerry Seinfeld for the school paper come to believe he is gay. When Jerry, a serial heterosexual dater and mater throughout the run of the series, finds out he is horrified. Seinfeld is nothing if not a single male heterosexual. Thus, he offers a tolerant but firm insistence that he is not gay, followed by the now famous line "not that there's anything wrong with that," to which his friends respond "of course not, people's sexual preference is their own business." In doing so, they underscore their tolerance for sexual deviance, while vigorously affirming their place on the legitimate side of the sexual order.

The dissents of Justice David Souter, Justice Ginsburg, and Justice Stephen Breyer follow a similar pattern. While they all contend that the Florida Supreme Court's decision is legitimate and should be respected on the grounds that the interpretation of Florida law is Florida's business, none of them directly embraces the Florida court's interpretation as their own, maintaining a stance of respectful distance throughout their opinions.

Thus, while Justice Souter argues that many interpretations of the Florida statute governing presidential elections are lawful, including the one adopted by the Florida Supreme Court, and adds that other interpretations are not only possible, but perhaps better, he nevertheless maintains that the Florida Supreme Court's interpretation is legitimate and respectable.

> Whatever people of good will and good sense may argue about the merits of the Florida Court's reading, there is no warrant for saying that it transcends the limits of reasonable statutory interpretation to the point of supplanting the statute enacted by the 'legislature.' (*Bush* 2000, 544)

Similarly, Justice Ginsburg argues that the Florida Supreme Court should be respected, rather than maligned. "There is no cause here to believe that the members of Florida's high court have done less than 'their mortal best to discharge their oath of office,' and no cause to upset their reasoned interpretation of Florida law." Like Souter, she tolerantly contends that even though she may disagree with the Florida Supreme Court's interpretation, it is nevertheless a reasonable construction, and as such "does not warrant the [majority's] conclusion that the justices of that court have legislated" or the contempt that accompanied that conclusion. Nevertheless, she distances herself from the Florida Supreme Court, implying that Rehnquist's reading of the Florida statute may well be the best one. "I might join The Chief Justice were it my commission to interpret Florida law" (*Bush* 2000, 546). However, she restrains herself from doing so, on the grounds that interpreting state law is the state's business and that deference to states is consistent with precedent and fostering "'cooperative judicial federalism'" (*Bush* 2000, 548).[10] In doing so, she stakes a claim to a place on the legitimate side of the law/politics divide.

---

10 Here, Justice Ginsburg is quoting from *Lehman Brothers* v. *Schein*, 94 S.Ct. 1741 (1974).

Similar to Justices Souter and Ginsburg, Justice Breyer also argues that Rehnquist is wrong to say that the Florida Supreme Court distorted the law. While one could disagree with the Court's interpretation, Breyer argues, it is not unjudicial "or a usurpation of the authority of the state legislation" (*Bush* 2000, 554). Justice Stevens also argues that the Florida Supreme Court should be respected and left alone to interpret state law as it sees fit, and that, accordingly, the US Supreme Court should practice restraint. "If we assume—as I do—that the members of [the Florida Supreme Court] and the judges who would have carried out its mandate are impartial, its decision does not even raise a colorable federal question" (*Bush* 2000, 542).

Fear of Loss of Acceptance

Another standard reaction to coming out is a fear of loss of acceptance, respect, and legitimacy. Although the shame attached to gay and lesbian sexual identity clearly has its origins in societal rejection, gays and lesbians—particularly those who are closeted—often internalize this shame over time. While the threat of external shaming, retribution, and violence is undoubtedly real, the internalization of shame can lead closeted gays and lesbians to exaggerate the magnitude of the threats associated with coming out, thus reinforcing the strength of the closet. While those who are not out may exhibit respect and tolerance for gays and lesbians in principle, fears of loss of acceptance are likely to emerge when the relationships are closer, especially those in the family. The closer to home, the stronger the potential for fear. These fears, while perhaps understandable, are often blown out of proportion. In this sense, the gay and lesbian coming out narrative strongly parallels the narrative in *Bush* v. *Gore*. Despite the dissenters' tolerance of the Florida Supreme Court, when it comes to the political identity of the US Supreme Court, several Justices, perhaps as a result of internalized shame regarding political behavior, become very fearful of loss of public acceptance, anticipating a long term diminishment of judicial legitimacy.

Two Justices, Breyer and John Paul Stevens, seem particularly concerned that *Bush* v. *Gore* will lead to a loss of public acceptance of the US Supreme Court. Thus, Justice Breyer's dissent begins and ends by discussing legitimacy and risk. Citing Alexander Bickel, whose lifelong scholarly concern was that activism might diminish the Court's legitimacy, Breyer argues that "in this highly politicized matter, the appearance of a split decision runs the risk of undermining the public's confidence in the Court itself." He argues that judicial legitimacy hinges on public support and that "[t]hat confidence is a public treasure. It has been built slowly over many years, some of which were marked by a Civil War and the tragedy of segregation. It is a vitally necessary ingredient of any successful effort to protect basic liberty and, indeed, the rule of law itself" (*Bush* 2000, 557). While he concedes that the Court is strong enough to withstand the erosion of public confidence, he nevertheless is concerned that the majority's decision to behave politically will cause significant damage.

> We run no risk of returning to the days when a President (responding to this Court's efforts to protect the Cherokee Indians) might have said 'John Marshall has made his decision;

now let him enforce it!' But we do risk a self inflicted wound—a wound that may harm not just the Court, but the Nation.

Thus, he concludes his dissent with a call for restraint (from coming out): "The most important thing we do is not doing" (*Bush* 2000, 557).[11] He adds: "What it does today, the Court should have left undone. I would repair the damage done as best as we now can, by permitting the Florida recount to continue under uniform standards" (*Bush* 2000, 557).

Like Justice Breyer, Justice Stevens' main concern is that the majority's decision in this case will erode public confidence in the Court and thus diminish its legitimacy.

> What must underlie petitioners' entire federal assault on the Florida election procedures is an unstated lack of confidence in the impartiality and capacity of the state judges who would make the critical decisions if the vote count were to proceed...The endorsement of that position by the majority of this Court can only lend credence to the most cynical appraisal of the work of judges throughout the land. (*Bush* 2000, 542)

He argues that such confidence "is the true backbone of the rule of law" (*Bush* 2000, 542). Like Breyer, he maintains that the damage to judicial legitimacy is significant, though not fatal. In one of the most quoted lines of the case, Stevens asserts:

> Time will one day heal the wound to that confidence that will be inflicted by today's decision. One thing, however, is certain. Although we may never know with complete certainty the identity of the winner of this year's Presidential election, the identity of the loser is perfectly clear. It is the Nation's confidence in the judge as an impartial guardian of the rule of law. (*Bush* 2000, 542)

Yet, as students of gay and lesbian coming out narratives might have predicted, a recent study suggests that Breyer and Souter's fears about the fall-out from *Bush* v. *Gore* were largely unfounded. Survey research conducted by Gregory Caldiera, James Gibson, and Lester Spence has found "no diminution of Court legitimacy in the aftermath of *Bush* v. *Gore* even among African Americans" (*Bush* 2000, 535). Thus, the fall-out seems not to have been significant, at least in terms of public respect for and acceptance of the Court.

Gaydar and "Poldar"

Gays and lesbians have long been said to possess "gaydar"—a kind of gay radar or heightened interest and ability in detecting who might be gay or lesbian despite the presence of any straight façade. Thus, many queers were delighted, but not really surprised, when high profile celebrities like k.d. lang, Ellen DeGeneres, and Melissa Etheridge publicly came out as gay in the 1990s; their gaydar had tipped them off long before any official announcements were made. If the parallel holds, the Justices who are themselves most political would be most likely to possess a kind of political radar which could be called "poldar." Justices with poldar would be interested in and

---

11 Here Justice Breyer is quoting from Justice Louis Brandeis in *Butler* v. *U.S.*, as cited in Bickel (1962).

able to detect political behavior in others, despite the presence of any legal façade. Justices who are not quite fully out of the closet yet might be apt to recognize such behavior but still distance themselves from those whom they suspect are "really" political and characterize their political behavior as wrong or shameful.

Two dissenting Justices appear to possess poldar: Justice Souter and Justice Breyer. Both address the majority's political behavior most directly, claiming that it is wrong. The other four opinions in *Bush* v. *Gore* certainly discuss politics, but far less directly, usually addressing judicial activism as a stand-in for political behavior. Justice Souter is particularly interesting, because, as Deborah Price and Joyce Murdoch note, it has long been rumored that he is a closeted gay man (2001, 399–402).

Justice Souter begins his dissenting opinion by addressing the political nature of the majority's decision, blaming the majority for acting politically, rather than allowing Congress, an openly political branch, to resolve the situation. Arguing that the majority's actions force him to deal with issues he would rather not address, he argues that the Court should have practiced judicial restraint, rather than involving itself in a political matter: "If this Court had allowed the State to follow the course indicated by the opinions of its own Supreme Court, it is entirely possible that there would ultimately have been no issue requiring out review, and political tension could have worked itself out in the Congress" (*Bush* 2000, 542). Souter argues that the Court was wrong not only to take the case, but also that the case was wrongly decided. "This case being before us, however, its resolution by the majority is *another* erroneous decision" (*Bush* 2000, 542).

Justice Breyer also addresses the political aspect of the case explicitly and implies that the Court took the case with the cover of pretextual legal reasons. "The political implications of this case for the country are momentous. But the federal legal questions presented, with one exception, are insubstantial" (*Bush* 2000, 551). He also argues that the Court erred in hearing and deciding the case. "The Court was wrong to take this case. It was wrong to grant a stay. It should now vacate that stay and permit the Florida Supreme Court to decide whether the recount should resume" (*Bush* 2000, 552). Concluding that framers' intent, law, and political history suggest that Justices should not be part of resolving electoral controversies, and that such issues are fundamentally political rather than legal, Breyer states: "Of course the selection of the president is of fundamental national importance. But that importance is political, not legal. And this Court should resist the temptation unnecessarily to resolve tangential legal disputes, where doing so threatens to determine the outcome of the election" (*Bush* 2000, 555). This is because the issue is political, not legal, and acting in the political sphere threatens judicial legitimacy. "Congress, being a political body, expresses the people's will far more accurately than does an unelected Court" (*Bush* 2000, 556). In addition, "[t]he Constitution and federal statues themselves make clear that restraint is appropriate" (*Bush* 2000, 555). Finally, "there is no reason to believe that federal law either foresees or requires resolution of such a political issue by this Court" (*Bush* 2000, 555). Despite their current distancing behavior, Justices Souter and Breyer may be (relatively) more likely to come out as political in the future, following the "you spot it, you got it" theory of identity that underlies gaydar (and poldar).

Queer Theory and Performance: Rewriting Shame through Irony, Parody, and Drag

Keeping in mind Edmund White's comment about the 'moment of truth' in gay life, it is perhaps important to note that *Bush* v. *Gore* surely is not the Court's first time, and almost certainly is not its last. It may seem amazing to some, perhaps most, that the Court would continue at this late date to attempt to closet its political identity. Thus, Leslie Goldstein has said, "I find comical the idea that after *Bush* v. *Gore* ANYONE would be harboring the idea that the Court is not already politicized."[12] Nevertheless, the Court apparently feels compelled to insist exactly that on a fairly regular basis, particularly in highly visible, iconic cases of judicial activism such as *Brown* v. *Board*, *Roe* v. *Wade*, and now *Bush* v. *Gore*—which, ironically, are thought by many to be the most clearly political. In addition, the secondary literature on *Bush* v. *Gore* reproduces the coming out story of the case itself. For example, Alan Dershowitz and Vincent Bugliosi both argue that the *Bush* v. *Gore* majority shamelessly furthered their personal political preferences, and by doing so they revealed their previously closeted political identity. The tone in these works is one of angry contempt, including much name-calling and questioning of the Court's motives and competence. Others, such as Howard Gillman, adopt a more measured tone, but agree that the Supreme Court majority in *Bush* v. *Gore* failed to avoid the appearance of partisan wrangling, thus risking a severe loss of public acceptance. Even Richard Posner, one of the strongest defenders of the Court's decision in *Bush* v. *Gore*, structures his defense in a manner that mirrors the shame often associated with homosexuality. He argues that the Court acted legally (that is, not politically) and thus resists the notion that the Court came out at all in *Bush* v. *Gore*. While the definition of what counts as political may vary amongst these authors, visible political behavior, however defined, is met with shame, contempt, and fear.

The solution to the shame of the open secret that has typically been offered in the gay and lesbian community is to proudly come out. Openly identifying and taking pride in gay and lesbian sexuality has been offered as a means of escaping the closet and of transforming shame into personal and political power.[13] Pride replaces shame, as gay and lesbian sexuality are no longer seen as problematic.

The earnest enthusiasm associated with this approach at times seems unbounded. Annamarie Jagose notes, "gay liberationists promoted the coming out narrative—an unambiguous and public declaration of one's homosexuality—as a potent means of social transformation" (1996, 38). In this view, escape from the shame of the closet is said to foster pride and self-esteem not only in individual gays and lesbians but also in the gay and lesbian community. The anger associated with rejecting shame and the exhilaration associated with taking pride in gay and lesbian sexual identity is said to empower the community to act together as a more potent political force

---

12 Goldstein's comment was made in response to Keith Whittington, who continued to analyze the case as if legal categories controlled the decision. As discussed on lawcourts-l, the listserv of the Law and Courts Section of the American Political Science Association, 2 May 2001.

13 See, for example, D'Emilio (1983), Kaufman and Raphael (1996), Signorile (1995).

(Jagose 1996, 235). This leads to increased visibility, which leads greater numbers of straight people to become aware that some of their friends, relatives, and other intimates are gay and lesbian. This in turn is said to foster greater interpersonal and political tolerance in the mainstream community and thus diminish the need for the closet. The personal becomes political as gays and lesbians, as well as straight people, come to understand that they have a vested interest in promoting civil rights across sexual categories.

Surprisingly similar solutions have been offered by a variety of critical theorists outside of mainstream US constitutional theory. For example, speaking about the election controversy in the midst of the crisis, critical theorist Stanley Fish has argued that everyone should stop trying to hide their politics behind legal principles (2000, A31). "The only principle operating here is that each party thinks its candidate deserves to win." Owning up to politics would not mean "that the political landscape is populated by hypocrites who talk the noble language of principle but then go about practicing politics as usual." Rather, "practicing politics as usual is what everyone always does and should do" (Fish 2000, A31). As we saw in Chapter 4, critical race theorists such as Derrick Bell have long challenged the mainstream's practice of hiding its politics behind the façade of legal neutrality, as have scholars in the critical legal studies movement and feminist legal theory.[14] In various ways they have all urged that the political be brought out into the open, thus reinforcing (if inadvertently), a politics of shame.

Just as critical theorists call for a more real or truthful political representation, the standard gay and lesbian coming out narrative promises to reveal an authentic self that is hidden underneath the façade of compulsory heterosexuality. Coming out of the closet, or openly declaring a gay or lesbian sexual identity, has been described as "an acknowledgment of a previously hidden truth," which signals an acceptance and an embracing of one's identity. Queer theorists such as Shane Phelan have argued that this process may serve to stabilize identity, rather than reveal the irony of the search for the authentic self. In Phelan's view, newly outed gays and lesbians trade one rigid identity for another and unwittingly prop up heterosexuality, which needs homosexuality to continue to act as a foil so as to maintain heterosexuality's dominant position in the political *status quo*. If queer theorists like Phelan are right, mainstream and critical calls for the Court to straightforwardly and proudly embrace its political identity may serve to further stabilize rather than transform US constitutional discourse.

In addition, coming out loudly and proudly may not necessarily diminish shame. Just as heterosexuality needs homosexuality, so too pride may need shame. As I was writing the first draft of this chapter in the summer of 2002, my partner Kate and I, filled with pride, had a civil union performed in Vermont. As we were preparing for that celebration, we were also searching for a better deal on our house and auto insurance. Without any fuss, an agent agreed to have policies written jointly in our names. A few days later I received a call from her explaining that the home office had written the policies separately, and, as a consequence, we would have to pay several hundred dollars more for the same coverage. It's hard to describe how awash

---

14 See Williams (1992), MacKinnon (1987), Roberto Unger (1975; 1976; 1982).

in shame we felt, particularly because at that moment we were perhaps as visible and proud to be lesbians in a publicly sanctioned way as we've ever been, perhaps seduced by the tolerance offered by the state in the form of the civil union. Ironically, our pride didn't diminish the shame; rather, it exacerbated it. Pride served to outline shame. Absent pride, the outline of shame disappears.

Queer theory offers some clues as to why this might be, and in doing so suggests a way out of the Court's current impasse. Speaking in the context of sexuality, Judith Butler has argued that the compulsion to maintain heterosexuality as natural becomes stronger the more it becomes apparent that it just is not. That is, the more heterosexuality insists that it is natural, the more it becomes clear that it is performative. She argues: "Compulsory heterosexuality sets itself up as the original, the true, the authentic; the norm that determines the real implies that 'being' lesbian is always a kind of miming, a vain effort" to copy the real, the heterosexual (Butler 1990, 312). Authenticity requires a myth of origin. In Butler's view, both are fantastic. She argues: "In this sense, the 'reality' of heterosexual identities is performatively constituted through an imitation that sets itself up as the original and the ground of all imitations" (Butler 1990, 312). However, a myth of origin is doomed to fail repeatedly, even as it continues to try time and again to show that it is the original, the one, the true form of sexuality. Thus, she asserts that, "heterosexuality is always in the process of imitating and approximating its own phantasmatic idealization of itself—*and failing.* Precisely because it is bound to fail, and yet endeavors to succeed, the project of heterosexual identity is propelled into the endless repetition of itself" (Butler 1990, 313). Similarly, I would argue, the Court (as well as mainstream and critical constitutional theorists) presents legal identity as the true, the natural, and the original, setting up political identity as an inauthentic and pale imitation in contemporary constitutional discourse. Judicial restraint and judicial activism reflect the law/politics binary and are based on the myth of origin that grounds it. Following Butler, the Court's legal façade is, then, a fiction or a performance that the Court feels compelled to repeat regularly (and that observers feel compelled to reflect) in order to further naturalize legal identity, despite all evidence to the contrary. As we saw in earlier chapters, contemporary constitutional discourse's various narratives, left to their own devices, also seem destined to fail repeatedly, even as each continues to lay claim to integrating the true source of original understanding into its theory of judicial review.

If coming out seems to reinforce this dynamic (at least somewhat), then the very reasonable solutions of Fish and other critical theorists are not likely to adequately disrupt contemporary constitutional discourse enough to allow the further integration of political sources of democratic authority. In fact, they may inadvertently serve to prop up contemporary constitutional discourse, impasse and all. As Butler argues,

> It may be that the very categories of sex, of sexual identity, of gender are produced or maintained in the *effects* of this compulsory performance, effects which are disingenuously renamed as causes, origins, disingenuously lined up within a causal or expressive sequence that the heterosexual norm produces to legitimate itself as the origin of all sex. (Butler 1990, 318)

Following Butler, the categories that structure contemporary constitutional discourse (judicial restraint and judicial activism, originalism and non-originalism, and so on) may well be the effects of the compulsory performance of the law/politics binary, even though they claim to be the foundation of the entire debate. Legality produces the myth of the founding fathers as the original of all constitutional discourse in order to legitimate itself contra politics. Ironically, the greater the skepticism that there is no authentic origin to which we can wed contemporary constitutional discourse, the greater such a connection appears to be needed to legitimate our current practice of judicial review. Hence, there is the compulsion to perform the standard narratives that dominate contemporary constitutional discourse over and over and over again, to the apparent satisfaction of few except the true believers. The result is a vigorous assertion of the legality of one narrative, followed by a charge (made from the standpoint of another narrative) that the first narrative has politicized the judiciary; this charge is met with strenuous defenses to the contrary, and so on, and so on, and so on. No wonder Fish and other critical scholars have become skeptical that contemporary constitutional discourse could ever be reimagined to a more transformative end. For their part, they simply continue to urge the Court to come out politically, as if that simple act would conclusively resolve the problem. Yet, to do so is to welcome yet another performance of the politics of shame. Such a performance may differ somewhat from the stories we are used to and thus may seem somewhat unfamiliar. But such performances, grounded as they are in reaction to the alleged original, are still likely to represent a politics of shame in one form or another.

Queer theory suggests a different approach to this problem, a different kind of narrative, which offers more than simply unmasking the messiness of the supposed purity of the legal/political and heterosexual/homosexual binaries. Coming out may well be important, but it doesn't signal the end of the struggle. The point is not to "be" authentically legal or political, or any other stable identity once and for all. Rather, the aim is to abandon attachment to the myths of origin that form the basis of naturalizing assumptions of all stripes regarding law and politics, restraint and activism, heterosexuality and homosexuality, and so forth. These props obscure constitutional contestation and democratic transformation, the drama occurring behind the façade of the predictable (tired?) and apparently dead-ended narratives produced on the basis of these assumptions.

In order to dislodge the shaky grounds upon which sex and gender rest, drag queens offer a theatrical, exaggerated, and humorous send-up of the sex and gender system as we know it, having the effect of revealing the performative and unstable basis of the original construction of gender and sex that is being mimicked.[15] Relatedly, camp typically parodies the "naturalness" of various aspects of the "middle class heterosexual lifestyle."[16] In this regard, rhetorical parody may serve as the drag of legal culture as it offers a way to disrupt the naturalness of contemporary constitutional discourse.

---

15 See for example, Rupp and Taylor (2003).
16 For a path-breaking piece on camp, see Sontag (1990, 275–92).

Queer theorists argue that drag and camp may not only parody particular forms of sex and gender, but also the very idea that there is an original, stable sex and gender to be copied. Similarly, I am suggesting that parody may be used not only to send-up specific narrative forms of constitutional discourse such as Whittington's romance or Dworkin's comedy, but that it may also be used, as in this chapter, to send-up the desire to identify an authoritative, authentic, and stable judicial identity in reference to the original whether it be grounded in legal or political behavior situated in the past, present, or the future. Despite some variation in form, all such attempts at stabilizing identity serve to circumscribe the parameters of constitutional contestation, foreclosing rather than opening up new discursive possibilities, such as imagining *Bush* v. *Gore* as a coming out narrative. While stabilization serves to circumscribe the parameters of constitutional contestation, parody seeks to identify openings to the end of destabilizing power as we know it, thereby fostering new possibilities.

Complicating the struggle for transformation further is queer theory's unfortunate propensity to adopt a serious and reasoned performative style that may be even straighter than that which it seeks to criticize. After all, academics gain authority as academics through meticulously reasoned argument. Working from the margins with respect to content, queer theorists would have all the more reason to display their chops in terms of form. In this light, Butler's concluding question becomes all the more telling, even as it becomes all the more pressing:

> How then to expose the causal lines as retrospectively and performatively produced fabrications, and to engage gender itself as an inevitable fabrication, to fabricate gender in terms which reveal every claim to the original, the inner, the true, and the real as nothing other than the effects of *drag*, whose subversive possibilities ought to be played and replayed to make the 'sex' of gender not a site of insistent political play? (Butler 1990, 318)

How can queer theory be so substantively on target, and yet so performatively straight?

As we have seen in previous chapters, transformative possibilities exist at the level of both form and content, and there is typically a relationship between the two. Academics generally and queer theorists in particular typically overlook this relationship and fail to question the way that their own very serious and earnest performances may impede change. Accordingly, there is a need to parody not only the straight reasoning of the Court, but also the performative styles of academic writing as well.

Esther Newton, a longtime researcher of drag queen communities, recommends rewriting moments of shame through performance. In this regard, I'd suggest a re-reading of Holly Hughes's outrageous queer performance in "Clit Notes," with a special focus on the passage that follows, in which Hughes uses drama and performance to get behind traditional façade.[17] As punishment for sexual deviance during her adolescence, Hughes's character, ironically, is forced to participate for the first time in the performance art for which she later became famous as one of the NEA Four, the group of artists whose funding by the National Endowment for the

---

17 Hughes (1996). Also see Hughes and Roman (1998). One might also attend, where available, a performance of "Preaching to the Perverted," Hughes's take on the Court's reaction to the NEA Four. This work is not yet available in print.

Arts came under fire when Jesse Helms sought to revoke their grants on the grounds of indecency.[18] She explains:

> I was under psychiatric orders to work on a production of *The Sound of Music*. This wasn't just any production, oh, no. This was a production under the direction of the most renowned thespian in the entire Thumb region of Michigan. She'd won kudos for her previous season's one-woman *Man of La Mancha*.
>
> I wasn't allowed to act. Instead, I was expected to work on the set crew. I was entirely responsible for the Alps. The Alps are pretty damn important in *The Sound of Music*. You got no Alps, you got no music. I was also expected, during the run of the show, to lower a microphone during 'Edelweiss' so the Von Trapp children could be plainly heard making that touching homage to those little fascist flowers.
>
> Opening night.
>
> By some fluke, I've managed to get the Alps up on their hind legs. I lower the microphone on cue. But one of the Von Trapp children has another idea. Instead of belting out 'Edelweiss,' he pivots and farts. Into the microphone.
>
> I have no idea how many of you, if any, have experienced, first-hand, the sheer destructive power of amplified flatulence. But let me assure you, it's nothing to sneeze at. The one thing we had in Saginaw was a damn good sound system.
>
> Pandemonium broke out, praise the Lord. The first thing to go were the Alps. You'd think I'd be upset because they were *my* Alps, after all. But I was delighted. Because all of a sudden you could look backstage and see:
>
> *The nuns and the Nazis were the same people!*
>
> It was just a question of costumes and phony accents.
>
> Finally the play made sense.
>
> I thought: 'This is what I want to do with the rest of my life.' (Hughes 1996, 202–203)

If Holly Hughes can rework the performance in *The Sound of Music* to this end, surely contemporary constitutional discourse and judicial identity could be redone to better effect. Of course, the first thing to go would have to be the props or façade that prevents us from seeing what's going on backstage.

To some, this may seem an extremely risky strategy in light of the recent ruling in *Lawrence* v. *Texas*, in which the Court overturned the notorious case of *Bowers* v. *Hardwick*, declaring that the Constitution affords protection from state laws that criminalize private acts of homosexual sodomy. Admittedly, there is no way of knowing in advance whether or not the pitfalls associated with integrating a queer approach into contemporary constitutional discourse would ultimately be damning politically. After all, queer theory anticipates the continued persistence of dominant power, regardless

---

18 In 1990, under the leadership of Senator Jessie Helms (R - North Carolina), Congress revoked federal support for the performance art of each of the NEA Four (Karen Finley, John Fleck, Holly Hughes, and Tim Miller), even though the artists' proposals had successfully passed through a peer-reviewed process. The artists sued for reinstatement, winning their case in 1993, and were awarded the grant monies in question. Shortly thereafter, the NEA ceased to fund the work of individual artists.

of the apparent political gains that might accrue from time to time. Transformation might lay not so much in altering this material reality in some sort of permanent fashion, as much as it may offer some imaginative escape from it—which may alter our experience of power subsequent to such an escape. Leaving home, as Modleski notes, allows us to imagine new narrative possibilities and in so doing allows us to reimagine our own relation to power as we know it. This seems to me to be exactly the move that needs to be made, lest we are seduced back into the myth of origin and the focus on paternity that keep leading back to the same old narrative impasses.

Unlike comedy, romance, and tragedy, which offer certain kinds of endings that foreclose broader possibilities, a queer analysis reminds us that there is no tidy resolution of the problem of political power for the court any more than coming out solves the problem of sexual identity for gays and lesbians, to say nothing of the problem of academic identity for queer theorists. Looking at *Bush* v. *Gore* as a coming out narrative suggests that while queer parody doesn't promise to resolve these problems permanently, it does offer the escape afforded by laughter in the face of the ongoing struggle, and that matters enormously in terms of being able to imagine a world of new, more democratically-based possibilities. Rather than foreclosing certain kinds of endings, as narratives that begin with a myth of origin do, a narrative that parodies both the stability of identity and the persistence of power opens up new storylines that were not possible within romance, comedy, and tragedy. In this sense, parody may ironically turn out to be the most democratically "empowering" alternative of those that we have considered. Thus, in response to the question "who's your daddy?" queer theory rejects the quest to discover a stable identity based on an authentic origin or the paternal desires that would ground it. Rather, queer theory embraces the politics of contestation as central to the ongoing construction of human identity and community. In doing so, queer theory foregrounds the ironic necessity of continued struggle in the face of the persistence of dominant power, which is both ridiculed and embraced, fueling the imagination of creative alternatives (rather than hopeless resignation) to business as usual.

However, in his debate with Dworkin, Fish reminds us of the problem of audience and the need that many have for the apparent stability associated with the familiar. In addition, the material realities of power make staying with what is known necessary for many, however desirable it may be to entertain the possibility of leaving home from time to time. Accordingly, the following chapter offers a parody of the drama of contemporary constitutional discourse, summarizing the various narrative forms available and concluding with a send-up the practice of contemporary judicial review. Using the popular reality television show *Queer Eye for the Straight Guy*'s makeover of sexual identity as a model, I offer a parody of the Court's makeover of *Bowers* into *Lawrence* that both supports and challenges the *status quo*, acknowledging but not centralizing the power of the founding myth.

Chapter 6

The Drama of Contemporary Constitutional Discourse: *Lawrence* v. *Texas* as a Makeover of *Bowers* v. *Hardwick*

This chapter stays with the narrative forms of contemporary constitutional discourse, myth of origin and all, challenging its limits and pushing its boundaries as far as possible from the inside out. It offers a parody of judicial power, as played out in the context of *Lawrence* v. *Texas* and *Bowers* v. *Hardwick*, using *Queer Eye for the Straight Guy*'s parody of sexual identity as a model. Drawing on the queer performance in *Queer Eye*, I characterize *Lawrence* as a makeover of *Bowers*. While *Lawrence* is typically read as an example of judicial activism, and *Bowers* as judicial restraint, I provide an alternative reading which suggests that *Lawrence* reveals the country to be living by the rule of *Bowers*, which no longer works. As in *Queer Eye*, the justices review the old rule in *Bowers* and improve it through a five-step makeover. *Lawrence* begins to transform the parochial, undesirable, and straight narrative that one finds in *Bowers* into the worldly and desirable (yet still largely straight) version that one finds in *Lawrence*. This analysis appropriates and reconfigures the standards of conventional constitutional discourse, aiming to move beyond its current impasse by destabilizing the judicial restraint/activism debate and imagining a different way to think about judicial review in the context of the persistence of power.

As Paul Brest, Robert Cover, and a number of other scholars have noted, even on its own account contemporary constitutional discourse has long been stymied at a serious impasse. Although a variety of arguments have been offered to legitimize both judicial activism as well as judicial restraint, none has been widely accepted as the standard upon which to ground judicial power.[1] The standard terms of the debate—activism, restraint, and legitimacy—have remained largely uncontested. This is in no small part due to the fixity of the comedic and romantic meta-narratives that ground mainstream constitutional debates.

As we have seen, romantic narratives tend to be nostalgic, typically seeking to remove obstacles that prevent a return to an idealized golden age. They typically begin wistfully, with the hero yearning to recapture an idyllic past. The hero of this story often feels alienated from his true self and must battle several formidable adversaries who would prevent him from attaining the ultimate goal of a return to the

---

1 For a detailed discussion of these debates see, for example, Burgess (1992), Keck (2004), and Perretti (1999).

edenic natural state which allows for pure self-expression. In this narrative the activist Court that ushers in change and progress is not the hero, but rather the adversary that makes it ever more difficult to recapture a connection with an uncorrupted past, as represented by the founding fathers. Thus, conservatives like Justice Antonin Scalia on the Court and Keith Whittington in the academy seek to restrain judicial power, relying on a purer understanding of constitutional meaning grounded in past pronouncements of the founders and previous Courts. However, romance is limited by its resistance to acknowledging significant brutality in the past and its inability to anticipate the possibility of significant transformation in the future. It also tends to lack humor and proportion, foregrounding self-seriousness above all else.

By contrast, comedic narratives tend to be forward-looking. They usually begin unhappily, with the hero earnestly seeking to overcome a significant dilemma that obstructs progress toward social change. Typically, the hero triumphs in the end, effectuating a desirable, if somewhat implausible, happy ending. In the post-World War II era, liberals such as Chief Justice Earl Warren on the Court and Ronald Dworkin in the academy have employed comedic narratives in support of judicial activism. They have each argued, for example, that the racial politics of the founding and the post-Civil War period create a dilemma that obstructs progress toward equal rights and tolerance for all, regardless of race. In their comedic narratives, an active Court serves as a hero that can overcome the racial politics of the past and effect progressive social change, as in the case of *Brown* v. *Board of Education*.[2] Unlike romance, comedy anticipates significant transformation, seeking to transform the founding fathers into figures worthy of reverence. Employing various *deus ex machina* devices to secure a happy ending, such as amnesia (forgetting self-interested acts of the founding fathers) and resurrection (raising the founders from the dead), comedy recentralizes the founders, thereby stabilizing rather than reconfiguring constitutional discourse as we know it. Like romance, however, comedy is remarkably self-serious in its effort to reconnect with the founders. Also like romance, comedy is unable to meaningfully acknowledge self-interest and brutality as a central part of the founders' identity.

Tragic narratives offer an alternative to the romantic and comedic narratives that dominate mainstream constitutional debate. Where romance nostalgically seeks to reconnect with an idealized past, and comedy seeks to reconfigure the less than desirable effects of the past, tragedy accepts the past as unchangeable, however undesirable it may be. Accordingly, tragic narratives tend to be quite sober, with the hero resisting powers well beyond his or her control, ending in potentially meaningful change, but also certain calamity. While small victories might result from battles won here and there, the war will inevitably be lost, and the tragic hero knows it. Due to a fundamental error in judgment, the tragic hero is limited in his or her ability to effectuate substantial change.

Thus Derrick Bell's epic tragic narrative explores the permanence of racism in American constitutional development from the founding to the present. In Bell's narrative, black heroes who adopt civil rights strategies and rely on judicial review

---

2   Whether *Brown* ultimately represents a happy ending of this sort remains a matter of controversy to this day, even amongst those who admire the decision. See for example, Sunstein (2004) and Rosenberg (1991).

to better their lot are ultimately doomed to failure, earnestly but errantly believing that law can effectuate meaningful social and political change. In the end, racism is a permanent feature of American law, due to the founding fathers' fundamental error in trading African-American rights for the promise of national and economic stability, an error whose specter continues to haunt contemporary constitutional debates. As we've seen, such dissent does not, in and of itself, serve to transform contemporary constitutional discourse or to empower those seeking social and political justice. Ironically, tragedy seems to aggrandize dominant power and undercut mobilization for active resistance. In doing so, this form seems to foreclose the creation of new, more populist narratives that would challenge and perhaps transform contemporary constitutional discourse, the very narratives for which its protagonists appear to yearn so deeply.

While *Bowers* v. *Hardwick* may certainly be read as romantic judicial restraint, and *Lawrence* v. *Texas* as comedic judicial activism, the parody of judicial review offered in this chapter suggests a different kind of alternative, an ironic reading of judicial review. Rather than seeking either a romantic stabilization or a comedic liberation from the past, or halting in a tragic acknowledgment of the brutality of power, this chapter employs irony and parody to disrupt the standard terms and forms of contemporary constitutional discourse, redirecting the discussion to a more theoretically promising and politically productive discussion of judicial review that accounts for constitutional change in the context of persistent power.

While Chapter 5 on *Bush* v. *Gore* removed the myth of (paternal) origin entirely, allowing space for an alternative narrative of judicial identity to emerge, this chapter acknowledges the persistence of power by decentering, but not abandoning, the myth of origin. It follows the lead of *Queer Eye for the Straight Guy*, which embraces that which it seeks to challenge, namely, the centrality of sexual identity and the heterosexual/homosexual binary. In doing so, *Queer Eye* suggests that identity is performative rather than stable; that political and legal struggle are better understood as ironic parody rather than earnest liberation; and that popular culture provides a unique insight into the everyday operation of political power, which may under certain circumstances transform rather than simply mirror *status quo* power relations. Using *Queer Eye*'s parody of sexual identity as a model, I offer a similar parody of judicial power, arguing that it offers a better account of the complexity of constitutional change and a more savvy understanding of the persistence of power in constitutional discourse.

Queer (Theory) Eye for the Straight (Legal) Guy

There are many parallels between *Queer Eye* and *Lawrence*. Both premiered in the Summer of 2003.[3] Proudly out with regard to their sexuality, the five homosexual men (the Fab Five) of *Queer Eye* are defined as homosexual in every way, and the heterosexual men they makeover are presented as their distinct opposites. In fact,

---

3 *Queer Eye for the Straight Guy* premiered on 15 July 2003. *Lawrence* v. *Texas* premiered on 26 June 2003.

every activity of both the homosexuals and heterosexuals on the show is presumed to be inflected with sexuality, even in categories that seem to have nothing whatsoever to do with sex, including food, grooming, and culture. Absent the distinction between heterosexuality and homosexuality, the show does not have meaning.

In its third season on the Bravo channel as of July 2005, *Queer Eye* contributes to the trend in television toward reality and makeover programming, as well as to the recent centralization of out gay characters. Each episode of *Queer Eye* features a heterosexual man who lives by a rule that, for a variety of reasons, no longer works for him. The Fab Five review the rule and update it in five selected areas (food, grooming, fashion, decorating, and culture), providing along the way an accessible, entertaining, and somewhat critical send-up of mainstream straight life.

Every episode of *Queer Eye* offers a makeover split up into five segments, each of which can be used to construct a parallel parody of the Court's use of judicial power in *Lawrence*. These are: reviewing the facts of the case, deciding which aspects of the old rule will be discarded, obtaining comments from family and friends, constructing a new rule, and evaluating the implementation of the new rule. The following sections discuss the structure of these segments and then apply that structure to produce a new analysis of *Lawrence*'s makeover of *Bowers*, alternatively rejecting, appropriating, and, taken as a whole, parodying the conventional understanding of sexual identity, including its alleged fixity, in politics and popular culture. In this manner, I begin the very serious task of challenging traditional beliefs and practices regarding sexuality, setting the stage for an ironic transformation of *Lawrence* into a playful parody.

The Fab Five's makeover of the straight guy highlights various slippages in the heterosexual/homosexual binary that reveal the instability of identity. These slippages are parodied through the Fab Five's queer performance, which challenges and ridicules the political advantages and disadvantages that respectively accrue to each identity. While sexual identity is centralized in *Queer Eye*, it is not stabilized. For the Fab Five on *Queer Eye* it is not necessary to claim a stable gay identity in order to construct a queer analysis. They argue that a "queer 'eye' doesn't mean a queer look. It's a point of view, receptiveness to looking at what works and what doesn't, instead of just accepting things as they are" (Allen 2004, 12). Anyone can offer a queer performance, given the right attitude. As we shall see, many of the queer attitudes prescribed for straight guys by *Queer Eye*'s Fab Five may also be used to characterize the performance of the Judicial Fab Five in *Lawrence* (Justices Anthony Kennedy, Ruth Bader Ginsburg, David Souter, John Paul Stevens, and Sandra Day O'Connor), particularly as compared to the decidedly unfabulous performance of the Phobic Five (namely, Justices Byron White, Warren Burger, Sandra Day O'Connor, Lewis Franklin Powell, William Rehnquist) who are responsible for the majority opinion in *Bowers*.[4]

On *Queer Eye*, even reality is not stabilized. The "reality" that is shown in each episode of *Queer Eye* is clearly presented with a box around it (literally, the television box). The box, as well as the illusion that the makeover takes place in one day, serves as the entertainment version of scare quotes, both of which signal

---

4   Regarding the instability of identity, note that Justice O'Connor's behavior gains her entry into both the Fab and the Phobic Five.

the constructedness of what is being represented. Consistent with queer theory, the makeover of the straight guy is presented in an entertaining and parodic manner in which the originality of heterosexuality is both acknowledged and mocked. As will become clear, much of the entertainment can be read as coming from the spectacle of five gay men poking fun at a straight man's lifestyle, a reversal if there ever was one. Taken as a whole, *Queer Eye*'s parody of sexual identity ironically enacts both a sunny façade regarding the fluidity of sexual identity, as well as a sober skepticism about the staying power of the makeover that bespeaks a savvy understanding of the persistence of power.

Segment One: Reviewing the Facts of the Case

Each episode of *Queer Eye* begins with the Fab Five responding to a straight guy who needs an emergency makeover. The opening sequence portrays each of the Fab Five as simply going about their business—cooking, shopping, decorating, and so forth—when suddenly each of their cell phones rings, signaling a *Queer Eye* emergency. They each drop what they're doing, put on sunglasses, grab a tool that is emblematic of their role (for example, a whisk, a paintbrush, shopping bags), and come together in order to help out the straight man in crisis. Motivated by the motto, "[i]f there was a straight guy in need, they'd rush to his rescue!" they pass the intersection of Gay and Straight streets as they move through the city to the strong back beat of the theme song, "All Things Just Keep Getting Better," which centers on the earnest lyric: "You came into my life/and things never looked so bright...All things/just keep getting better" (Allen 2004, 5). The straight guy featured in each episode has been chosen from thousands of petitions that are received each season from straight men and/or their families and friends, each of whom have filed a fairly detailed and structured preliminary questionnaire that petitions the Fab Five to take on their case.[5]

Immediately following the opening sequence, the Fab Five get to work. They are shown deliberating in their chamber, a black SUV, as they begin to review a file that has been composed in advance for them about the straight guy who will be made-over that week. The facts of the case are presented including vital information such as the straight guy's name, occupation, hobbies, waist and inseam, marital and dating status, and so on. For example, in an episode originally aired in the second season of the show, the Fab Five come to the rescue of Kevin Downey Jr, age 37, 6'0", 165 lbs, 33W 32L, switchboard manager by day, hipster comedian by night, with stage show experience in Long Island and Youngstown, Ohio.[6] Downey seeks to take his career as a comedian to the next level and has a strong interest in vintage clothes and novelties. He is presented as having been an awkward, pimply teen with an obsessive compulsive disorder that leads him to buy and store huge amounts of junk and vintage materials in his tiny apartment. Currently living in Brooklyn, Downey has been dating his girlfriend Matilda for six and a half years. Due to the appallingly

---

    5   See <http://www.thequeereye.com/Be_on_the_Show/>.
    6   For a synopsis of this episode see: <http://www.bravotv.com/Queer_Eye_for_the_ Straight_Guy/Episodes/118/>.

disordered state of his apartment, Matilda has refused to visit Downey there for the last five months. This is a particularly serious problem, since Downey would like to ask Matilda to marry him.

In the standard *Queer Eye* narrative, the heterosexual is often presented as a somewhat lovable yet pathetic loser with a problem that homosexuals can help him solve. The old rule under which the straight guy is living typically occasions some sympathy as well as some light ridicule from the Fab Five, some of which, consistent with the form of parody, is in questionable taste. For example, when it becomes clear that Downey has obsessive compulsive disorder, all of the Fab Five start opening and shutting files, repeating themselves, checking the car door locks and engaging in other behaviors that are usually associated with that disability. When information about Downey's girlfriend is introduced, Carson, the fashion expert and often the snarkiest commentator of the five, repeats her name a few times saying "Matilda Downey Jr, Matilda Downey Jr—sounds like a drag queen with a drug problem." In doing so, Carson and the others foreshadow the full-scale send-up that will occur when they visit the straight guy's extremely disordered home in the next segment of the show. The review of the facts of Downey's case concludes with a mission for the makeover that will include discarding the old rule governing Downey's life and, once that space is cleared out, ushering in a new rule. Thus, the Fab Five identify their mission, "to change a pack rat into a rat packer." This will include formulating a plan to take his career to the next level, redecorating his apartment, and getting Matilda to marry him.

Like the Fab Five, the US Supreme Court receives large numbers of urgent petitions for redress that follow a fairly standard format. The Justices meet in their deliberating chamber on a regularly scheduled basis, dressed in black robes, in order to discuss prepared files and the facts of cases that have been chosen to receive a full hearing. Just as in *Queer Eye*, the Judicial Fab Five begin by reviewing the facts of the case. They note: "The facts in *Bowers* had some similarities to [the facts in *Lawrence*]" (*Lawrence* 2003, 566). *Bowers* v. *Hardwick* is a case that upheld a Georgia statute criminalizing sodomy (but only as applied to homosexuals, despite the broad wording of the law). After police entered his bedroom unannounced, Michael Hardwick was charged with committing criminal sodomy, and he subsequently challenged the constitutionality of the statute. In *Bowers*, the Phobic Five dismissed Hardwick's challenge, finding that "the Constitution does not confer a fundamental right upon homosexuals to engage in sodomy" (*Bowers* 1986, 186). Seventeen years later, the Judicial Fab Five were poised to consider the viability of this rule in *Lawrence*.

Although the facts of *Lawrence* are quite similar to those of *Bowers*, the Judicial Fab Five of *Lawrence* read them quite differently from the Phobic Five of *Bowers*. Having received a report of a weapons disturbance, police in Houston entered the home of John Geddes Lawrence. Finding him having anal sex with another man, Tyrone Garner, the police arrested them both for abridging a Texas law that prohibited "deviate sexual intercourse with another individual of the same sex" (*Lawrence* 2003, 558). Blurring the line between the two identities, the Judicial Fab Five point out that sodomy can be practiced by both homosexuals and heterosexuals. They note: "One difference between [*Bowers* and *Lawrence*] is that the Georgia statute prohibited the conduct whether or not the participants were of the same sex, while the Texas statute, as we have seen, applies only to participants of the same sex" (*Lawrence* 2003, 566). Lawrence and Garner had been convicted, and their convictions were affirmed despite constitutional challenges to the Texas law made on both equal protection and due process grounds. Should Lawrence and Garner have been convicted? Is the Texas law constitutional? To answer these questions, the Judicial Fab Five identifies its mission as follows: "For this inquiry we deem it necessary to reconsider the Court's holding in *Bowers*" (*Lawrence* 2003, 558). They add: "The central holding of *Bowers* has been brought into question by this case, and it should be addressed" (*Lawrence* 2003, 560). Like *Queer Eye*'s Fab Five, the Judicial Fab Five have identified a mission that will require discarding the old rule of *Bowers* and constructing a new one in its place. Following the pattern established in *Queer Eye*, their mission can be read as transforming the policing of sexual perversity into a celebration of sexual diversity. The Judicial Fab Five faces a difficulty similar to that which *Queer Eye*'s Fab Five must confront. The rather disordered state of mainstream constitutional theory must be reviewed, and the Fab Five must consider what to discard and what to keep before a new rule can be established to replace the old rule, *Bowers* v. *Hardwick*.

Segment Two: Tearing Down the Old Rule

In the second segment of *Queer Eye*, the Fab Five visit the home of the straight guy to get a better sense of who he is and how to solve his problem. The home, and particularly the bedroom, is central to the *Queer Eye* makeover. The makeover includes five areas of focus, namely, food, grooming, decorating, fashion, and culture. Taken together, the work in these areas results in an overall makeover of the straight guy.

In this segment, the key question is: what must be discarded in order to forward the straight guy's mission and effectuate a happy ending? This question is particularly acute in the case of Kevin Downey, Jr, given that his home has become such a junk-filled mess that his girlfriend won't even visit, let alone consider living with him. The process of discarding material, behavioral, psychological, and cultural clutter is designed to undo the havoc wrought by the old rule as well as to create the space necessary to establish a new rule that better addresses the Fab Five's mission for the straight guy.

Entering the straight guy's world, particularly his home, the Fab Five typically begin to realize the extent of the dilemma they are facing by encountering various aspects of the straight guy's lifestyle that significantly obstruct his goals and the Fab Five's mission. Thus, they begin to make decisions about what needs to be discarded. This segment typically includes a portrayal of the Fab Five's disgust at the filthy state of the straight guy's bathroom, while wardrobes and bedrooms are often singled out for being either too bland or too outrageous. Astonishment at the paltry (and often moldy) offerings in the kitchen and surprise at the lack of attention being paid to personal grooming are also included in the ridicule. Offending bric-a-brac and clutter of various shapes and sizes is often made fun of and subsequently tossed out—often literally out of the window into the street or front yard. Finally, the straight guy's interests, or lack thereof, are often playfully mocked.

In the case of Kevin Downey, Jr, the Fab Five are particularly critical of the state of his apartment. Thom Filicia, *Queer Eye*'s interior designer, states, "[t]his is the grossest place I have ever seen in my life." Lifting up a copy of a book entitled *Please Kill Me*, Ted Allen, the show's food expert, quips: "This is what [Downey] wrote after living here for a year." Moving into the bedroom, Carson Kressley, the show's fashion expert, asks: "You actually have sex in this room?" Downey sheepishly admits what they undoubtedly already knew, that "my girlfriend hasn't been here for a long time." Restoring regular sex is an important part of the Fab Five's mission, but it is not the only issue at stake here. Referring to Downey's habit of collecting junk, Filicia proclaims that Downey's apartment is filled with "80 per cent crap and 20 per cent fun and interesting things." As the segment ends, the Fab Five ask Downey how his apartment came to be such a wreck. He replies that it was clean, it got dirty, he cleaned it again and it got dirty again until finally he was unable to even touch it anymore to clean it. "It's grotesque," he states, concluding, "I hate it." Clearly the straight guy has reached an impasse and is in dire need of help to transform the situation. Consistent with queer theory, the straight guy's apparent liberation lies in reconceptualizing identity as performative rather than given.

Decisions about what to discard and what to keep provide an opportunity for the Fab Five to gently spoof home and family life as we know it. In the process, the Fab Five wind up both reinforcing and challenging many of the stereotypes about gay and straight lifestyles that are part and parcel of the heterosexual/homosexual binary, thereby destabilizing these identities and the power relations that constitute them. The Fab Five don't just get rid of the straight guy's unnecessary junk, they playfully and often rather bitchily mock it, even as they fulfill stereotypical roles performed by gay men (food, decorating, fashion, and so on) in a fabulously flamboyant style. A large part of the entertainment and pleasure of *Queer Eye* stems from gay men laughing at the straight guy and his lifestyle, rather than *vice versa*. As Jai Rodriguez, the culture expert on *Queer Eye*, has said: "When we descend upon a straight guy's house like the Gay Cavalry, we pick apart every nasty, unkempt part of their home and life. Yes, it's fun. And, yes, it can be scary." David Bergman, an independent critic, adds, "despite the rather backward stereotypes that *Queer Eye* reinforces, it does remind the viewer that straight people haven't a clue how to live. They are trapped in homes full of junk...The show is a reminder that maybe the models for a full and satisfying life are not to be found exclusively in what heterosexuals have done" (Bergman 2004, 18).

Similar to *Queer Eye*'s Fab Five, the central question for the Judicial Fab Five is: what to discard and what to keep from *Bowers*, in order to alleviate the havoc wrought by the old rule and to accomplish a successful makeover in the form of *Lawrence*? As in *Queer Eye*, the mission that the Judicial Fab Five have identified leads them to centralize sexuality, evaluating the old rule regarding the home, including the bedroom, in order to gain a better sense of what should be discarded in order to make room for a new rule. This leads them to reexamine *Bowers*, and it is there that the Judicial Fab Five discover the extent of the dilemma they are facing as they begin to make decisions about what needs to be discarded in order to move beyond the impasse. The description of Downey's apartment by *Queer Eye*'s interior decorator as "80 per cent crap and 20 per cent interesting things" implies that 80 per cent of Downey's belongings will be discarded, while 20 per cent will be retained. So too will the Court discard most, but not all, of what they find in *Bowers* in order to restore legitimate sex to the homosexuals of Texas. Several familiar areas of constitutional discourse focused on in *Bowers* are retained in *Lawrence*. However, much of what is kept is redone in a manner that furthers the transformative mission of the Judicial Fab Five. Similar to *Queer Eye*, the Judicial Fab Five's makeover of *Bowers* focuses on five areas, namely: text, history, precedent, moral/ethical standards, and framers' intent.

In *Lawrence*, the Judicial Fab Five discard the textual interpretation of the Due Process Clause of the Fourteenth Amendment found in *Bowers*, which states that liberty does not include "a right of privacy that extends to homosexual sodomy" (*Bowers* 1986, 190). As opposed to the light mockery that *Queer Eye*'s Fab Five use to clear out space for the new rule, the Judicial Fab Five adopt a very serious and somewhat combative tone:

> That statement, we now conclude, discloses the Court's own failure to appreciate the extent of the liberty at stake. To say that the issue in *Bowers* was simply the right to engage in certain sexual conduct demeans the claim the individuals put forward, just as it would demean a married couple were it to be said marriage is simply about the right to have sexual intercourse. (*Lawrence* 2003, 558)

As in *Queer Eye*, sex remains central to the successful makeover, although it is substantially remade in subsequent segments of the case (and this chapter).

Additionally, the Court discards *Bowers*' interpretation of precedent, which distinguishes "homosexual sodomy" from privacy cases such as *Carey* v. *Population Services International*, *Pierce* v. *Society of Sisters*, *Meyer* v. *Nebraska*, *Prince* v. *Massachusetts*, *Skinner* v. *Oklahoma*, *Loving* v. *Virginia*, *Griswold* v. *Connecticut*, *Eisenstadt* v. *Baird*, and *Roe* v. *Wade*. According to *Bowers*, these cases protect family relationships, marriage, and procreation. The Judicial Phobic Five assert that they

> ...think it evident that none of the rights announced in those cases bears any resemblance to the claimed constitutional right of homosexuals to engage in acts of sodomy...No connection between family, marriage, or procreation on the one hand and homosexual activity on the other has been demonstrated. (*Bowers* 1986, 190)

In *Lawrence*, the Judicial Fab Five reject this reading of precedent, offering an alternative interpretation of these cases that includes rather than excludes the adult decisions to engage in private, consensual, same-sex sexual behavior.

The Judicial Fab Five also discard *Bowers*' interpretation of history and tradition. *Bowers* suggests that "[p]roscriptions against [homosexual sodomy] have ancient roots" and that "[a]gainst this background, to claim that a right to engage in such conduct is 'deeply rooted in this Nation's history and tradition' or 'implicit in the concept of ordered liberty' is, at best facetious" (*Bowers* 1986, 192). The stability of sexual identity itself is questioned in *Lawrence*, as the Judicial Fab Five reject *Bowers*' claim, arguing that homosexual identity is a relatively recent societal construction.

From this they conclude that "there is no longstanding history in this country of laws directed at homosexual conduct as a distinct matter." Further, they add, "the historical grounds relied upon in *Bowers* are more complex...Their historical premises are not without doubt and, at the very least, are overstated" (*Lawrence* 2003, 571).

Consistent with what one would expect of a queer parody, the traditional moral and ethical standards of *Bowers* are also discarded by the Judicial Fab Five in *Lawrence*. They begin by noting that "the Court in *Bowers* was making the broader point that for centuries there have been powerful voices to condemn homosexual conduct as immoral. The condemnation has been shaped by religious beliefs, conceptions of right and acceptable behavior, and respect for the traditional family" (*Lawrence* 2003, 571). Acknowledging that "[f]or many persons these are not trivial concerns but profound and deep convictions accepted as ethical and moral principles to which they aspire and which thus determine the course of their lives," the Judicial Fab Five nevertheless discard this viewpoint outright as a legitimate basis for the old rule. Adding that "[t]he sweeping references by Chief Justice Berger [in *Bowers*] to the history of Western civilization and to Judeo-Christian moral and ethical standards did not take account of other authorities pointing in the opposite direction" (*Lawrence* 2003, 573), *Lawrence* discards *Bowers'* view that "[t]he law... is constantly based on notions of morality" (*Bowers* 1986, 196), directly citing a newer precedent established in the wake of *Bowers*, namely *Planned Parenthood* v. *Casey*, which states: "Our obligation is to define the liberty of all, not to mandate our own moral code" (*Planned Parenthood* 1992, 10).

Finally, *Lawrence*'s Judicial Fab Five reject a more conventional understanding of the founders, appropriating their authority in order to support the outcome of the makeover. The last words of *Lawrence* argue that the founding fathers would not have wanted future generations to blindly defer neither to their views nor the opinions of successive legislative leaders in perpetuity. Thus, the Judicial Fab Five reject *Bowers'* assertion that fidelity to the framers requires deference to state legislatures in this area. *Bowers'* interpretation of framers' intent is fixed in the state of the law at the time of the founding. Noting that "[s]odomy was a criminal offense at common law and was forbidden by the laws of the original 13 States when they ratified the Bill of Rights," *Bowers* concludes that a right to homosexual sodomy would "have little or no cognizable roots in the language or design of the Constitution," thus making the Court vulnerable and open to charges of illegitimacy (1986, 195). As a consequence, *Bowers* argues for judicial deference to state legislative decision-making in this area. The Judicial Fab Five in *Lawrence* wholly discard this view of the founders, as well as the judicial deference it prescribes, in favor of a far more modest, and far less romantic, view of the founding fathers, arguing that "had those who drew and ratified the Due Process Clauses of the Fifth Amendment or the Fourteenth Amendment known the components of liberty in its manifold possibilities, they might have been more specific. They did not presume to have this insight" (*Lawrence* 2003, 578). Consequently, the Judicial Fab Five conclude, the framers were open to the participation of future generations in working out the meaning of the Constitution for themselves, with due reference to, but not blind reverence for, the founding fathers.

Taken together, the rejection of *Bowers*' interpretation of the constitutional text, precedent, history, moral standards, and framers' intent leads to the discarding of *Bowers* as a whole. Thus the Judicial Fab Five conclude: "*Bowers* was not correct when it was decided, and it is not correct today. It ought not to remain binding precedent. *Bowers* v. *Hardwick* should be and now is overruled" (*Lawrence* 2003, 578). Just as *Queer Eye*'s Fab Five discarded Downey's junk in order to make room for a new set of practices better designed to further his goals, the Judicial Fab Five's rejection of various arguments in *Bowers* provides the space for a makeover of contemporary constitutional discourse that will include a new rule, constructed with an eye to furthering the mission statement enunciated earlier: transforming the policing of sexual perversity into the celebration of sexual diversity.

Segment Three: Obtaining Comments from Family and Friends

Before and after many of the commercial breaks in *Queer Eye*, family and friends offer both supportive and critical reactions to the Fab Five's project. Downey's brother, girlfriend, and best friend all comment on the pathetic state of his clothes, apartment, and hair. For example, his girlfriend, Matilda, jokes that his bedroom is so messy "it looks like the room threw up on itself." Yet, in a later "friends and family" segment, she says that Downey's great sense of humor attracted her to him, and that he is "the love of her life."

Just as friends and family comment on the Fab Five's project in *Queer Eye*, so too do the judicial brethren comment upon the Fab Five's project in *Lawrence*—sometimes supportively and sometimes critically. For example, although Justice O'Connor does not join the others in overruling *Bowers*, she does "concur in the Court's judgment that Texas' sodomy law banning 'deviate sexual intercourse' between consenting adults of the same sex is unconstitutional" (*Lawrence* 2003, 585). Thus, she appears supportive of the project of changing the policing of sexual perversity into the celebration of sexual diversity, even though she thinks that the Equal Protection Clause provides a better basis for the makeover. As we saw in Chapter 3, Justice Scalia, on the other hand, is entirely cynical about the Judicial Fab Five's makeover of *Bowers*. Sarcastically noting that while the Court in *Planned Parenthood* v. *Casey* readily resisted making over *Roe* on the grounds that "[l]iberty finds no refuge in a jurisprudence of doubt, it failed to exercise such virtuous restraint while making over *Bowers* in *Lawrence*," he casts doubt upon the entire project, asserting that "[m]ost of the rest of today's opinion has no relevance to its actual holding" (*Lawrence* 2003, 586). Ironically, not even the archly conservative Scalia is able to resist the pull of parody.

Interestingly, an unusually large number of amicus curiae or "friends of the court" briefs were filed in this case, both supportive and critical of making over *Bowers*, including 13 briefs representing 113 organizations and individuals against the makeover, and 15 briefs representing 135 organizations and individuals for the makeover.[7] In addition, numerous parties outside of the Court including interest

---

7   <http://supreme.lp.findlaw.com/supreme_court/docket/2002/march.html#02-102>.

groups, pundits, and politicians also weighed in on the makeover at this time. Perhaps the most widely publicized "friends and family" comment came from Sen. Rick Santorum (R-PA) who asserted: "If the Supreme Court says that you have the right to consensual [gay] sex within your home, then you have the right to bigamy, you have the right to polygamy, you have the right to incest, you have the right to adultery. You have the right to anything."[8]

Segment Four: (Re)Constructing a New Rule

After they finish discarding all the unnecessary junk that impedes progress towards completing their project, the Fab Five start to reconstruct a new rule for the straight guy that will better enable him to reach his goals without sacrificing his core aesthetic. That is, they simultaneously reject and appropriate the straight guy's frame of reference. As Rodriguez, the culture maven, puts it, "it's time to put back the pieces and rebuild our straight guy" (Allen 2004, 209). Decisions about what is kept are animated by the Fab Five's views of what is practicable. While the Fab Five assert that "[i]t's about believing that everything is possible," they also clearly accept the limitations placed upon them regarding the material they have to work with (Allen 2004, 7). Thus, they clarify:

> We want you to look *your* best. That means taking who you are, emphasizing the best, eliminating the worst, and tweaking the rest. And that means checking out what you've already got working for you, what you *can* get working for you, and figuring out how to make that journey from A to B. (Allen 2004, 12)

Appropriating or tweaking what's there, or what the Fab Five call tszujing, is central to a successful makeover. Tszujing means "taking something and tweaking it, fluffing it, nudging or finessing it to be a little more fabulous and fun" (Allen 2004, 11). As Allen says, "Queer Eye is all about tszujing—about taking a classic and injecting it with a little something extra, a little thought and effort" (2004, 54). Consistent with the parameters of queer parody, the Fab Five seem both to accept the limitations of straight society while subtly camping it up as best they can. Taking the mainstream frame of reference as a given, they push it as far as they can without abandoning it, appropriating it to serve their own ends as much as possible.

Thus, Filicia recommends anchoring the makeover by checking out "the factual, structural situation you're living in" and then picking a favorite thing, allowing that to determine how the rest of the room will come together (Allen 2004, 122, 144). As Kressley states: "Start with classic pieces and tszuj it from there" (Allen 2004, 161). He adds that this will prevent the straight guy "from looking like a complete jackass" (Allen 2004, 161). That is, he will retain a fashion frame of reference that will provide a familiar basis that will ground all subsequent change. *Queer Eye's* personal groomer, Kyan Douglas, notes that gay and straight men alike now have the freedom to take care of themselves and to express themselves "through their personal aesthetic" (Allen 2004, 88). He emphasizes that this requires a certain

---

8   <http://www.sodomylaws.org/santorum/snnews006.htm>.

amount of attention and time. Cautioning that there are few practices that straight men needlessly rush through more than shaving, Douglas highlights the centrality of sex to everything, including the mundane practice of shaving, emphasizing the importance of thoroughness and attention to detail: "As with sex, faster is almost never better" (Allen 2004, 115).

Consistent with queer theory, Allen rejects stability in favor of a more open-ended approach, arguing that, "[b]eing open-minded and curious is sexy and interesting, unlike being stuck in your ways, which is not" (Allen 2004, 17). This entails "curiosity and the humility to ask intelligent questions" and relying on the advice of well-trained experts for assistance. "Queer eye is all about giving guys license to ask other guys for help" (Allen 2004, 43). Maintaining an open mind also requires avoiding getting stuck in a bygone era. Kressley cautions, precedent should not necessarily be authoritative:

> A lot of guys are in a time warp. They hold in their memories a particular moment when they think they were at their peak—usually right out of college, the twenty-five-ish period. They (a) never throw anything out, and (b) never look for anything new. You discovered Bass Weejuns in '87 and you're still wearing them today? It's ridiculous—fashion's answer to Rip Van Winkle. Hold on to what works, but open your mind—and your closet—to new ideas. (Allen 2004, 163)

Kressley recommends that the straight guy identify and pattern himself after a fashion role model in order to guide his open mind (Allen 2004, 163). Finally, Rodriguez counsels straight men to take care of their souls by being attentive inwardly as well as focusing outwardly as they get a better sense of themselves. "[G]et attuned to looking and thinking in new directions, which will make [them] more interesting and, therefore, more desirable" (Allen 2004, 208). He notes that this will necessitate a more cosmopolitan, outward-looking attitude that combines familiarity with change. "[T]here's nothing wrong with...comfort. But there's a bigger world out there, and the only way you get to discover it is to say yes" (Allen 2004, 210).

Beginning with the home, the Fab Five incorporate several of these principles, attitudes, and practices into Downey's makeover, which is anchored in his longstanding kitsch aesthetic. Tszujing his vintage rotating bar to anchor the room, they name Downey's personal aesthetic the "boom-boom vibe" after his lounge, which he calls the boom-boom room. Filicia, the interior designer, adds "new" pieces that are consistent with this aesthetic, such as a vintage black leather lounge couch. Similarly, Kressley, the fashion advisor, uses Downey's classic tuxedo pants, as well as several vintage shirts, to anchor his wardrobe. He also tszujes other items, transforming Downey's vintage ties into "new" belts, and adds new pieces such as a hipster corduroy blazer that is consistent with his kitschy style. Douglas, the show's groomer, instructs Downey on "advanced" hair and grooming techniques, attention to which requires time and commitment. Allen, the show's food and wine expert, introduces Downey to a variety of international champagnes and caviars, which he is to prepare for his girlfriend's visit to his apartment, during which time he will ask her to marry him. Advising him to choose a less strong, pink champagne, he jokingly parodies the heterosexual/homosexual binary, telling Downey, "I'm all about the fruit, you're all about the Brut." Rodriguez, the show's cultural advisor, sets Downey up with a comedian mentor, who advises Downey to be open to including more of himself in his act, including material about his girlfriend. He also arranges for Downey to perform that night at his mentor's downtown club with the new material.

Finally, Rodriguez also sits on the "boom-boom" bed with Downey, and, in a nostalgic yet somewhat surreal nod to tradition that also highlights the instability of identity, a gay man earnestly instructs a straight man how to propose to his girlfriend, saying that he should do it in such a way that will "signify to the family that this is a guy they can trust to take care of their daughter." He also advises Downey to speak slowly and carefully as "this is going to be the greatest thing she'll ever hear." "I know," Downey earnestly replies, looking straightly and sincerely into Rodriguez's eyes.

In short, the Fab Five have taken Downey's aesthetic and tszujed it in order to better achieve their goal of turning a pack rat into a rat packer, which includes a more effective wooing of his girlfriend and moving his career to the next level. His response is enthusiastic, to say the least. When the Fab Five bring Downey back to his newly redecorated apartment, he is overwhelmed, exclaiming, "Wow! Oh my God! Shit! This fucking rocks! I just want to fuck this room!" True to form, Filicia, the interior decorator drolly retorts, "Don't fuck the chairs because they're really expensive and the fabric is new." Downey concludes, "This is more than a remake, more like a rebirth...Gay guys rock!"

As in *Queer Eye*, now that the old rule has been discarded, the Judicial Fab Five have more space in *Lawrence* to articulate a new rule, which relies on a successful makeover of *Bowers* in five key areas, namely: text, precedent, history, moral standards, and framers' intent. Consistent with *Queer Eye*, the success of the makeover relies upon both the simultaneous rejection and appropriation of *Bowers'* frame of reference, which requires the adoption of a new set of attitudes, principles, and practices regarding anchoring, tszujing, remaining open-minded, asking for help, seeking an appropriate role model, and looking outward.

Under *Lawrence*'s new rule, "liberty gives substantial protection to adult persons in deciding how to conduct their private lives in matters pertaining to sex" (*Lawrence* 2003, 11). Unlike *Bowers'* characterization of homosexual sex as perverse and therefore worthy of policing, the new rule issued by the Fab Five in *Lawrence* includes homosexuals in such protection and thus seems to celebrate sexual diversity. As long as they are not being harmed or exchanging money, consenting adults are free to conduct sexual relationships as they see fit in private (*Lawrence* 2003, 558). "This, as a general rule, should counsel against attempts by the State, or a court, to define the meaning of the relationship or to set its boundaries absent injury to a person or abuse of an institution the law protects" Anything less, the Judicial Fab Five conclude, would be demeaning, or, to put it in Kressley's words, this rule is designed to prevent the Court from looking like "a complete jackass."

The new rule begins in the home and is firmly anchored in a classic constitutional text that has long been associated with sexual, familial, and lifestyle freedoms, the Due Process Clause of the Fourteenth Amendment. "We conclude that the case should be resolved by determining whether the petitioners were free as adults to engage in the private conduct in the exercise of their liberty under the Due Process Clause of the Fourteenth Amendment of the Constitution" (*Lawrence* 2003, 558). Just as in *Queer Eye*, the Judicial Fab Five take stock of the classics that have survived the discard phase and tszuj or appropriate them to better serve the new rule.

> It suffices for us to acknowledge that adults may choose to enter in this relationship in the confines of their homes and their own private lives and still retain their dignity as free persons...The liberty protected by the Constitution allows homosexual persons the right to make this choice. (*Lawrence* 2003, 567)

Similarly, classic precedents that were used to support the ruling in *Bowers* are tszujed to different effect here in *Lawrence*. Many of these precedents follow the *Queer Eye* pattern of pertaining specifically to the home and the bedroom, as well as the soul. The Judicial Fab Five interpret precedents such as *Griswold, Eisenstadt, Roe*, and *Casey* as addressing not only privacy in various aspects of both marital and single relationships but also as protecting "liberty in both its spatial and more transcendent dimensions" including the right "to make certain fundamental decisions" that affect one's destiny (*Lawrence* 2003, 562, 560).

These older precedents are mixed with new ones to foster a constitutional rhetoric that combines classic and contemporary arguments. Accordingly, the Judicial Fab Five integrate cases decided after *Bowers* into their makeover of precedent, as, for example, in the case of *Planned Parenthood of Southeastern Pa.* v. *Casey* decided in 1992. Quoting from *Casey* extensively, they makeover precedent in this area to include same-sex sexuality, arguing liberty protects matters that

> ...involve the most intimate and personal choices a person may make in a lifetime, choices central to personal dignity and autonomy, [which] are central to the liberty protected by the Fourteenth Amendment. At the heart of that liberty is the right to define one's own concept of existence, of meaning, of the universe, and of the mystery of life. (*Lawrence* 2003, 574)

Further, the Judicial Fab Five maintain an open-minded and outward-looking stance by integrating more cosmopolitan, international case law into their discussion of precedent as a model for decision-making in the American context. They note that "almost five years before *Bowers* was decided the European Court of Human Rights considered a case with parallels to *Bowers* and to today's case," and then use this case, *Dudgeon* v. *United Kingdom*, as a model for invalidating laws of the sort that are at issue in *Lawrence* (*Lawrence* 2003, 573). Citing several additional international cases, the Judicial Fab Five also note that since *Bowers* many cases have been decided that reject its narrow reasoning.

The Judicial Fab Five also use international sources such as *Dudgeon* v. *United Kingdom* (1981) to makeover *Bowers'* narrow interpretation of history and tradition. Whether it's the straight guy humbly asking the sommelier for assistance in choosing an appropriate wine for dinner, as in *Queer Eye*, or relying on the expert authority of gay historians for a different take on sexuality and family life through the ages, as in *Lawrence*, the Fab Five's prescription regarding the attitude necessary for a successful makeover is being followed. Rejecting *Bowers'* claim that "proscriptions against [homosexual] conduct have ancient roots," the *Lawrence* Court notes that

Dudgeon is "authoritative in all countries that are members of the Council of Europe (21 nations then, 45 nations now)," and that as such it "is at odds with the premise in *Bowers* that the claim put forward was insubstantial in our Western civilization" (*Lawrence* 2003, 573). Refusing to remain stuck with an old and no longer viable interpretation of the past, the Judicial Fab Five argue that "there is no longer-standing history in this county of laws directed at homosexual conduct as a distinct matter" (*Lawrence* 2003, 559).

Consistent with *Queer Eye*'s suggestion to rely on the help of experts, the Judicial Fab Five affirm the view of prominent queer theorists (such as the gay and lesbian historians Professors Jonathan Ned Katz, John D'Emilio, and Estelle Freedman) that homosexual identity is historically contingent. The Judicial Fab Five note that "the concept of the homosexual as a distinct category of person did not emerge until the late 19th century." Thus they conclude that sodomy laws prior to that time could not have been specifically targeted at prohibiting or regulating homosexual sex (*Lawrence* 2003, 568). Laws specifically prohibiting homosexual sodomy did not emerge "until the last third of the 20th century," and even these were often unevenly enforced. In addition, many were repealed following *Bowers*. Relying upon experts such as the noted legal scholar Professor William Eskridge, the Judicial Fab Five argue that "laws prohibiting sodomy do not seem to have been enforced against consenting adults acting in private," but rather were specifically targeted against predatory sexual behavior involving "minors...force...disparity in status...or relations between men and animals" (*Lawrence* 2003, 559). Intimating a slippage between the lines of sexual identity set up by the heterosexual/homosexual binary, the Judicial Fab Five conclude that the criminalization of sodomy is as "consistent with a general condemnation of non-procreative sex as it is with an established tradition of prosecuting acts because of their homosexual character" (*Lawrence* 2003, 559).

Maintaining an open mind toward shifting moral and ethical standards, the Judicial Fab Five argue that liberty for all rather than the morality of some should be pivotal in judicial decision-making. As opposed to *Bowers'* moral condemnation of homosexuality, *Lawrence* relies on an "emerging awareness that liberty gives substantial protection to adult persons in deciding how to conduct their private lives in matters pertaining to sex" (*Lawrence* 2003, 559).

Finally, seeking appropriate role models in a tszujed or appropriated version of the founding fathers, the Judicial Fab Five envision them as humble statesman, quite aware of human prejudice and self-interest. In their view, the founders "knew times can blind us to certain truths and later generations can see that laws once thought necessary and proper in fact serve only to oppress" (*Lawrence* 2003, 579). Rather than adopting a stable set of well-defined rights in 1787, the Fab Five's founding myth includes framers who were motivated by historically contingent and expanding freedoms, thus suggesting openness to changing interpretations of the Constitution in the future. "As the Constitution endures, persons in every generation could invoke its principles in their own search for greater freedom" (*Lawrence* 2003, 579). In short, the Judicial Fab Five work within the familiar parameters of mainstream constitutional discourse. Rather than discarding the myth of origin, the Judicial Fab Five rework it, expanding it to accommodate the new rule established in *Lawrence*. The Judicial Fab Five remake the standard categories of mainstream constitutional discourse (that is, text, precedent, history, moral standards, and framers' intent), reworking *Bowers* into *Lawrence* and transforming the policing of sexual perversity into a celebration of sexual diversity.

Segment Five: Implementation and Evaluation

In the last segment of *Queer Eye*, the Fab Five evaluate whether the straight guy is able to implement the new rule. Leaving the straight guy's home, the Fab Five evaluate the staying power of the makeover by watching the rest of the straight guy's day on a television screen over drinks in their hip downtown loft. Consistent with queer theory, the Fab Five reject a comic viewpoint that leads to a seemingly definitive, if improbable, happy ending, adopting in its stead a more ironic standpoint that both appropriates the comedic form while subtly suggesting the likelihood of a persistent struggle rather than a tidy conclusion: "This is a *journey*, not a firm destination with confirmed reservations for the best penthouse suite" (Allen 2004, 13; emphasis in original). Sometimes the mission cannot be effectively realized, given the straight guy's persistent inability to change the rule by which he lives—even when it is clearly preventing him from fulfilling his goals as he understands them. Thus, it is an open question as to whether the straight guy will be able to pull this off. In the case of Downey, we have to wonder whether his apartment will fall back into a state of disrepair after the Fab Five move on to their next case.

At least initially, Downey appears to pass the Fab Five's evaluation with flying colors. They watch him as he follows to a tee the new rule that they have formulated for him, dressing and grooming exactly according to their instructions. He then begins his proposal process by following the very traditional practice of calling his girlfriend's parents and asking for their permission, even before he has discussed it with Matilda herself. Immediately after this call, Matilda arrives at Downey's apartment and is as astounded to see the changes as Downey was during his first viewing. As soon as Matilda appears on their screen, the Fab Five gush repeatedly about how beautiful she is. According to plan, Downey serves her champagne and caviar, while the Fab Five comment on how great they look together. In the meantime, Downey and Matilda travel downtown to the nightclub in which he'll be performing his new act. After seating Matilda at a table with other friends (and after more comments from the Fab Five about how lovely she is), Downey goes backstage to prepare for the show. As instructed, he integrates material about Matilda into his set, which meets with great approval from the crowd despite its rather off-color nature.

After a toast at the friends' table, he brings Matilda into a private area backstage. On one knee, and letting her know that he has already gained her parents' approval, he asks her to marry him. She cries, answers yes, and they each declare the other to be their best friend. The Fab Five cry, cheer, and toast from afar. Kressley, the fashion expert, notes that if they're going to have a wedding to go to he had better start looking for a dress to wear. Always the bridesmaid, never the bride, apparently. Walking out of the club hand in hand into the lights of the city, and referencing the "boom-boom room," Downey and Matilda say "I love you" and the screen fades to black. The makeover seems to have been a stunning success, with the mission of transforming a pack rat to rat packer complete, including moving up to the next level at work as a comic and at home with an accepted marriage proposal. The Fab Five offer Downey a final toast, proclaiming him a "gold nugget" hidden under a pile of junk, as if in an archaeological dig. Yet, they also wryly note that Downey's case is definitely one that they'll want to revisit in a few months, just to see how things worked out.

One can imagine the Judicial Fab Five similarly evaluating the implementation of *Lawrence* from a distance. As in *Queer Eye*, *Lawrence* gives the appearance of resolution while at the same time leaving viewers hanging. While the Judicial Fab Five and their supporters seemed to be celebrating the immediate success of their makeover,[9] the response of the general public after the opinion was issued gives the discerning observer cause to wonder how the makeover will be implemented when the Judicial Fab Five are no longer around, given the persistence of power. Will the case eventuate in a successful or a failed makeover of the policing of perversity or something else entirely? Will *Lawrence* be read as a comic, romantic, or ironic narrative? Or will the brutality that regularly effects the gay community take center stage, as it did when Matthew Shepard was killed, thus suggesting the need for a more tragic narrative frame? Certainly the fanfare directly after the Court issued its decision suggested a comedic, happy ending, with *Lawrence* anchoring gay and lesbian rights and liberties in much the same way that *Brown* has been said to have anchored the rights and liberties of African-Americans.

Yet, as was the case with Downey on *Queer Eye*, it may be too soon to tell for sure. One intervention may not make for a permanent transformation. While *Lawrence* claimed "not to involve whether the government must give formal recognition to any relationship that homosexual persons seek to enter," the debates about same-sex marriage that have since emerged in various venues across the United States have certainly raised questions about the implementation of the new rule of rights and liberties enunciated by the Judicial Fab Five in this case (*Lawrence* 2003, 578). It remains to be seen whether the Judicial Fab Five's television monitor will soon include two gay men (to say nothing of two lesbians) walking off into the sunset together before the screen fades to black.

Conclusion

As the Fab Five put it, "*Queer Eye* is not a make-*over* show; it's a make-*better* show" (Allen 2004, 13). At the end of the day, the straight guy might be dressing better, behaving better, living better, looking better, and cooking better, but he of course remains a straight guy with a particular set of problems that must be solved within the context of his specific life. In each episode, part of the mission includes effectuating a (more or less) happy pairing of the straight guy with a straight girl in order to take their place in a (more or less) straight family life. The apparent fixity of identity that the show reinforces in this manner places serious limitations

---

9   Justice Kennedy's voice was said to break while he read the majority opinion from the bench, and gay and lesbian lawyers who were present were said to be visibly weeping.

on the makeover. At this level, the show reinforces the dominant position of the straight guy and the implementation of his goals within his personal aesthetic. In other words, it serves to support, or perhaps perfect, *status quo* power relations in a tidy comedic narrative. As Bergman has argued, while the complicated lives of straight men may count for a lot on *Queer Eye*, the real lives of gay men are virtually invisible, or at best caricatured, reinforcing a stereotypical view of gay men as experts in hairdressing, interiors, fashion, and cooking. Conceding that "[w]e can be delighted that the Fab Five of *Queer Eye for the Straight Guy* don't pretend to be straight," he cautions that "[t]he Fab Five aren't allowed a life of their own. Only the love lives of straight people count, and gay men become the little fairies that transform their pumpkins into coaches, put glass slippers on those newly pedicured feet" (Bergman 2004, 18).

Yet, that's not quite the whole story. The Fab Five are in fact central to this story, if only for a moment here and there. In the process of the makeover, *Queer Eye* centralizes (albeit temporarily) these five gay men and their (albeit sometimes stereotypical) take on the world. It matters, and it complicates the analysis of what is possible to know that this can happen, if only for a minute. Almost without our realizing it, the relation between heterosexuality and homosexuality has shifted. The heterosexual frame of reference is appropriated and fashioned, as it were, to a different end. Something transformative has occurred, even if we are returned almost immediately to the mainstream world where queer perspectives are invisible, marginal, or appropriated. In this sense, pop culture offers a more realistic take on the problem of persistent power—how it expresses itself and how it might be cleverly yet cautiously subverted—and this may be useful for understanding the politics of law and social change as played out not only in *Lawrence*, but in contemporary constitutional discourse more generally.

Admittedly, *Queer Eye* contains elements of comedy, focusing on solving everyday problems that arise within typically straight family life and holding out the promise of addressing any and all dilemmas that obstruct progress toward a happy ending. *Queer Eye* not only embeds itself in straight family life, but also romanticizes it, embracing traditional notions of gender—at least when it comes to straight women. Yet *Queer Eye* also offers an ironic parody of heterosexuality, homosexuality, and the relationship between the two.

We all know that the Fab Five do not actually wait for emergency phone calls and then spontaneously spring into action. Despite appearances to the contrary, each case has of course been chosen well in advance, the show is carefully scripted and each shot set up beforehand. Presumably we also know that all gay men don't really know everything there is to know about cooking, grooming, fashion, and so forth. Even the choices that the Fab Five make for their straight men are clearly questionable at times.[10] And we all know that the Fab Five could never possibly complete an extensive makeover and solve in one day all the problems the straight

---

10 For example, British writer Mark Simpson, who coined the term metrosexual, has archly asserted: "The gay fashion 'expert' on *Queer Eye* dispenses sartorial advice while dressed like the children snatcher in *Chitty Chitty Bang Bang*." As reported in *The Advocate*, 17 February 2004, p. 10.

guy has managed to create over the course of his adult life, just as much as we all know that a reality/makeover show is never going to overcome homophobia in one day or even in a year of days. As the theme song of the show suggests, things may keep getting better for straight men. But will they keep getting better for gay men? Will the Fab Five ever be able to walk off into a full life, even if it is a hard day's night that follows a long day's work of making over straight men?

Just as neither closeting nor coming out resolves the problem of sexual identity for the Fab Five, neither *Bowers* nor *Lawrence*, neither judicial restraint nor judicial activism, resolves the problem of judicial power in contemporary constitutional discourse. Parodying judicial review by comparing it with popular culture may, however, provide an opportunity to expand the familiar reference points of contemporary constitutional discourse, as well as the occasional moment of escape from power as we know it. This may in turn help us to experience moments of democratic transformation, which create new frames of reference that offer imaginative alternative narratives. These narratives, ironically, challenge the persistence of power and in so doing help us to reimagine our relation to it. Just as parodying the relationship between heterosexuality and homosexuality in *Queer Eye* provides a richer understanding of the complex politics of sexual identity, parodies of judicial review may provide a richer understanding of the complex politics of judicial identity and constitutional change than the standard characterization of *Lawrence* actively overturning *Bowers*. As noted in Chapter 5, they may also provide an alternative way to understand contemporary constitutional discourse that moves beyond perpetuating the ceaseless bickering between advocates of judicial restraint and activism about who is and isn't really political. The more ironic aspects offered by *Queer Eye* may provide a grounds for resisting the false hope promised by the seductive comedy of judicial activism and the nostalgic romance of judicial restraint or the despair that has been associated with tragic resignation to the persistent impasse between the two in contemporary constitutional discourse. Offering neither liberation or resolution, irony can provide the basis for a more complicated and savvy conception of judicial power and constitutional change that resists tragic resignation and provides an alternative narrative of judicial identity that has the potential to move contemporary constitutional discourse beyond its current comedy/romance, activism/restraint divide.

As I noted in Chapter 5, turning to irony and parody may seem to be an extremely risky strategy in light of the recent ruling in *Lawrence* v. *Texas* (or any other important case that seems to support one's particular political preferences, whatever they may be). Who needs irony and parody when rights and liberties are finally being recognized? Who needs alternative narratives that challenge judicial power? Those questions ignore the ongoing political and legal struggles that are characteristic of the implementation and evaluation phase. While irony and parody based on popular culture and democratic authority don't promise to resolve these struggles in the way that comedy does—or hold out the possibility of returning to an uncorrupted past the way that romance does, or capitulate in a resigned fashion the way that tragedy seems to—they do promise, at a minimum, sustaining laughter in the face of what is sure to be a long and ongoing struggle between the forces of regress and progress, law and politics, convention and justice. The escape afforded by this laughter may lead to the creation of slightly different frames of reference, which may form the basis of new narratives that strategically combine familiarity and change, expansiveness and reconstitution, in entertaining and politically savvy stories of judicial power. Such stories may in turn fundamentally alter constitutional meaning as we have come to know it, such that we won't ever look at it again in the same way or take its constituent components for granted as given.

Chapter 7

Conclusion

The aim of this book has been to reformulate how we think about contemporary constitutional discourse using the tools of cultural studies. The contemporary debate has, on its own account, been dead-ended at the impasse of legal principle versus political preference for years on end; the cultural studies approach presented here allows the debate to be reimagined as a series of competing narratives such as romance, comedy, and tragedy. Taken together, these narratives provide the main rhetorical forms that produce the drama of contemporary constitutional discourse. Left to their own devices, romance and comedy lack the critical dissent, democratic authority, and imaginative vision necessary to dislodge the longstanding impasse that has long befuddled conservatives and liberals, activists, and restraintists. Indeed, the law/politics divide on which these narratives are based reinforces the impasse. I have argued that these narratives are best understood and reconstituted by integrating popular culture and parody into the ongoing debate about constitutional meaning. As we have seen, popular culture can reflect, critique, and reconstitute power in a manner that is much more accessible than the standard constitutional narratives, if left to their own devices, could ever hope to be. Some scholars have been critical of the integration of popular culture and law, arguing that it diminishes critical capacity and legal stability, undermining legitimacy and fostering disenchantment with the law (Sherwin 2000). I, on the other hand, have argued that parody, especially when it is grounded in popular culture, can enhance critical capacity by generating alternative, democratically grounded narratives that represent but also move beyond the original, using humor not only to acknowledge the persistence of power, as is the case with tragedy, but also to reconstitute it. While this may lead us to question legitimacy, such questioning may ultimately strengthen the law, by allowing it to serve as a resource for resisting power as we know it and reimagining our relation to it.

Such an approach allows us to ask the following question: What if the founding fathers meant for the Constitution to be read satirically? Once the limits of romance become clear and the founders are no longer thought to control the text in a conventional sense, that is to say, once paternal authority is reconstituted through popular culture and parody, it becomes possible, perhaps even compelling, to explore such a question.

To this end, Chapter 2 casts a romantic myth of origin as the default narrative in the drama of contemporary constitutional discourse. True to form, Keith Whittington's romantic originalism has at least three significant limitations. First, the idealization of the beloved founding fathers prevents the romantic narrative from adequately addressing past brutality or anticipating the possibility of its re-emergence in the future. As Joseph Roach puts it, "the relentless search for the purity of origins is a voyage not of discovery but of erasure" (1988, 6). Second, because significant transformation is thought to end with betrothal, romantic narratives cannot acknowledge or anticipate significant change in the future. If alternative narratives emerge that challenge the union, such plurality is inevitably interpreted as evidence of corruption rather than progress, a threat to the monolithic simplicity offered by the romantic narrative. Thus, while the rise of legal realism and political jurisprudence in the twentieth century fundamentally alters the course of constitutional interpretation and judicial power, the romantic response is, and can only be, retrenchment. Third, romantic narratives typically lack the sense of humor that is necessary to make an adequate transition from infatuation to a more complex and developed relationship that will sustain over time. As a consequence, they remain a compelling story over time only to those true believers whose infatuation with the founders seems boundless. As a consequence, romance offers little to the rest of us, those who are no longer, or perhaps never were, enamored of the founding fathers as the loadstone of constitutional discourse.

Once these limits become clear, romance is ripe for criticism, expansion, and reconstitution through parody, as attested to by the examples of *The Wide Sargasso Sea*, *Gone with the Wind*, and *The Wind Done Gone*. These works foreground the brutal antecedents that undergird white patriarchal power, extend the standard romance beyond its initial union, and disrupt the apparent stability of the myth of origin.

Could there be a better place to begin a satirical reading of the Constitution than romantic originalism, the very site that bemoans the loss of the authentic and resists multiple readings as a matter of principle? Originalism brings the values of the Enlightenment, especially reason, to bear on constitutional interpretation. Try as constitutional scholars and jurists might, attempting to recover authenticity through reason again and again is not likely to resolve the impasse in contemporary constitutional discourse, as it seems to be caused in no small part by a lack of consensus over what counts as reasonable. Whatever the society of the founding era may (or may not) have been, few would argue that contemporary society in general and popular culture in particular are entirely rational. As such, popular culture presents an intriguing alternative to the standard way of approaching the impasse in contemporary constitutional discourse.

Ironically, turning to popular culture might be more in step with the founding than the hyper-rational approach that currently dominates constitutional debate. After all, foundings are not simply about beginnings, but also about repudiations. Supposing we could locate *the* founding moment, it is entirely plausible to think that it would partake of both consent and dissent, as suggested by the events surrounding the Stamp Act, the example which many point to as the beginning of the American Revolution. That is, being true to the founding might entail embracing both the birth and death of political order, both legitimacy and repudiation, in a manner that parallels popular culture's embrace of both consent and dissent to dominant power. Despite its preoccupation with the founding fathers, contemporary constitutional discourse strongly foregrounds consent and legitimacy as its central problem, to the virtual exclusion of the equally important problems of dissent and repudiation. However, a satirical interpretation of the Constitution based in parody can incorporate both consent and dissent and thus holds great promise for moving contemporary constitutional discourse beyond its current impasse.

As Chapter 3 suggested, even though Ronald Dworkin's work seeks to move beyond romantic originalism and to transform the founding fathers into inclusive liberals, it is still typically read as focusing on legitimizing rather than dissenting from the founding order. While romance seeks to join the past with the present as protagonists work together to establish a union with the fathers, comedic protagonists typically must overcome the ills of their fathers in order to enjoy full freedom in the future. Although they acknowledge that the founding fathers perpetuated profound political problems which need to be overcome, they still centralize and stabilize paternal power, undercutting their transformative goal.

Using interpretive strategies drawn from cultural studies allows us to read Dworkin as transforming our conception of the founding fathers to include not simply legitimacy but also repudiation, not only consent but also dissent. Adopting a strategy of parody that has been modeled in popular culture and soap operas, Chapter 3 suggests that comedic constitutional narratives such as Dworkin's can be read as a repudiation and reconstitution of the founding fathers, rather than simply as a defense of them. In this manner, Dworkin's work has the potential to transform contemporary constitutional discourse by contesting, rather than assuming, the stability of its most basic term—legitimacy—and the role that the founding fathers play in establishing and maintaining it. Read in this way, Dworkin's work has greater transformative potential, as parody creates an alternative story that parallels the original, even as it contests the apparent stability of its constitutive terms: paternity, legitimacy, law, and power. This in turn may help us to contest the apparent stability of other central terms in contemporary constitutional discourse, such as judicial activism and judicial restraint, as suggested by the discussion of Justice Scalia's dissent in *Lawrence* v. *Texas*. Despite their almost obsessive preoccupation with legitimizing the founders and judicial power, reading Dworkin and Scalia through the lens of dissent yields a parody of both comedic judicial activism and romantic judicial restraint that suggests that law and legitimacy may be as unstable in constitutional discourse as they regularly appear to be in the soaps.

Reading Dworkin's and Scalia's narratives through the lens of populist sources of interpretation such as soap operas transforms their elite theories, making it unlikely that either will be viewed in quite the same way ever again. Read in this way, Dworkin's narrative can account for brutal abuses of power, and the seemingly perpetual rivalry between judicial restraint and activism can be reconstituted. Such a reading can open up the meaning of legitimacy, destabilize the standard narrative of paternal power, and present new narrative possibilities in the drama of contemporary constitutional discourse, particularly as regards the ongoing conflict between advocates of judicial activism and restraint.

However, read straight rather than through parody, Dworkin's work simply legitimates the founding fathers' continued influence in contemporary constitutional discourse without any clear transformative payoff. Read in this way, Dworkin's continued attachment to the founding fathers impedes a full recognition of their brutality, reinforces the debate's central impasse, and obstructs the very transformation that comedy appears to desire so desperately.

Tragedy, on the other hand, is explicitly grounded in dissent against the powers that be, however futile a task that may seem. As such, it offers an alternative to the romantic and comedic narratives that dominate mainstream constitutional debate. Where romance nostalgically seeks to reconnect with an idealized past and comedy seeks to reconfigure the less than desirable effects of the past, tragedy accepts the past as unchangeable, foregrounding the brutal abuse of power and its senseless but certain consequences. Tragic narratives tend to be quite sober and nearly overwhelming due to their propensity to acknowledge brutality in an unvarnished manner and to underscore the hero's limited ability to effect substantial change.

As we saw in Chapter 4, critical race theorist Derek Bell's work exemplifies the tragic approach, presenting an epic narrative about the permanence of racism that emanates from the founding fathers tragically errant decision to constitutionalize slavery. Despite his repudiation of this decision and his use of popular culture to challenge both the form and content of mainstream constitutional discourse, due to the dictates of the tragic form Bell appears to remain subject to the authority of the founding fathers in the end. His work seems to offer no escape from this fateful decision of the founding fathers. Their power appears as complete as the racism that they seeded at the founding seems eradicable.

Focusing on three stories that represent the beginning, the end, and the postscript of the narrative of race in the American constitutional narrative, Bell's work challenges both the form and content of mainstream constitutional discourse by incorporating popular culture and science fiction into a story of time travel, alien visitation, and alien abduction. Suggesting that racism has been a permanent feature of constitutional discourse since the founding, Bell's tragic narrative integrates elements of realism and the fantastic, to the end of exploring the hypocrisy of government and the failure of the civil rights movement.

The problem with tragedy is that it tends, however inadvertently, to aggrandize dominant power and to undercut mobilization for active resistance. Because of this, many have faulted Bell's work for lacking hope and failing to provide a productive alternative to the current political and legal culture that it criticizes so incisively. Put differently, Bell's tragedy seems to foreclose the very thing that it most desires, namely, the creation of an alternative populist narrative that might challenge and transform contemporary constitutional discourse in both form and content.

Bell rejects humor because it may incorporate humiliation in a manner that resonates with past abuses of power. Nevertheless, his work urges us to investigate the relationship between form and content. In this light, it makes sense to explore the tools associated with every alternative form available to escape persistent power, including tools associated with irony, such as humor and parody, in order to explore the urgent question that Bell's work raises: in light of the persistence of power and the permanence of racism in this constitutional order should we stay or should we go? Should we stay and embrace contemporary constitutional discourse as we know it, myth of origin and all? Or should we leave and investigate what contemporary constitutional discourse might look like without a myth of origin and other familiar signposts to ground it?

As we saw in Chapter 5, leaving with humor can destabilize judicial identity in a manner that can produce an alternative narrative that moves beyond the impasse in contemporary constitutional discourse. *Bush* v. *Gore* abandons the myth of origin while hilariously insisting, despite all evidence to the contrary, that the Court's work is legal, not political, in character. In doing so, the Court's behavior parallels the open secret stage of a classic coming out story, where one behaves as if one were gay while insisting that one is not. Accordingly, judicial identity is read as a coming out narrative in which the Court leaves home, abandoning presumptively normative legal behavior in favor of a deviant political behavior, while still resisting the change in identity that would seem to follow. In doing so the Court reveals, however inadvertently, the constructedness of the law/politics binary upon which judicial identity appears to be (rather unstably) based.

Unlike comedy, romance, and tragedy, which offer certain kinds of endings that foreclose broader possibilities, a queer analysis foregrounds the instability of desire and identity, which opens up new narrative possibilities that do not necessarily seek or lead to closure. Thus, coming out as political doesn't resolve the problem of judicial power anymore than coming out gay or lesbian solves the problem of persistent power for the previously closeted. Parodying the false hope that underlies an unreflective view of the coming out process serves to reconstitute the basic terms of the debate such that resolving the tension between legal principle and political preference is no longer the central goal. In place of airy dreams of reconnecting with a purportedly simpler time that may never have really existed for all but a privileged few, this approach offers savvy resistance in place of the false hope of future liberation, laughter in place of resignation, and straightforward realism about the brutal effects of power. It offers new storylines that acknowledge but reconstitute the persistence of power in an accessible and entertaining manner, opening up a world of new, more democratically-based possibilities.

While the novelty of this approach may make it well-suited to overcome the dead-endedness of contemporary constitutional discourse, it may also create some new difficulties. Audience is central to parody. Parody always works at two levels, so that those out of power can laugh at it, while those in power who cannot countenance laughing at themselves or the absurdity of power can remain assured enough of their own position so as not to seek reprisals against the others. Thus, if it is working correctly, both levels of parody will always be incomprehensible for some portion of the audience. That is, some will not get the joke by design. In addition, the novelty of parody may cause it to seem too unfamiliar and hence incomprehensible even to those it is trying to make laugh. Put differently, the danger is that few will get the joke, and that the parody will be read as inadvertently supporting power as we know it. Additionally, others might not have the resources, material or otherwise, to make the leap. Some parodies might be too far out there, too outrageous, and too destabilizing to work for some audiences. In such circumstances, it might make better sense for parody to be offered within familiar frameworks, a performance where the old and the new coexist simultaneously, offering the comfort of familiarity and the disorder of alterity.

Accordingly, Chapter 6 offers a parody of the drama of contemporary constitutional discourse that stays with and reconstitutes its major forms, myth of origin and all. Using the popular reality television show *Queer Eye for the Straight Guy*'s makeover of sexual identity as a model, this chapter parodies the transformation of *Bowers* v. *Hardwick* into *Lawrence* v. *Texas*, both supporting and challenging the *status quo*, acknowledging but not centralizing the power of the founding myth. Just as *Lawrence* begins to transform the parochial, undesirable, and straight narrative that one finds in *Bowers* into the worldly and desirable (yet still largely straight) version that one finds in *Lawrence*, Chapter 6's use of *Queer Eye* summarizes and parodies the various practices of judicial review currently available in contemporary constitutional discourse, concluding that the straightforward and earnest search for legitimacy is not the only way or the best way that the discourse can be read. When contemporary constitutional theory is viewed through the lens of popular culture and parody it can also be read as a familiar, yet theoretically promising and politically savvy, discourse of populist dissent. The result is a new way to read and evaluate contemporary constitutional discourse that provides an example of how to transform the consciousness of its audience, so that it might be viewed not only as a serious, elitist discourse of legitimacy, but also as an entertaining and accessible source of democratic dissent. Reformulated in this way, democratic authority is based not simply in consent, but also in dissent. Such dissent is a necessary precondition for legal, political, and social transformation, particularly given the dominance of consent and conformity in contemporary constitutional discourse, to say nothing of the culture more generally. The creative tension between consent and dissent, legitimacy and repudiation, can produce the movement necessary to (re)centralize democratically-based change as part of our constitutional discourse.

As some scholars have begun to note, this approach may also raise new problems, which I have aimed to address throughout this work. Is parody an ill-suited strategy for this particular political context? Why abandon legal liberalism when it seems like it offers greater inclusion than ever before (Keck 2006)? While these kinds of questions have the potential of pulling us squarely back into the familiar parameters of the mainstream debate, they might also lead to other, more productive questions (Bybee 2006).

What is the most productive admixture of familiarity and alterity, legitimacy and repudiation? While the *Bush* v. *Gore* parody may be too unfamiliar for some, the *Queer Eye* parody may be too familiar for others. Perhaps most central is the question of audience reception in relation to parody. Is it ever appropriate to laugh at power and its brutalities? What if some don't understand that power is the butt of such humor? Might parody reinforce rather than challenge power as we know it? The 2006 mockumentary *Borat: Cultural Learnings of America for Make Benefit Glorious Nation of Kazakhstan* exemplifies the controversial relationship between audience reception and the success of parody. This frenetic, excessively over-the-top reality-based movie parodies traditional prejudices expressed by the fictional character Borat and the real anti-Semitic, homophobic, racist, and sexist allies that he encounters in his journey across America. One scene features Borat talking with a cowboy at a rodeo about homosexuals saying, "In my country, we kill the homosexuals." "We're trying to get that here too," the cowboy responds. Another scene features Borat singing a country and western song with the lyrics "throw the Jew down the well," joined by enthusiastic audience members in Tuscon, Arizona. This type of audience response has led some to critique the film on the grounds that it may support rather than challenge longstanding biases, by encouraging audiences to laugh at those subject to such prejudices rather than at the ignorance and hatred of their oppressors.

Sacha Baron Cohen, the creator of Borat and a grandson of a Holocaust survivor, has said that his work aims to expose indifference to hatred. He argues that anti-Semitism thrived in Nazi Germany due to rampant, but unexposed, indifference (Baron Cohen 2007). He hopes that audiences will become aware of their own indifference in the company of people who express such rancor openly (Baron Cohen 2007). Baron Cohen's satire exposes contemporary indifference to a wide variety of traditional prejudices, exploring the ignorance and hatred that underlay the views of Borat and his allies. But might his work foster such hatred rather than simply expose it?

Once we begin to explore these kinds of problems and their import for the use of parody in contemporary constitutional discourse, our focus has already shifted in a new direction, moving beyond the law/politics impasse that has stymied constitutional debate for years. This shift itself suggests that a more populist, cultural studies approach to constitutional matters has strong potential to transform the basic focus of contemporary constitutional discourse and provide hope for thinking that additional questions will emerge that we have yet to even imagine.

If, as leading jurists and scholars continue to insist, the central problem of contemporary constitutional discourse is judicial legitimacy and a lack of democratic authority, an obvious solution is to integrate populist interpretations into the debate. Adopting a cultural studies approach to the problem can assist us in moving away from a simple focus on traditional (that is, elite) understandings of legitimacy. Rather than offering yet another theory that attempts to legitimize either an active or restrained use of judicial review, this book has explored how narrative analysis, popular culture, parody, and queer theory can foster democratic authority and open up these debates to dissenting, alternative interpretations of constitutional meaning and judicial power. While a cultural studies approach may or may not serve to legitimize elite decision-making, it does foreground populist interpretations and the very different perspectives that they can bring to bear on constitutional discourse. It also demonstrates the linkage between fatherhood and law, illustrating the problems and prospects of the romantic, comedic, tragic, and ironic narratives that address these themes in elite and popular culture. As we have seen, integrating these narratives yields entertaining and humorous parodies that have the power to destabilize and transform constitutional discourse as we know it.

If the interpretations presented here seem unusual or outlandish, that may be due to the longstanding exclusion of populist sources of interpretation from these debates. Romance novels, soap operas, science fiction, coming out narratives, and reality television shows have not typically been thought to be central to constitutional interpretation, despite the fact that they regularly explore law, fatherhood, legitimacy, identity, and other issues central to such discourse. Ironically, these overlooked sources of populist meaning may provide the very basis of democratic authority for which constitutional scholars and jurists have long been searching. I have inserted them here to begin to alter how we think about constitutional interpretation, consistent with Robert Cover, Paul Brest, and Derrick Bell's calls to devise new stories, based on new practices, to bring new worlds into being that move us beyond our current impasse. If they did not appear at least somewhat out of place, perhaps at times even jarring in their difference at times, they could not possibly contribute to such a vision. Through their disruption, they offer a way to view contemporary constitutional debate not simply as a serious, elite discourse of legitimacy, but also as an accessible, entertaining, and even an occasionally transformative source of democratic authority.

By appropriating and reformulating the terms of the mainstream debate, parody challenges the dominance of elite constitutional interpretation and its expert analysis of the relationship between law and politics and provides a populist basis upon which to fundamentally alter contemporary constitutional discourse as we know it, thus producing new storylines with new problems and possibilities. In this manner, the discourse can begin to be transformed from a dreary parsing of scholarly and juristic argot into a vibrant discussion with points of access and understanding for all.

Bibliography

Abelove, Henry, Michele Aina Barale, and David Halperin (eds) (1993), *The Gay and Lesbian Studies Reader* (New York: Routledge).

Allen, Ted, et al. (2004), *Queer Eye for the Straight Guy: The Fab 5's Guide to Looking Better, Cooking Better, Dressing Better, Behaving Better, and Living Better* (New York: Clarkson-Potter).

Apostilidis, Paul (2001), "Homosexuality and 'Compassionate' Conservatism in the Discourse of the Post-Reaganite Right," *Constellations* 8: 78–105.

Bakhtin, Mikhail M. (1984a), *Rabelais and His World*, translated by Helene Iswolsky (Bloomington, IN: Indiana University Press).

—— (1984b), *Problems of Dostoevsky's Poetics*, translated by Caryl Emerson (Minneapolis, MN: University of Minnesota Press).

Baron Cohen, Sasha, interviewed by Terry Gross on National Public Radio program *Fresh Air* on 4 January 2007; replayed 30 March 2007.

Baumgartner, Jay, and Jody Morris (2006), "The Daily Show Effect," *American Politics Research* 34: 341–67.

Bell, Derrick (1987), *And We Are Not Saved: The Elusive Quest for Racial Justice* (New York: Basic Books).

—— (1992), *Faces at the Bottom of the Well: The Permanence of Racism* (New York: Basic Books).

—— (1996), *Gospel Choirs: Psalms of Survival in an Alien Land Called Home* (New York: Basic Books).

Benhabib, Seyla (ed.) (1996), *Democracy and Difference: Contesting the Boundaries of the Political* (Princeton, NJ: Princeton University Press).

Berger, Raoul (1977), *Government by Judiciary: The Transformation of the Fourteenth Amendment* (Cambridge, MA: Harvard University Press).

Bergman, David (2004), *Gay and Lesbian Review Worldwide* 10: 18.

Berube, Allan (1990), *Coming Out Under Fire: The History of Gay Men and Women in World War Two* (New York: Plume).

Bickel, Alexander (1962), *The Least Dangerous Branch: The Supreme Court at the Bar of American Politics* (New York: Bobbs-Merrill).

Bird, S. Elizabeth (1992), *For Enquiring Minds: A Cultural Study of Supermarket Tabloids* (Knoxville, TN: University of Tennessee Press).

Black, J. David (2002), *The Politics of Enchantment: Romanticism, Media, and Cultural Studies* (Waterloo, Ontario: Wilfred Laurier University Press).

Blasius, Mark (1994), *Gay and Lesbian Politics: Sexuality and the Emergence of a New Ethic* (Princeton, NJ: Princeton University Press).

Bork, Robert H. (1990), *The Tempting of America: The Political Seduction of the Law* (New York: Free Press).

—— (1996), *Slouching Towards Gommorah: Liberalism in Decline* (New York: Regan Books).

Bower, Lisa (1994), "Queer Acts and the Politics of 'Direct Address': Rethinking Law, Culture, and Community," *Law and Society Review* 28: 1009–34.

Bowers v. *Hardwick* (1986), 478 U.S. 186.

Brest, Paul (1981), "The Fundamental Rights Controversy: The Essential Contradictions of Normative Constitutional Scholarship," *Yale Law Journal* 90: 1063–109.

Brettschneider, Marla (2004), "Questing for Heart in a Heartless World: On the Question of Same-Sex Marriage," *PEGS: Journal of the Good Society*.

Brigham, John (1987), *The Cult of the Court* (Philadelphia, PA: Temple University Press).

—— (1990), "Bad Attitudes: The Consequences of Survey Research for Constitutional Practice," *Review of Politics* 52: 582–602.

—— (1996), *The Constitution of Interests* (New York: New York University Press).

—— (2002), "Original Intent and Other Cult Classics," *PEGS: The Good Society* 11: 13–17.

Brookhiser, Richard (2006), *What Would the Founders Do? Our Questions, Their Answers* (New York, Perseus).

Brooks, Peter, and Paul Gerwitz (1998), *Law's Stories: Narrative and Rhetoric in Law* (New Haven, CT: Yale University Press).

Brown v. *Board of Education* (1954), 347 U.S. 483.

Brown, Wendy (2006), *Regulating Aversion: Tolerance in the Age of Identity and Empire* (Princeton, NJ: Princeton University Press).

Bugliosi, Vincent (2001), *The Betrayal of America: How the Supreme Court Undermined the Constitution and Chose Our President* (New York: Thunder's Mouth Press).

Burgess, Susan (1992), *Contest for Constitutional Authority: The Abortion and War Powers Debates* (Lawrence, KS: University of Kansas Press).

—— (1999), "Queer New Institutionalism: Notes on the Naked Power Organ in Mainstream Constitutional Theory and Law," in Howard Gillman and Cornell Clayton (eds) (1999), 199–218.

—— (2001), "A Fine Romance: Keith Whittington's Originalism and the Drama of US Constitutional Theory," *Law and Society Review* 35: 931–42.

—— (2002), "Who Killed Politics? The Case of Cass Sunstein: Queer Theory Meets Mainstream US Constitutional Theory," *Studies in Law Politics and Society* 26: 25–42.

—— (2005), "Did the Supreme Court Come Out in *Bush* v. *Gore?* Queer Theory on the Performance of the Politics of Shame," *Differences: A Journal of Feminist Cultural Studies* 16: 126–46.

—— (2006), "Queer (Theory) Eye for the Straight (Legal) Guy: *Lawrence* v. *Texas'* Makeover of *Bowers* v. *Hardwick*," *Political Research Quarterly* 59: 401–414.

—— (2007), "Who's Your Daddy? Legitimacy, Parody, and Soap Operas in Contemporary Constitutional Discourse," *Law, Culture, and the Humanities* 3: 55–81.

Bush v. *Gore* (2000), 121 S.Ct. 525.

Butler v. *U.S.* (1963), 317 F.2d 249.

Butler, Judith (1990), *Gender Trouble: Feminism and the Subversion of Identity* (New York: Routledge).

—— (1993), "Imitation and Gender Insubordination" in Henry Abelove, Michele Aina Barale, and David Halperin (eds) (1993), 307–320.

Bybee, Keith (2006), "Law in Action," *Political Research Quarterly* 59: 415.

Caldiera, Gregory, James Gibson, and Lester Spence (2003), "The Supreme Court and the US Presidential Election of 2000: Wounds, Self-Inflicted or Otherwise?" *British Journal of Political Science* 33: 535–56.

Califia, Pat (1994), *Public Sex: The Culture of Radical Sex* (Pittsburgh, PA: Cleis Press).

Carey v. *Population Services International* (1977), 431 U.S. 678.

Clinton, Robert Lowry (1989), *Marbury* v. *Madison and Judicial Review* (Lawrence, KS: University Press of Kansas).

Cover, Robert (1983), "Nomos and Narrative," *Harvard Law Review* 97.

—— (1986), "Violence and the Word," *Yale Law Journal* 95: 1601–29.

Cuddon, J.A. (1998), *The Penguin Dictionary of Literary Terms and Literary Theory* (New York: Penguin).

Dean, Jodi (1998), *Aliens in America: Cultural Conspiracies from Outerspace to Cyberspace* (Ithaca, NY: Cornell University Press).

Delgado, Richard (1995), *The Rodrigo Chronicles: Conversations About America and Race* (New York: New York University Press).

—— (2001), *Critical Race Theory: The Cutting Edge* (Philadelphia, PA: Temple University Press).

D'Emilio, John (1983), *Sexual Politics, Sexual Communities: The Making of a Homosexual Minority in the United States, 1940–1970* (Chicago, IL: University of Chicago Press).

Dershowitz, Alan (2001), *Supreme Injustice: How the High Court High-jacked the Election* (Oxford: Oxford University Press).

Donadio, Rachel (2006), "The Chick-Lit Pandemic," *New York Times*, 26 March 2006.

Doty, Alexander (1993), *Making Things Perfectly Queer: Interpreting Mass Culture* (Minneapolis, MN: University of Minnesota Press).

Dudgeon v. *United Kingdom* (1981), 7525 ECHR.

Duggan, Lisa (1992), "Making it Perfectly Queer," *Socialist Review* 22.

—— and Nan D. Hunter (1995), *Sex Wars: Sexual Dissent and Political Culture* (New York: Routledge).

Dworkin, Ronald (1977), *Taking Rights Seriously* (Cambridge, MA: Harvard University Press).

—— (1985), *A Matter of Principle* (Cambridge, MA: Harvard University Press).

—— (1986), *Law's Empire* (Cambridge, MA: Harvard University Press).

—— (1993), *Life's Dominion: An Argument about Abortion, Euthanasia, and Individual Freedom* (Cambridge, MA: Harvard University Press).

—— (1996), *Freedom's Law: The Moral Reading of the American Constitution* (Cambridge, MA: Harvard University Press).

—— (2000), *Sovereign Virtue: The Theory and Practice of Equality* (Cambridge, MA: Harvard University Press).

—— (2006), *Justices in Robes* (Cambridge, MA: Harvard University Press).

Eisenstadt v. *Baird* (1972), 405 U.S. 438.

Ely, John Hart (1973), "The Wages of Crying Wolf: A Comment on *Roe* v. *Wade*," *Yale Law Journal* 82: 920.

—— (1980), *Democracy and Distrust: A Theory of Judicial Review* (Cambridge, MA: Harvard University Press).

Ewick, Patricia and Susan Silbey (1995), "Subversive Stories and Hegemonic Tales: Toward a Sociology of Narrative," *Law and Society Review* 29: 197–226.

Farhi, Paul. "Conception of a Question: Who's Your Daddy?" *Washington Post*, 4 January 2005, C1.

Fineman, Martha (1995), *The Neutered Mother, the Sexual Family, and other Twentieth Century Tragedies* (New York: Routledge).

Fish, Stanley (1982), "Working on the Chain Gang: Interpretation in Law and Literature," *Texas Literature Review* 60: 551–67.

—— (2000), "The High-Minded Fight Over Florida," *New York Times*, 15 November 2000, A31.

Fiske, John (1989a), *Reading Popular Culture* (New York: Routledge).

—— (1989b), *Understanding Popular Culture* (New York: Routledge).

Forrester, Joel, interviewed by Terry Gross for National Public Radio program *Fresh Air*, 28 November 2006.

Geraghty, Christine (1991), *Women and Soap Opera* (Cambridge: Polity Press).

Gilbert, Sandra M., and Susan Gubar (1979), *The Madwoman in the Attic: The Woman Writer and the Nineteenth-Century Literary Imagination* (New Haven, CT: Yale University Press).

Gillman, Howard (2001), *The Votes that Counted: How the Court Decided the 2000 Presidential Election* (Chicago, IL: University of Chicago Press).

—— and Cornell Clayton (eds) (1999), *The Supreme Court and American Politics: New Institutionalist Interpretations* (Lawrence, KS: University of Kansas Press).

Gledhill, Christine (1997), "Genre and Gender: The Case of the Soap Opera," in Stuart Hall (ed.), *Representation: Cultural Representations and Signifying Practices* (New York: Sage Publications).

Glynn, Kevin (2000), *Tabloid Culture: Trash Taste, Popular Power, and the Transformation of American Television* (Durham, NC: Duke University Press).

Goldstein, Leslie Friedman (1991), *In Defense of the Text: Democracy and Constitutional Theory* (Savage, MD: Rowman and Littlefield).

Goss, Fred (2001), "The Wind Done Gone," *The Advocate*, 11 September 2001.

Griswold v. *Connecticut* (1965), 381 U.S. 479.

Halley, Janet (1989), "The Politics of the Closet: Towards Equal Protection for Gay, Lesbian, and Bisexual Identity," *UCLA Law Review* 36: 915.

—— (1993), "The Construction of Heterosexuality," in Michael Warner (ed.) (1993).

Harris, Wendell V. (1992), *Dictionary of Concepts in Literary Criticism and Theory* (New York: Greenwood Press).

Hatcher, Laura (2006), "What is the Federalist Society?" paper presented at the annual meeting of the Law and Society Association.

Honig, Bonnie (2003), *Democracy and the Foreigner* (Princeton, NJ: Princeton University Press).

Hughes, Holly (1996), *Clit Notes: A Sapphic Sampler* (New York: Grove Press).

—— and David Roman (eds) (1998), *O Solo Homo: The New Queer Performance* (New York: Grove Press).

Jagose, Annamarie (1996), *Queer Theory: An Introduction* (New York: New York University Press).

Kaufman, Gershen, and Lev Raphael (1996), *Coming Out of Shame: Transforming Gay and Lesbian Lives* (New York: Doubleday).

Keck, Thomas (2004), *The Most Active Supreme Court in History: The Road to Modern Judicial Conservatism* (Chicago, IL: University of Chicago Press).

—— (2006), "Queering the Rehnquist Court," *Political Research Quarterly* 59: 417–18.

Keith, Toby (2002), "Who's Your Daddy," from *Unleashed* CD (Nashville, TN: Dreamworks).

Kozlowski, Mark (2003), *The Myth of the Imperial Judiciary: Why the Right is Wrong About the Courts* (New York: New York University Press).

Lawrence v. *Texas* (2003), 539 U.S. 558.

Lehman Brothers v. *Schein* (1974) 94 S.Ct. 1741.

Loving v. *Virginia* (1967), 388 U.S. 1.

MacKinnon, Catherine (1987), *Feminism Unmodified: Discourses on Life and Law* (Cambridge, MA: Harvard University Press).

Meyer v. *Nebraska* (1923), 262 U.S. 390.

Miller, D.A. (1988), *The Novel and the Police* (Berkeley, CA: University of California Press).

Millman, Joyce (2006), "She Has a Thing for Older Doctors. Especially Jerks," *New York Times*, 26 March 2006.

Modleski, Tania (1982), *Loving With a Vengeance: Mass Produced Fantasies for Women* (Hamden, CT: Archon Press).

Morton, Robert (ed.) (1997), *Worlds Without End: The Art and History of the Soap Opera* (New York: Henry Abrams).

Mumford, Laura (1997), "Taking Issue: Social Themes in the Soaps," in Robert Morton (ed.) (1997).

Newton, Esther (1972), *Mother Camp: Female Impersonators in America* (Englewood Cliffs, NJ: Prentice-Hall).

—— (2000), *Margaret Mead Made Me Gay: Personal Essays, Public Ideas* (Durham, NC: Duke University Press).

Nichols, John (2006), "Bob Hagan's Modest Proposal," *The Nation*, retrieved 29 December 2007 from <http://www.thenation.com/blogs/thebeat?pid=64227>.

Norton, Anne (2004), *Leo Strauss and the Politics of Empire* (New Haven, CT: Yale University Press).

Nussbaum, Martha (2004), "Danger to Human Dignity: The Revival of Disgust and Shame in the Law," *Chronicle of Higher Education*, 6 August, B4–9.

O'Neill, Johnathan (2005), *Originalism in American Law and Politics: A Constitutional History* (Baltimore, MD: Johns Hopkins University Press).

Patriot, The (2000), Sony Pictures Studio.

Perel, David (2005), *Bat Boy Lives: The Weekly World News Guide to Politics, Culture, Celebrities, Alien Abductions, and the Mutant Freaks that Shape Our World* (New York: Sterling).

Perretti, Terri (1999), *In Defense of a Political Court* (Princeton, NJ: Princeton University Press).

Perry, Michael (1999), *We the People: The Fourteenth Amendment and the Supreme Court* (New York: Oxford University Press).

Phalen, Peggy (1993), *Unmarked: The Politics of Performance* (New York: Routledge).

Phelan, Shane (1994), *Getting Specific: Lesbian Postmodern Politics* (Minneapolis, MN: University of Minnesota Press).

Pierce v. *Society of Sisters* (1925), 268 U.S. 510.

Planned Parenthood v. *Casey* (1992), 505 U.S. 833.

Posner, Richard (2001), *Breaking the Deadlock: The 2000 Election, the Constitution, and the Court* (Princeton, NJ: Princeton University Press).

Powell, Jefferson (2002), *A Community Built on Words: The Constitution in History and Politics* (Chicago, IL: University of Chicago Press).

Preminger, Alex (1965), *Princeton Encyclopedia of Poetry and Poetics* (Princeton, NJ: Princeton University Press).

Price, Debra, and Joyce Murdoch (2001), *Courting Justice: Gay Men and Lesbians* v. *The Supreme Court* (New York: Basic Books).

Prince v. *Massachusetts* (1944), 321 U.S. 158.

Queer Eye for the Straight Guy, <www.bravotv.com/Queer_Eye_for_the_Straight_Guy/>.

Radway, Janice (1984), *Reading the Romance: Women, Patriarchy, and Popular Literature* (Chapel Hill, NC: University of North Carolina Press).

Rand, Erica (1995), *Barbie's Queer Accessories* (Durham, NC: Duke University Press).

Randall, Alice (2001), *The Wind Done Gone* (Boston, MA: Houghton Mifflin).

Regis, Pamela (2003), *A Natural History of the Romance Novel* (Philadelphia, PA: University of Pennsylvania Press).

Roach, Joseph (1988), "Cities of the Dead: Circum-Atlantic Performance," *TDR* 41: 163–71.

Roe v. *Wade* (1973), 410 U.S. 113.

Rollins, Joe (2004), *AIDS and the Sexuality of Law: Ironic Jurisprudence* (New York: Palgrave/Macmillan).

Rosenberg, Gerald (1991), *The Hollow Hope: Can Courts Bring about Social Change* (Chicago, IL: University of Chicago Press).

Rubin, Edward (2005), *Beyond Camelot: Rethinking Politics and Law for the Modern State* (Princeton, NJ: Princeton University Press).

Rupp, Leila, and Verta Taylor (2003), *Drag Queens at the 801 Cabaret* (Chicago, IL: University of Chicago Press).

Sarat, Austin (2000), "Imagining the Law of the Father: Loss, Dread, and Mourning in *The Sweet Hereafter*," *Law and Society Review* 34: 3–45.

Schafer, Roy (1970), 'The Psychoanalytic Vision of Reality,' *International Journal of Psychoanalysis* 51: 279–97.

Schein v. *Chasen* (1975), 519 F.2d 453.

Scott, James (1985), *Weapons of the Weak: Everyday Forms of Peasant Resistance* (New Haven, CT: Yale University Press).

Sedgwick, Eve (1985), *Between Men: English Literature and Homosocial Desire* (Berkeley, CA: University of California Press).

—— (1990), *Epistemology of the Closet* (Berkeley, CA: University of California Press).

—— (1993), *Tendencies* (Durham, NC: Duke University Press).

Sherwin, Richard (2000), *When Law Goes Pop: The Vanishing Line between Law and Popular Culture* (Chicago, IL: University of Chicago).

—— (ed.) (2006), *Popular Culture and Law* (Aldershot: Ashgate).

Shields, Carol (2001), *Jane Austen* (New York: Penguin).

Signorile, Michaelangelo (1995), *Outing Yourself* (New York: Simon and Schuster).

Silbey, Jessica (2002), "What We Do When We Do Law and Pop Culture," *Law and Social Inquiry* 27: 139–68.

Simpson, Mark, *The Advocate*, 17 February 2004: 10.

Skinner v. *Oklahoma* (1942), 316 U.S. 535.

—— (1967), 388 U.S. 1.

Sontag, Susan (1990), "Notes on 'Camp'," in *Against Interpretation* (New York: Anchor Books), 275–92.

Storing, Herbert (1981), *What the AntiFederalists Were For: The Political Thought of the Opponents of the Constitution* (Chicago, IL: University of Chicago Press).

Stychin, Carl (1995), *Law's Desire: Sexuality and the Limits of Justice* (New York: Routledge).

Sunstein, Cass (1984), "Naked Preferences and the Constitution," *Columbia Law Review*, 84: 1689–732.

—— (1994), *The Partial Constitution* (Cambridge, MA: Harvard University Press).

—— (1999), *One Case at a Time: Judicial Minimalism on the Supreme Court* (Cambridge, MA: Harvard University Press).

—— (2004), "Did Brown Matter?" *New Yorker*, 28 April 2004.

—— (2005), *Radicals in Robes: Why Extreme Right Wing Courts Are Wrong for America* (New York: Basic Books).

Tribe, Laurence (2002), *Bush* v. *Gore: The Question of Legitimacy* (New Haven, CT: Yale University Press).

Unger, Roberto (1975), *Knowledge and Politics* (New York: Free Press).

—— (1976), *Law in Modern Society* (New York: Free Press).

—— (1982), *The Critical Legal Studies Movement* (Cambridge, MA: Harvard University Press).

Warner, Gary (1998), *One Life to Live: Thirty Years of Memories* (New York: Hyperion).

Warner, Michael (ed.) (1993), *Fear of a Queer Planet* (Minneapolis, MN: University of Minnesota Press).

Wechsler, Herbert (1959), "Toward Neutral Principles of Constitutional Law," *Harvard Law Review* 23: 1–27.

White, Edmund (2002), "Representative Freaks," *Out*, June: 20–21.

White, Hayden (1973), *Metahistory* (Baltimore, MD: Johns Hopkins University Press).

—— (1978), *Tropics of Discourse* (Baltimore, MD: Johns Hopkins University Press).

—— (1987), *The Content of the Form: Narrative Discourse and Historical Representation* (Baltimore, MD: Johns Hopkins University Press).

Whittington, Keith (1999a), *Constitutional Construction: Divided Powers and Constitutional Meaning* (Lawrence, KS: University Press of Kansas).

—— (1999b), *Constitutional Interpretation: Textual Meaning, Original Intent, and Judicial Review* (Cambridge, MA: Harvard University Press).

Williams, Patricia (1992), *The Alchemy of Race and Rights: Diary of a Law Professor* (Cambridge, MA: Harvard University Press).

—— (1995), *The Rooster's Egg* (Cambridge, MA: Harvard University Press).

—— (1998), *Seeing a Color Blind Future: The Paradox of Race* (New York: Noonday Press).

Wilson, Anna (1996), "Death and the Mainstream: Lesbian Detective Fiction and the Killing of the Coming-Out Story," *Feminist Studies* 22: 251–78.

Winterson, Jeanette (1998), *Oranges Are Not the Only Fruit* (New York: Vintage).

Wolfe, Christopher (1986), *The Rise of Modern Judicial Review: From Constitutional Interpretation to Judge-Made Law* (New York: Basic Books).

Young, Iris Marion (1996), "Communication and the Other: Beyond Deliberative Democracy," in Seyla Benhabib (ed.) (1996): 120–36.

Index